McGraw-Hill Education

500 Review Questions for the MCAT: Physics

D0112626

Also in McGraw-Hill's 500 Questions Series

McGraw-Hill Education

500 Review Questions for the MCAT: Physics

Connie J. Wells

Mc
Graw
Hill
Education

New York Chicago San Francisco Athens London Madrid
Mexico City Milan New Delhi Singapore Sydney Toronto

Copyright © 2015, 2012 by McGraw-Hill Education. All rights reserved. Printed in the
United States of America. Except as permitted under the United States Copyright Act of
1976, no part of this publication may be reproduced or distributed in any form or by any
means, or stored in a database or retrieval system, without the prior written permission
of the publisher.

1 2 3 4 5 6 7 8 9 10   DOC/DOC   1 2 1 0 9 8 7 6 5

ISBN   978-0-07-183623-4
MHID   0-07-183623-3

e-ISBN   978-0-07-183624-1
e-MHID   0-07-183624-1

MCAT is a registered trademark of the Association of American Medical Colleges,
which was not involved in the production of, and does not endorse, this product.

McGraw-Hill Education products are available at special quantity discounts to use as
premiums and sales promotions or for use in corporate training programs. To contact a
representative, please visit the Contact Us pages at www.mhprofessional.com.

CONTENTS

INTRODUCTION

The new MCAT Examination reflects an assessment of students' knowledge of concepts and scientific skills, along with the ability to apply those skills and concepts to the analysis of problems and questions related to biological systems. The 375-minute exam evaluates this knowledge in four major areas: (1) Biological and Biochemical Foundations of Living Systems (95 minutes), (2) Chemical and Physical Foundations of Biological Systems (95 minutes), (3) Psychological, Social, and Biological Foundations of Behavior (95 minutes), and (4) Critical Analysis and Reasoning Skills (90 minutes). Ten Foundational Concepts outline the topics included within these major areas. This book addresses Foundational Concept 4 under Chemical and Physical Foundations of Biological Systems, including those areas of physics that underlie an understanding of questions related to these areas:

Foundational Concept 4: *Complex living organisms transport materials, sense their environment, process signals, and respond to changes using processes understood in terms of physical principles.*

The content categories for this foundational concept that are included in this book are:

4A. Translational motion, forces, work, energy, and equilibrium in living systems
4B. Importance of fluids for the circulation of blood, gas movement, and gas exchange
4C. Electrical circuits and their elements
4D. How light and sound interact with matter
4E. Atoms, nuclear decay, and electronic structure

In testing students' scientific inquiry and reasoning skills, MCAT questions will ask them to combine their knowledge with these inquiry and reasoning skills: (1) Knowledge of Scientific Concepts and Principles, (2) Scientific Reasoning and Problem Solving, (3) Reasoning About the Design and Execution of Research, and (4) Data-Based and Statistical Reasoning. Questions in this book emphasize these skills from all areas of inquiry and reasoning: identifying scientific principles and the relationships between them, using various representations (verbal, symbolic, and graphical), identifying observations and applications related to physics concepts, using mathematical equations to solve problems, reasoning about physics concepts, evaluating explanations and predictions, drawing conclusions from observations and evidence, identifying independent and dependent variables, analyzing graphical information to draw conclusions, and using data to make predictions or explain relationships between variables.

The chemistry and physics multiple-choice section of the examination is composed of 59 questions to answer in 95 minutes. It is advisable for the student preparing for this examination not only to use the questions and explained answers to review the material, but also to use selected sections to take as timed tests, setting a clock to get a feel for the rate at which questions need to be answered in order to complete the exam. At this rate, each set of 10 questions should take 16 minutes. Additionally, since calculators are not allowed on the examination, the student should practice techniques to determine numerical answers, such as (1) setting up the expression or formula and canceling values in the numerator and denominator that are close in value, (2) writing larger numerical values in scientific notation and using powers of 10 to simplify, and (3) looking for the most reasonable solution among the answer choices.

The 500 questions in this book are organized in chapters by topic along the lines of the MCAT guidelines. Explained answers follow at the end of the book, arranged by chapter and by question number. The questions will give you valuable independent practice to supplement your review. Good luck!

McGraw-Hill Education

500 Review Questions for the MCAT: Physics

PART 1

Translational Motion, Forces, Work, Energy, and Equilibrium

CHAPTER 1

Translational Motion

1. Which of the following equations describing acceleration (a), displacement (s), time (t), and velocity (v) for a moving object could be dimensionally correct?

    (A) $a = \dfrac{vt^3}{s^2}$

    (B) $v = \dfrac{as}{t^2}$

    (C) $v^2 = as$

    (D) $t = \dfrac{v^2}{as}$

2. Which of the four graphs below best represents a graph of "y as a function of x^2"?

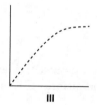
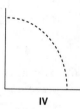

| I | II | III | IV |

    (A) I
    (B) II
    (C) III
    (D) IV

3. On a graph that has a quantity measured in newtons on the y axis and a quantity measured in meters on the x axis, what units would identify the quantities associated with the slope and with the area?

   (A) The slope would have units of N/m, and the area would have units of N·m.
   (B) The slope would have units of N·m, and the area would have units of N/m.
   (C) The slope would have units of N, and the area would have units of N·m.
   (D) The slope would have units of m/N, and the area would have units of N·m.

4. Work is determined by multiplying force times distance. One joule of work is the equivalent of one newton of force multiplied by one meter. Which of the following is equivalent to one joule?

   (A) Force = 5 N and distance = 200 cm
   (B) Force = 5 N and distance = 20 cm
   (C) Force = 50 N and distance = 0.2 cm
   (D) Force = 5 N and distance = 2 cm

5. Quantities in everyday applications often have the prefixes *mega-* and *micro-*. How many micrometers (μm, sometimes called microns) are equivalent to one megameter (Mm)?

   (A) 1×10^3
   (B) 1×10^6
   (C) 1×10^{12}
   (D) 1×10^{15}

6. If quantity X is measured in kilograms, quantity Y is measured in meters per second, and quantity Z is measured in meters, determine the units for the calculated quantity $\dfrac{XY^2}{Z}$.

   (A) $\dfrac{\text{kg} \cdot \text{m}}{\text{s}^2}$

   (B) $\dfrac{\text{kg} \cdot \text{m}^2}{\text{s}^2}$

   (C) $\dfrac{\text{kg} \cdot \text{m}}{\text{s}}$

   (D) $\dfrac{\text{kg} \cdot \text{m}^2}{\text{s}}$

7. If quantity X is measured in newtons and quantity Y is measured in kg/m, determine the units on the calculated quantity $\sqrt{\dfrac{X}{Y}}$.

(A) $\dfrac{\text{kg} \cdot \text{m}}{\text{s}}$

(B) $\sqrt{\dfrac{\text{kg} \cdot \text{m}}{\text{s}}}$

(C) $\sqrt{\dfrac{\text{kg} \cdot \text{m}^2}{\text{s}^2}}$

(D) $\dfrac{\text{m}}{\text{s}}$

8. The equation for the ideal gas law is $PV = nRT$, where P is pressure, V is volume, n is the number of moles of gas, R is the ideal gas constant, and T is temperature. Which of the four graphs below best represents the plot of pressure vs. volume, where n, R, and T are constant?

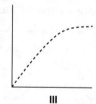
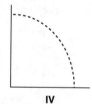

| I | II | III | IV |

(A) I
(B) II
(C) III
(D) IV

9. The equation for the period, T, of a pendulum with length L is $T = 2\pi\sqrt{\dfrac{L}{g}}$.

Which of the diagrams below best represents data gathered for a pendulum with length as the independent variable and period as the dependent variable?

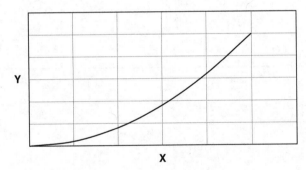

(A) I
(B) II
(C) III
(D) IV

10. Your professor provides you with data from an experiment. When you plot the data, it forms a curve of the shape below.

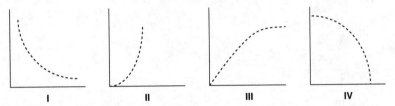

You are required to plot the data so that it forms a line (so that you can ultimately determine the slope of the line in order to find the equation of the line). How would you plot the data so that it forms a line?

(A) Y versus $1/X$
(B) Y versus X^2
(C) Y versus $\sqrt{X}$
(D) Y versus $1/X^2$

11. What is the vector sum of vector X and vector Y below?

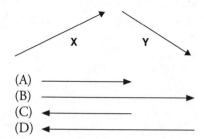

(A) ──────────►

(B) ──────────────►

(C) ◄────────

(D) ◄──────────────

12. An airplane takes off from airport A, flies 300 km north, then flies 1,400 km at 45° north of east. After it lands at airport B, what is the closest approximation of the magnitude of the airplane's displacement from airport A?

(A) 1,000 km north and 1,000 km east
(B) 1,300 km north and 1,000 km east
(C) 300 km north and 1,700 km east
(D) 1,300 km north and 1,300 km east

13. Two perpendicular forces, a 30 N force directed due north and a 40 N force directed due east, are exerted simultaneously on an object whose mass is 35 kg. What is the magnitude of the resultant acceleration of the object in m/s²?

(A) 155
(B) 3.5
(C) 1.4
(D) 0.70

14. An airplane is flying north with an airspeed of 200 km/h when it meets a crosswind of 70 km/h toward the east. Which of the following expressions determines the resultant speed of the airplane?

(A) $(200 + 70)$ km/h
(B) $(200 - 70)$ km/h
(C) $\sqrt{(200^2 + 70^2)}$ km/h
(D) $\sqrt{(200^2 - 70^2)}$ km/h

15. What is the resultant of vector A minus vector B below?

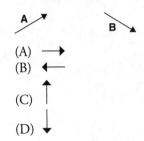

(A) →

(B) ←

(C) ↑

(D) ↓

16. The graph below illustrates the velocity of an object as a function of time.

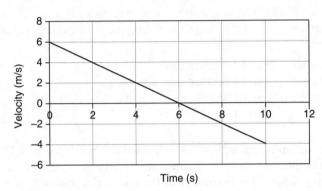

What is the object's instantaneous acceleration at $t = 5$ s?

(A) 0

(B) −2.5 m/s²

(C) 1 m/s²

(D) −1 m/s²

17. An object starts from rest at $x = 0$ m and accelerates at a constant rate, moving from a position of $x = 0$ m to $x = 2$ m in 4 s. How far will the object move in the next 4 s (i.e., from t = 4 s to t = 8 s)?

(A) 3 m

(B) 4 m

(C) 5 m

(D) 6 m

18. The slope of a point on a Velocity as a Function of Time graph is:

(A) change in position.

(B) average acceleration.

(C) instantaneous acceleration.

(D) change in velocity.

19. Which of the following could be true of an object moving with constant acceleration?

(A) It moves in a circle.
(B) It increases its velocity.
(C) It decreases its velocity.
(D) All of the above.

20. A plot of Velocity as a Function of Time for a moving object is a straight line. Which of the following could be true?

(A) The velocity is constant.
(B) The acceleration is constant.
(C) The acceleration and velocity are both zero.
(D) All of the above.

21. The path of an object's motion will be parabolic if it undergoes:

(A) constant velocity in two dimensions.
(B) constant acceleration in two dimensions.
(C) constant acceleration in one dimension and constant velocity in a second dimension.
(D) increasing acceleration in one dimension.

22. Using the following graph of Velocity as a Function of Time for an object in motion, determine the change in position of the object over the first 6 s of its motion.

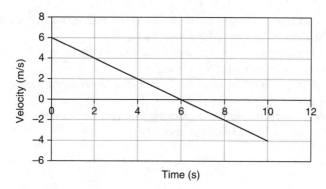

(A) 0 m
(B) 6 m
(C) 18 m
(D) 36 m

Refer to the following graph for questions 23 and 24.

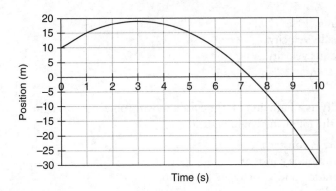

23. The graph above describes the motion of an object as Position as a Function of Time. What is the best estimate of the velocity of the object at time $t = 7$ s?

    (A) 2 m/s
    (B) −2 m/s
    (C) 7 m/s
    (D) −7 m/s

24. In the above graph of Position as a Function of Time, assume that the forward direction of the object is positive. What best describes the motion of the object?

    (A) The object moves forward for about 7 s, reverses direction at $t = 7$ s, and then moves backward for about 3 s.
    (B) The object moves forward for about 3 s, reverses direction at $t = 3$ s, and then moves backward for about 7 s.
    (C) The object speeds up for the first 3 s and then slows down during the period from $t = 3$ s to $t = 7$ s.
    (D) The object starts its motion by moving forward, then reverses its direction at $t = 3$ s and again at about $t = 7$ s.

25. Which of the following best describes the acceleration and velocity vectors for an air rocket fired straight upward from the ground, from the moment just after it leaves the ground until it hits the ground again? Assume that the upward direction is positive.

    (A) The acceleration is always negative, and the velocity is positive on the way up and negative on the way down.
    (B) The acceleration and velocity vectors are both positive on the way up and both negative on the way down.
    (C) The acceleration and velocity vectors are both positive on the way up and on the way down.
    (D) The acceleration is always negative, and the velocity is always positive.

26. A ball is thrown into the air at a velocity of 20 m/s and at a 60° angle to the ground. The ball takes a parabolic path and is in the air for a total of 4 s. If the upward direction from the ground is positive, what is the ball's velocity at a time 2 s after it leaves the ground?

    (A) +10 m/s
    (B) 0
    (C) −10 m/s
    (D) −15 m/s

27. A stone thrown straight upward has an acceleration that is:

    (A) smaller than that of a stone thrown straight downward.
    (B) the same as that of a stone thrown straight downward.
    (C) greater than that of a stone thrown straight downward.
    (D) zero until it reaches the highest point in its path.

28. An airplane is flying horizontally at an altitude of 500 m when a wheel falls from it. If there were no air resistance, the wheel would strike the ground in:

    (A) 10 s.
    (B) 20 s.
    (C) 50 s.
    (D) 80 s.

29. An air rocket is fired vertically at velocity v, rises to a height from the ground h, and remains in the air for a time t. When the same rocket is fired at v at an angle of 60° above the ground,

    (A) the rocket reaches an altitude greater than h and is in the air for a time greater than t.
    (B) the rocket reaches an altitude less than h and is in the air for a time greater than t.
    (C) the rocket reaches an altitude less than h and is in the air for the same time as t.
    (D) the rocket reaches an altitude less than h and is in the air for a time less than t.

30. The graph below plots Displacement as a Function of Time for a mass oscillating on a spring. At what time are the displacement and acceleration in opposite directions?

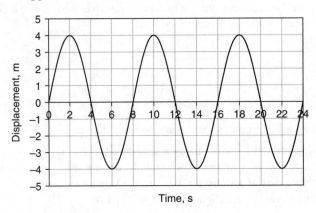

    (A) $t = 0$
    (B) $t = 4$ s
    (C) $t = 6$ s
    (D) All of the above

31. A rock is thrown at velocity v horizontally from the top of a building of height h. How much time does it take the rock to travel from the edge of the building to the ground?

    (A) $\sqrt{hv}$
    (B) h/v
    (C) $2h/g$
    (D) $\sqrt{2h/g}$

32. The drawing below shows the path of a projectile that is launched at an angle from the ground at point A and lands on the ground at point E. Assuming negligible air friction, at which points would you find an acceleration of zero, a maximum speed, and the maximum height?

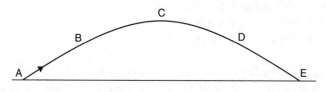

	_a_ = 0	**_v_ = max**	**_h_ = max**
(A)	B	E	E
(B)	No point	C	D
(C)	C	B	C
(D)	No point	A	C

33. An airplane starts on a course due north at an airspeed of 100 km/h and encounters a crosswind from the west at 10 km/h. Which is the most likely resultant flight path of the airplane?

(A) 110 km/h on a path due northwest
(B) 110 km/h on a path due northeast
(C) 101 km/h on a path east of north
(D) 101 km/h on a path west of north

34. A boat that has a still-water speed of 8 m/s attempts to motor straight across a river that is flowing at a speed of 6 m/s. If the boat leaves the shore at point A, which of the vectors in the illustration below represents the path of the boat?

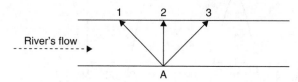

(A) Path 1
(B) Path 2
(C) Path 3
(D) It is impossible for the boat to reach the other side of the river.

35. A block slides across a table and off the edge. What are the horizontal and vertical components of the block's acceleration from the time it leaves the table until it hits the floor?

(A) $a_H = 0$ and $a_V = 9.8$ m/s^2
(B) $a_H = 9.8$ m/s^2 and $a_V = 0$
(C) $a_H = 4.9$ m/s^2 and $a_V = 4.9$ m/s^2
(D) $a_H = 4.9$ m/s^2 and $a_V = 9.8$ m/s^2

36. A block slides across a flat roof that is 5 m from the ground and leaves the edge moving horizontally at a speed of 2 m/s. What are the horizontal and vertical components of the block's velocity when it hits the ground below?

(A) $v_H = 0$ and $v_V = 2$ m/s
(B) $v_H = 10$ m/s and $v_V = 10$ m/s
(C) $v_H = 2$ m/s and $v_V = 10$ m/s
(D) $v_H = 2$ m/s and $v_V = 14$ m/s

37. A simple pendulum oscillates with a period of T seconds. The length of the pendulum is doubled, and the mass attached to the pendulum is doubled. What will be the new period of the pendulum's oscillation?

(A) ¼T
(B) ½T
(C) $\sqrt{2}T$
(D) $2T$

38. The graph below plots Displacement as a Function of Time for a mass oscillating on a spring. At what time(s) is the velocity of the oscillating mass equal to zero?

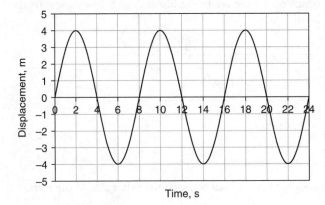

(A) 2 s and 10 s
(B) 4 s and 12 s
(C) $t = 0$ only
(D) 6 s and 14 s

CHAPTER 2

Forces, Torque, and Equilibrium

39. A 500 kg test car finishes a race and, because its brakes have failed completely, engages a parachute from the rear of the vehicle to slow down. Initially, it is traveling at 70 m/s, and in 4 s it has slowed down to 30 m/s. What is the magnitude of the average force exerted on the car by the parachute?

(A) 150 N
(B) 300 N
(C) 3,000 N
(D) 5,000 N

40. The graph below plots data for the acceleration of an object as a function of the net force exerted on the object. What is the mass of the object?

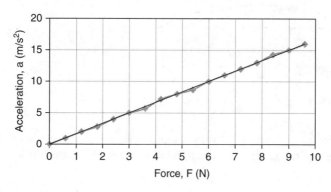

(A) 0.2 kg
(B) 0.6 kg
(C) 1.7 kg
(D) 2.4 kg

41. An automobile towing a trailer accelerates on a level road. The force that the automobile exerts on the trailer is:

    (A) equal to the force that the trailer exerts on the road.
    (B) greater than the force that the trailer exerts on the automobile.
    (C) equal to the force that the trailer exerts on the automobile.
    (D) equal to the force that the road exerts on the trailer.

42. A 2 kg cart is pulled across a horizontal surface. If the horizontal pulling force on the cart is 12 N when $a = 5$ m/s^2, what is the friction force?

    (A) 0
    (B) 0.5 N
    (C) 1.0 N
    (D) 2.0 N

43. A box is held stationary on a ramp by a string connected to the wall. The forces on the box are labeled in the diagram below. Which of the following statements is true?

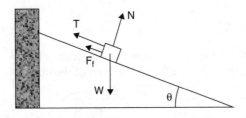

    (A) $T = -F_F$
    (B) $T = W \cos \theta + F_F$
    (C) $W \sin \theta = T + F_F$
    (D) $T + F_F = W$

44. A block is held by a string on a tilted ramp so that the block cannot slide. If the angle of the ramp is increased, how do the forces on the block change?

	Normal Force from Ramp	Static Friction	Tension from String
(A)	Increases	Increases	Increases
(B)	Decreases	Decreases	Decreases
(C)	Increases	Increases	Decreases
(D)	Decreases	Decreases	Increases

45. An elevator car weighing 10,000 N is supported by a steel cable. What is the tension in the cable when the elevator is being accelerated upward at a rate of 3 m/s²?

(A) 13,000 N
(B) 10,000 N
(C) 7,000 N
(D) 4,000 N

46. An object with a mass of 15 kg has a net force of 10 N exerted on it. What will be the acceleration of the object in m/s²?

(A) 150
(B) 15
(C) 1.5
(D) 0.67

47. A force of 10 N, applied for 5 s to a mass of 2 kg, will change the speed of the mass:

(A) from rest to 12 m/s.
(B) from 10 m/s to 25 m/s.
(C) from 20 m/s to 50 m/s.
(D) from 20 m/s to 45 m/s.

48. Two perpendicular forces, one of 30 N directed due north and the second of 40 N directed due east, are exerted simultaneously on an object with a mass of 35 kg. Determine the magnitude of the resultant acceleration of the object in m/s².

(A) 155
(B) 3.5
(C) 2.1
(D) 1.4

49. A string of negligible mass connects three blocks on a level surface, as shown in the illustration below. A force of 12 N acts on the system. Assuming no surface friction, what is the acceleration of the blocks and the tension in the string attached to the 1 kg block?

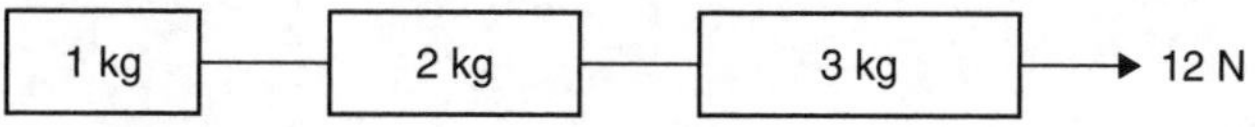

	Acceleration	Tension
(A)	4 m/s²	6 N
(B)	2 m/s²	2 N
(C)	2 m/s²	12 N
(D)	12 m/s²	6 N

50. A person is standing on a scale in an elevator car that is accelerating upward. Compare the reading on the scale to the person's actual weight (the gravitational force on the person by Earth).

(A) The scale reading will always be the same as the person's weight.
(B) The scale reading will be greater than the person's weight.
(C) The scale reading will be less than the person's weight.
(D) The scale will always read zero when the elevator is moving.

51. In the illustration below, a picture frame suspended by two cords is at rest. Determine the value of the tension in cord 1.

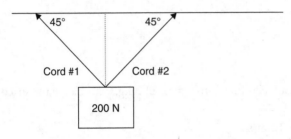

(A) 50 N
(B) 70 N
(C) 140 N
(D) 100 N

52. A force of 10 N is applied to a mass of 2 kg for 5 s. The speed of the mass will change from:

(A) rest to 12 m/s.
(B) 10 m/s to 25 m/s.
(C) 20 m/s to 45 m/s.
(D) 20 m/s to 70 m/s.

53. A hypothetical planet has four times the mass of Earth but the same radius as Earth. If a rock weighs 12 N on the surface of Earth, how much would it weigh on the surface of the hypothetical planet?

(A) 2 N
(B) 6 N
(C) 48 N
(D) 12 N

54. A hypothetical planet has a mass half that of Earth (which has the gravitational acceleration g at the surface) and a radius twice that of Earth. What is g on the hypothetical planet?

   (A) $2g$
   (B) $g/8$
   (C) $g/2$
   (D) $g/4$

55. At a distance of 12,800 km from Earth's center, the acceleration due to gravity is about 2.5 m/s². What is the closest estimate of the acceleration due to gravity at a point 25,000 km from Earth's center?

   (A) 10.0 m/s^2
   (B) 0.6 m/s^2
   (C) 2.5 m/s^2
   (D) 1.2 m/s^2

56. Earth has a radius r. A satellite with a mass of 100 kg is inserted into an orbit at a point $4r$ above Earth's surface. What is the weight of the satellite at this point?

   (A) 1,000 N
   (B) 500 N
   (C) 400 N
   (D) 40 N

57. Three objects are shown on the grid below, with the mass and coordinates of each object labeled. What are the coordinates of the center of mass of the system of the three objects?

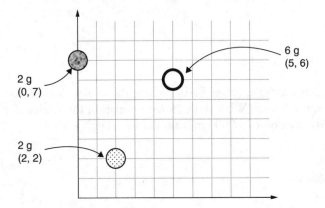

(A) 2.2, 4.0
(B) 3.4, 4.0
(C) 2.8, 5.0
(D) 3.4, 5.4

58. An object slides across a level surface and then down an incline. The kinetic energy of the object at the bottom of the incline is:

(A) equal to the gravitational potential energy at the top of the incline.
(B) equal to the gravitational potential energy at the top of the incline plus the energy lost to thermal energy due to friction.
(C) equal to the gravitational potential energy at the top of the incline minus the energy lost to thermal energy due to friction.
(D) equal to the kinetic energy plus potential energy at the top minus the energy lost to thermal energy due to friction.

59. How much energy is stored in a spring ($k = 200$ N/m) when it is compressed by 0.05 m from its rest position?

(A) 6.0 J
(B) 0.25 J
(C) 0.375 J
(D) 15.0 J

60. A string of negligible mass connects three blocks on a level surface, as shown in the illustration below. A force of 12 N acts on the 3 kg block, and the friction force on each block is 1 N. What is the acceleration of the blocks and the tension in the string attached to the 1 kg block?

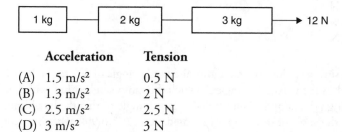

Acceleration	**Tension**
(A) 1.5 m/s²	0.5 N
(B) 1.3 m/s²	2 N
(C) 2.5 m/s²	2.5 N
(D) 3 m/s²	3 N

61. In the illustration below, a 20 kg box sits on a level table and is connected by a string to a hanging box with a mass of 10 kg. The coefficient of kinetic friction between the 20 kg mass and the table is 0.2. Assuming that the pulley has negligible mass and is essentially frictionless as it rotates, what is the tension in the string connecting the two boxes after the boxes start to move?

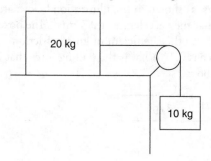

(A) 80 N
(B) 60 N
(C) 20 N
(D) 5 N

62. Which of the following statements is true regarding the coefficient of friction between an object and a level surface?

(A) The coefficient of friction is generally less than 1 if the object is moving and more than 1 if the object is stationary.
(B) As the object moves across the surface, the coefficient of friction decreases as the object slows down.
(C) The coefficient of friction is generally less if the object rolls than if the object slides across the surface.
(D) The coefficient of static friction is generally less than the coefficient of kinetic friction.

63. A 100 N box is pulled across a level floor with a constant horizontal force of 30 N so that it accelerates uniformly at 2 m/s². Determine the friction force between the box and the floor.

(A) 5 N
(B) 10 N
(C) 15 N
(D) 30 N

64. A box is sitting stationary on a ramp tilted at an angle of 30° to the horizontal, which is the maximum angle at which the ramp can be tilted without the box sliding. The ramp is then tilted to a larger angle so that the box begins to slide. As the angle of the ramp is increased from 31° to 90°, what happens to the kinetic friction force and the normal force of the ramp on the box?

(A) The friction force decreases, and the normal force decreases.
(B) The friction force increases, and the normal force increases.
(C) The friction force remains constant, and the normal force decreases.
(D) The friction force remains constant, and the normal force remains constant.

65. Three boxes connected by strings, as shown in the illustration below, are pulled across a level surface so that they accelerate at 0.5 m/s². The boxes are all made of the same material, so the coefficient of kinetic friction between each box and the surface is 0.1. What is the pulling force that is applied to the right of the 3 kg box?

(A) 3 N
(B) 6 N
(C) 9 N
(D) 12 N

66. When a falling parachutist reaches terminal velocity, she is no longer accelerating. Which of the following statements is true about the parachutist?

(A) The gravitational force on the parachutist is equal to the friction force of the air on the parachutist.
(B) The gravitational force on the parachutist is still greater than the friction force of the air, so the parachutist continues to fall.
(C) The friction force of the air on the parachutist has become greater than the gravitational force on the parachutist, so the parachutist no longer accelerates.
(D) The friction force of the air on the parachutist has reached a point where it no longer has an effect, so the parachutist falls at constant speed.

67. A force of 40 N is needed to set a 10 kg steel box moving across a wooden floor. Determine the coefficient of static friction.

    (A) 0.08
    (B) 0.25
    (C) 0.40
    (D) 0.80

68. A box is sliding at constant speed down an inclined surface. Which of the following correctly expresses the coefficient of kinetic friction between the two surfaces?

    (A) $20 \sin 40°$
    (B) $20 \cos 40°$

    (C) $\dfrac{20 \sin 40°}{20 \cos 40°}$

    (D) $\dfrac{20 \cos 40°}{20 \sin 40°}$

69. A lever is set up to lift a heavy box, as in the illustration above. The box is set on one end of a board, and a large rock is placed under the board to act as a fulcrum. A force is applied downward at the opposite end of the board to lift the box. The box is at a distance l from the rock, and the force is applied at a distance of $3l$ from the rock. When the box is lifted a distance d at a speed v, what are the distance and speed for the force at the other end?

    (A) The distance is d, and the speed is v.
    (B) The distance is $3d$, and the speed is v.
    (C) The distance is $3d$, and the speed is $3v$.
    (D) The distance is d, and the speed is $3v$.

70. The illustration below shows a pulley system with a fixed pulley attached at the top and a movable pulley at the bottom to which a weight W is attached. A rope is attached to the top pulley, wound around the bottom pulley, and then run up and around the top pulley. Pulling down on the rope in the direction shown with a force F causes the weight to be lifted upward. Assume constant speed and neglect the masses of the pulleys and the rope. When the force F moves downward a distance d, how far upward does the weight move?

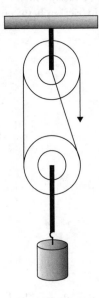

(A) d
(B) $\frac{1}{2}d$
(C) $\frac{1}{4}d$
(D) $2d$

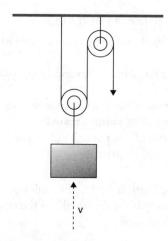

71. The illustration shows a pulley system designed to lift an object of mass m. The system consists of a fixed pulley attached to the ceiling and a movable pulley to which the object is attached. What is the force that a person has to exert downward on the rope in order to lift the object at constant speed?

(A) mg
(B) $\frac{1}{2}mg$
(C) $\frac{1}{4}mg$
(D) $2mg$

72. A father and his two children play a game in which the children sit in a tire swing attached to a single rope that goes over a pulley attached to a tree limb, as shown in the illustration below. The father stands on the ground, pulls down on one end of the rope, and lifts the children sitting in the swing. The children, with a total mass of 40 kg, sit in the swing. With what force does the father pull downward on the rope to lift the children at constant speed?

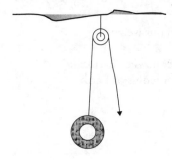

(A) 20 N
(B) 40 N
(C) 400 N
(D) 200 N

73. The gravitational acceleration g on the surface of a planet varies:

    (A) in direct proportion to the planet's mass and in inverse proportion to its radius squared.
    (B) in direct proportion to the planet's radius and in inverse proportion to its mass.
    (C) in direct proportion to the square root of the planet's mass and in inverse proportion to the square root of its radius squared.
    (D) in direct proportion to the square root of the planet's radius and in inverse proportion to the square root of its mass.

74. The weight of an object on the surface of Earth is 40 N. The radius of Earth is approximately 6,400 km. What would be the weight of the object if it were located 6,400 km above Earth's surface?

    (A) 40 N
    (B) 20 N
    (C) 10 N
    (D) 5 N

75. An object with a mass of 60 kg on the surface of Earth is taken to the moon, where the gravitational field value g is one-sixth that on Earth. What is the mass of the object on the surface of the moon?

    (A) 60 kg
    (B) 40 kg
    (C) 30 kg
    (D) 10 kg

76. The theoretical value of g on Earth's surface at the equator, based on the gravitational force between Earth and any object on its surface, is considered to be 9.8 m/s². However, the effective value of g is always slightly less, primarily due to:

    (A) the effects of the sun and moon on our weight.
    (B) the spin of Earth on its axis.
    (C) a lack of knowledge about the exact mass of Earth.
    (D) a lack of knowledge about the exact radius of Earth.

77. Two planets have the same density, but the radius of one of the planets is three times greater than that of the other. An object weighs 30 N on the surface of the smaller planet. What does it weigh on the surface of the larger planet?

    (A) 30 N
    (B) 60 N
    (C) 90 N
    (D) 270 N

78. Assume that the sun's mass is about 300,000 times the mass of Earth and that its radius is about 100 times Earth's radius. Compare the gravitational force on an object near the sun's surface to the gravitational force on the same object near Earth's surface.

    (A) 10,000 times
    (B) 3,000 times
    (C) 300 times
    (D) 30 times

79. Two objects have the same radius, but object B has twice the density of object A. A third object, C, is placed the same distance from object A as from object B. Compare the gravitational forces of objects A and B on object C.

    (A) Object B exerts twice the gravitational force on C.
    (B) Object B exerts half the gravitational force on C.
    (C) Objects A and B exert the same gravitational force on C.
    (D) Object B exerts four times the gravitational force on C.

80. Three objects are positioned along a line. Each has a mass of 2 kg and an x coordinate as shown in the illustration below. Which object has the greatest net gravitational force on it due to the other two objects?

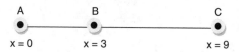

    (A) The net force on A is the greatest.
    (B) The net force on B is the greatest.
    (C) The net force on C is the greatest.
    (D) The net force on each object is the same.

81. Three objects are positioned along a line. Each has a mass and an x coordinate as shown in the illustration below. Where could object B be positioned on the line so that no net gravitational force is exerted on it due to the other two objects?

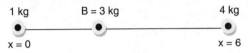

(A) At $x = 2$
(B) Somewhere between $x = 2$ and $x = 4$
(C) At $x = 4$
(D) Somewhere between $x = 4$ and $x = 6$

82. A satellite is in a circular orbit around Earth at an altitude of three Earth radii above the surface. Compare the gravitational force of Earth on the satellite at this altitude to the gravitational force of Earth on the satellite when it is sitting on the surface prior to launch.

(A) There is no gravitational force on the satellite when it is moving in orbit.
(B) The gravitational force is one-half as great in orbit as on the surface of Earth.
(C) The gravitational force is one-quarter as great in orbit as on the surface of Earth.
(D) The gravitational force is one-sixteenth as great in orbit as on the surface of Earth.

83. Binary stars A and B have masses of m and $2m$, respectively. Compare the magnitude of the gravitational force the smaller star exerts on the larger star to the gravitational force the larger star exerts on the smaller star.

(A) 1:1
(B) 1:2
(C) 2:1
(D) 4:1

84. When a satellite is in uniform circular orbit around Earth, what are the forces that must be exerted on the satellite to keep it in orbit?

(A) None; the satellite needs no forces exerted on it to remain in orbit.
(B) Only the gravitational force of Earth on the satellite.
(C) The gravitational force of Earth on the satellite and a horizontal force to keep it moving.
(D) The gravitational force of Earth on the satellite and a centripetal force.

85. A satellite is in circular orbit around Earth at an altitude of three Earth radii above the surface. If the satellite uses onboard retro rockets to cut its speed to one-half, at what distance from Earth can it establish a new stable circular orbit?

    (A) Between two Earth radii and three Earth radii above the surface
    (B) Between three Earth radii and four Earth radii above the surface
    (C) Less than two Earth radii above the surface
    (D) More than four Earth radii above the surface

86. An object is whirled in a vertical circular path by an attached string. For the speed of the object to remain constant at every point, the tension in the string must be:

    (A) kept constant.
    (B) greater when the object is at the top of its path.
    (C) greater when the object is at the bottom of its path.
    (D) zero at the top of its path.

87. As an automobile turns a corner on a level road, the centripetal force necessary to keep the automobile in the turn is provided by:

    (A) the gravitational force of Earth.
    (B) the normal force of the road.
    (C) the friction force of the road.
    (D) inertia.

88. A ball is whirled in a vertical circular path at a speed of 1 m/s. When the ball is at the bottom of the path, the string is cut. The ball will subsequently:

    (A) drop vertically to the floor and hit the floor at a speed greater than 1 m/s.
    (B) drop vertically to the floor and hit the floor at a speed less than 1 m/s.
    (C) take a parabolic path to the floor and hit the floor at 1 m/s.
    (D) take a parabolic path to the floor and hit the floor at a speed greater than 1 m/s.

89. Student A is given a ball of mass m attached to a string of length R and told to whirl the ball on the string in a vertical circle so that its velocity at the top is at a minimum. Student B is given a ball of mass $2m$ attached to a string of length $2R$ and told to whirl the ball so that its speed matches the minimum speed of the ball held by student A at the top of each ball's motion. In order to do this, student B must make sure that the string tension is:

    (A) twice the tension as that in the string held by student A.
    (B) the same as that in the string held by student A.
    (C) ½ the tension as that in the string held by student A.
    (D) It's not possible to match the velocities under these conditions.

90. A nickel is placed on a turntable at a distance 10 cm from the center. When the turntable is set at 60 revolutions per minute, the nickel makes one revolution per second. What is the speed at which the nickel is moving in the circular path?

    (A) $2\pi/3$ m/s
    (B) 0.2π m/s
    (C) $\pi/2$ m/s
    (D) 0.1π m/s

91. A satellite with a mass m is moving at velocity v in a stable circular orbit around Earth, whose radius is R and whose mass is M. Which of the following equations can be used to correctly determine the satellite's altitude h above Earth's surface?

    (A) $\dfrac{GM}{(R+h)} = v^2$

    (B) $\dfrac{GM}{(R+h)} = v$

    (C) $\dfrac{GM}{(R+h)^2} = v^2$

    (D) $\dfrac{GM}{R^2} = v^2$

92. Studies of traffic accidents on a particular curve lead to measures to reduce the number of vehicles going off the curve when the road is slick. Which of the following measures would be most effective in reducing such accidents?

(A) Reducing the speed limit for large vehicles, allowing only small vehicles to travel at regular speed.

(B) Creating a banked curve so that the road slopes downward on the outside of the curve.

(C) Decreasing the radius of the curve so that the distance around the curve is less.

(D) Creating a banked curve so that the road is higher on the outside of the curve.

93. As Earth rotates, the speed of a location on its equator is approximately 1,000 miles per hour. At what latitude would a location have half that speed?

(A) 30°

(B) 60°

(C) 45°

(D) 75°

94. A metal washer is placed on a turntable so that it just stays in place when the turntable is spinning. At this position, the washer is 10 cm from the center and is moving at constant speed. When the washer is positioned farther from the center, it slides off when the turntable is turned on. If the turntable continues to move at the same speed, what must be done to allow the washer to stay in place when it is moved to 12 cm from the center?

(A) Glue another washer on top of the first washer.

(B) Sand the top of the washer so that it has the same surface on the bottom but has less mass.

(C) Put a lubricating oil between the washer and the surface.

(D) There are no changes that can be made under these conditions that would allow the washer to move in a stable circle at a distance greater than 10 cm.

95. As a simple pendulum (an object that has mass and is attached to the end of a string) swings in a circular arc at an amplitude less than 90°, the tension in the string must:

(A) remain constant.

(B) be greatest when the object is at the bottom of its swing.

(C) be least when the object is at the bottom of its swing.

(D) be zero when the object reaches its maximum amplitude during the swing.

96. Which of the following is NOT true regarding a satellite in circular orbit at constant speed around a planet?

(A) The centripetal force on the satellite is always toward the center of the planet.

(B) The satellite exerts the same amount of force on the planet as the planet exerts on the satellite.

(C) The force that the satellite exerts on the planet is in the same ratio to the force that the planet exerts on the satellite as the ratio of their masses.

(D) The acceleration of the satellite as it moves in its orbit is not zero.

97. In the diagram below, a hollow cone is spinning horizontally on its tip and a small object inside the cone takes a circular path without sliding down the interior of the cone. Which of the following statements is a reasonable explanation for this situation?

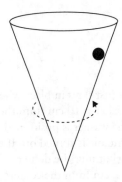

(A) The normal force of the cone on the object has a component toward the center that provides a centripetal force.

(B) The friction force of the cone on the object has a component that provides a centripetal force.

(C) The weight of the object has a component that provides a centripetal force.

(D) The combination of friction and the gravitational force on the object keeps it moving in a circle.

98. An object at the end of a string is whirled in a horizontal circle at constant speed, as in the diagram below. If the mass of the object is 250 g and the angle θ is equal to 60°, which of the following expressions allows you to solve for the tension (T) in the string in newtons?

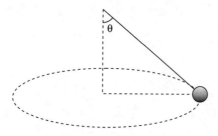

(A) $T = 0.25\, g$

(B) $T = \dfrac{0.25\, g}{\sin 60°}$

(C) $T = \dfrac{0.25\, g}{\cos 60°}$

(D) $T = 0.25\, g \,(\tan 60°)$

99. The moon's mass is about one-sixth that of Earth. Compared to the gravitational force that Earth exerts on the moon, the gravitational force that the moon exerts on Earth is:

(A) one-sixth as much.
(B) one-half as much.
(C) the same.
(D) twice as much.

100. A space shuttle in circular orbit needs to shift to a new orbit in which the astronauts experience a lower value of g. To accomplish this, the shuttle will stabilize in a new orbit:

(A) closer to Earth and at a higher speed.
(B) farther from Earth and at a lower speed.
(C) closer to Earth and at a lower speed.
(D) farther from Earth and at a higher speed.

101. Assume that a piece of space debris is in a circular orbit at a distance r above Earth's surface. If Earth's radius is R and the period of the orbit is T, what is the speed in orbit of the space debris?

(A) $\dfrac{2\pi R}{T}$

(B) $\dfrac{2\pi(R+r)}{T}$

(C) $\dfrac{2\pi r}{T}$

(D) $\dfrac{T}{2\pi r}$

102. A curve with a radius of 80 m is banked (angled with the horizontal) at 10°. Suppose that an ice storm hits and the curve is covered with ice so that it is effectively frictionless. What provides the centripetal force allowing a car to make the turn?

(A) The weight of the car
(B) A component of the friction force perpendicular to the road
(C) A component of the normal force
(D) Inertia

103. A string that is 1.2 m long will break under a force of 120 N. It is used to spin a 2 kg stone in a vertical circle. Which of the following expressions can be used to determine the maximum speed of the stone (without breaking the string)?

(A) $\dfrac{mv^2}{L} = mg$

(B) $120 - mg = \dfrac{mv^2}{L}$

(C) $mg - mv = 120$

(D) $120 = \dfrac{mv^2}{L}$

104. An object with a mass of 2,000 kg moves with a constant speed of 20 m/s on a circular track with a radius of 100 m. What is the magnitude of the acceleration of the object in m/s²?

(A) 400
(B) 80
(C) 40
(D) 4

105. A car goes around a curve of radius *r* at a constant speed *v*. Then it goes around a curve of radius 2*r* at speed 2*v*. What is the centripetal acceleration of the car as it goes around the second curve, compared to the first?

(A) The same.
(B) Twice as great.
(C) Four times greater.
(D) The acceleration cannot be determined without knowing the mass of the car.

106. A stone with a mass of 2 kg is attached to a strong string and whirled in a vertical circle of radius 0.2 m. At the exact bottom of the path, the speed of the stone is 4 m/s. Calculate the tension in the string at this point.

(A) 180 N
(B) 60 N
(C) 30 N
(D) 20 N

107. The radius of the path of an object in uniform circular motion is doubled. For its speed to remain the same, the centripetal force on the object must be:

(A) one-fourth as much as before.
(B) half as great as before.
(C) the same as before.
(D) twice as great as before.

108. An object traveling in a circle at constant speed has:

(A) a constant velocity.
(B) an inward radial acceleration.
(C) an outward radial acceleration.
(D) a constant tangential acceleration.

109. Consider two satellites in circular orbits around Earth but at different distances from Earth. Which of the following statements is true regarding the centripetal accelerations of the satellites?

(A) Both experience the same centripetal acceleration.
(B) The object nearer to Earth experiences the greater centripetal acceleration.
(C) The object farther from Earth experiences the greater centripetal acceleration.
(D) It depends on the masses of the satellites, which are not known.

110. An object has a mass of quantity m and a momentum of quantity p. If the momentum of the object doubles, its kinetic energy is:

(A) the same.
(B) half as much.
(C) twice as much.
(D) four times greater.

111. Which of the following correctly expresses change in velocity?

(A) p/t
(B) Ft
(C) ma/t
(D) p/m

112. On an air track, a 2 kg cart moving at 1 m/s to the right collides with a 1 kg cart moving at 3 m/s to the left. After the collision, the 2 kg cart is moving at 2 m/s to the left. What is the velocity of the 1 kg cart after the collision?

(A) 1 m/s to the right
(B) 1 m/s to the left
(C) 3 m/s to the right
(D) 2 m/s to the left

113. Object A, which is moving to the right at speed $2v$, collides head-on and totally inelastically with an identical object B moving to the left at speed $4v$. What occurs after the collision?

(A) Object A moves to the right at v, and object B moves to the left at $2v$.
(B) Object A moves to the right at $2v$, and object B moves to the left at v.
(C) The objects move together to the right at speed v.
(D) The objects move together to the left at speed v.

114. Two skaters stand face to face on the ice. Skater 1 has a mass of 40 kg, and skater 2 has a mass of 50 kg. They push off one another and move in opposite directions. What is the ratio of skater 1's speed to skater 2's speed?

(A) 1:1
(B) 1:2
(C) 4:5
(D) 5:4

115. A cart rolls across a level floor and strikes a wall elastically at 10 m/s. In a second trial, the cart strikes the wall at 20 m/s. Assuming that the contact time between the cart and the wall is the same in both cases, compare the force that the cart exerts on the wall in the second trial to the force that it exerts in the first trial.

(A) The same
(B) Half as much
(C) Twice as much
(D) Four times greater

116. A cart on a level air track is moving at +2 m/s when it strikes and connects to a stationary cart of the same mass. What is the final velocity of the connected carts?

(A) +4 m/s
(B) +2 m/s
(C) +1 m/s
(D) −1 m/s

117. An experiment is set up with motion sensor A at one end of an air track and motion sensor B at the other end. Chart A below shows velocity versus time for cart A, which has a mass of 1 kg and moves away from sensor A, and chart B below shows velocity versus time for chart B, which also has a mass of 1 kg and moves away from sensor B and toward cart A. What is the force exerted by the carts on each other?

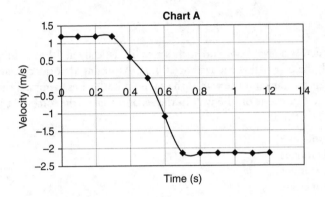

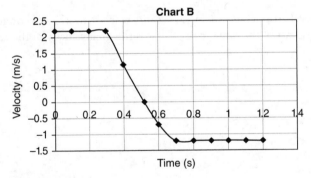

(A) 5.0 N
(B) 7.5 N
(C) 11.0 N
(D) 12.5 N

118. The rate at which momentum changes is:

(A) impulse.
(B) kinetic energy.
(C) force.
(D) acceleration.

119. The graph below shows the force exerted on a tennis ball during a collision with a tennis racket.

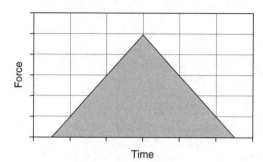

The area between the plot line and the time axis represents:

(A) the acceleration of the tennis ball while it is in contact with the racket.
(B) the change in momentum of the tennis ball when it hits the racket.
(C) the change in velocity of the tennis ball when it hits the racket.
(D) the work done by the tennis ball on the racket when it hits the racket.

120. A car moving at a speed v is brought to rest in time t by a force F_1. To stop the car in one-half the time (½t), what force F_2 is required?

(A) Force F_2 must be twice as large as F_1.
(B) Force F_2 must be half as large as F_1.
(C) Force F_2 must be one-fourth as large as F_1.
(D) The forces required to stop the car are the same in both situations.

121. When automobiles have to stop quickly, injury to occupants can be reduced by using air bags. What is the primary mechanism by which an air bag reduces injury?

(A) An air bag increases the time it takes to stop the person, so the force on the person is less.
(B) An air bag increases the distance over which the person comes to a stop, so the acceleration is smaller.
(C) An air bag is soft, so it absorbs the force of the impact.
(D) An air bag applies a force on the person in the opposite direction from the force that the car is exerting on the person, so the net force on the person is less.

122. The graph below represents the collision of an object of mass 0.25 kg with a wall. Determine the magnitude of the change in velocity of the object during the impact.

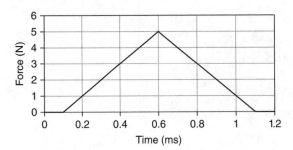

(A) 10 m/s
(B) 1.0 m/s
(C) 0.01 m/s
(D) 0.001 m/s

123. A baseball is thrown toward a target at a speed v and exerts a force F on the target when it collides with it. What is the force exerted on the target if the speed of the baseball is doubled on the second throw?

(A) $\frac{1}{2}F$
(B) F
(C) $2F$
(D) $4F$

124. Which of the following properties are conserved in a totally inelastic collision of two objects, in the absence of external forces on the system of objects?

(A) Only momentum
(B) Only kinetic energy
(C) Both momentum and kinetic energy
(D) Neither momentum nor kinetic energy

125. Which statement is NOT always true for changes in the linear momentum of a system?

(A) There is a change in the velocity of the system.
(B) A net external force must be exerted on the system.
(C) The center of mass of the system changes position.
(D) Either or both the magnitude and direction of momentum change.

126. Which of the following statements is always true for inelastic collisions, assuming that there is no external force applied in the direction of motion?

(A) Momentum is conserved, but kinetic energy is not conserved.
(B) Kinetic energy is conserved, but momentum is not conserved.
(C) Both momentum and kinetic energy are conserved.
(D) Energy is not conserved, but the objects exchange velocities during the collision.

127. In the illustration below, a particle of mass m_1 moving at speed v along the x axis collides elastically with a stationary particle that has a mass of m_2. After the collision, the mass m_1 is moving at speed v_1 at an angle θ above the x axis, and mass m_2 is moving at speed v_2 at an angle φ below the x axis. If the two masses are equal and there are no external forces exerted on the system of particles, then:

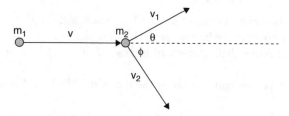

(A) speed v_1 must equal speed v_2.
(B) angle θ must equal angle φ.
(C) $\theta + \varphi$ must equal 90°.
(D) speed v must equal $v_1 + v_2$.

128. During an inelastic collision, kinetic energy of the system is lost because kinetic energy:

(A) is changed to other forms of energy.
(B) must decrease as momentum increases.
(C) cannot be conserved during any collision.
(D) decreases any time a force is applied to a system.

129. When two moving objects of equal mass collide head-on and elastically, they will:

(A) simultaneously come to a stop.
(B) exchange velocities during the collision.
(C) each have the same velocity after the collision as before the collision.
(D) move off at right angles to each other after the collision.

130. A photon of light collides with a stationary electron. Using conservation of linear momentum and conservation of mass-energy principles, what is the expected result?

    (A) The electron recoils with kinetic energy K, and a photon with a longer wavelength is produced.
    (B) The electron recoils with kinetic energy K, and a photon with a shorter wavelength is produced.
    (C) The electron recoils with kinetic energy K, and the photon retains its previous speed and wavelength after the collision.
    (D) The electron remains stationary, and the photon rebounds from it with a shorter wavelength.

131. You are given several small objects, all of the same mass, to throw at an upright block of wood in order to knock it over. To have the best chance of accomplishing this, you will choose:

    (A) a small dart, thrown at the top of the block so that it sticks in the wood.
    (B) a small dart, thrown at the bottom of the block so that it does not stick.
    (C) a small, elastic rubber ball, thrown at the base of the block so that it bounces.
    (D) a small, elastic rubber ball, thrown at the top of the block so that it bounces.

132. A rubber ball drops from a height of 2 m onto a concrete floor and rebounds to a height of 1 m. What is the coefficient of restitution between the ball and the floor?

    (A) 0.25
    (B) 0.50
    (C) 0.70
    (D) 0.90

133. In an experiment, students launch a ball with velocity v_0 so that it hits a force sensor horizontally. The sensor registers the force, F. Which of the following expressions could be used to determine the final velocity of the ball of mass m after it collides elastically with the sensor during a time t?

    (A) $v = \dfrac{Ft}{m} + v_0$

    (B) $v = \dfrac{Ftv_0}{m}$

    (C) $v = \dfrac{mF}{v_0 t}$

    (D) $v = \dfrac{Fm}{t} + v_0$

134. A small rocket is fired into the air and lands 30 m forward from the launch site. The rocket is fired a second time at the same velocity and angle. This time, the rocket splits into two pieces at the peak of its motion. The first piece lands on the ground 27 m forward from the launch site. Where would the second piece, which has half the mass of the first piece, land?

(A) 24 m forward from the launch site
(B) 30 m forward from the launch site
(C) 33 m forward from the launch site
(D) 36 m forward from the launch site

135. Ball 1, rolling on a level, frictionless table, strikes an identical stationary ball 2, which takes the path shown in the illustration below after the collision. What would be the path of ball 1 after the collision?

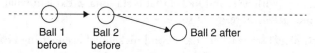

Ball 1   Ball 2   Ball 2 after
before   before

(A) →
(B) ↙
(C) ↗
(D) Ball 1 is stationary after the collision.

136. A ball is dropped onto the floor from height h and bounces with velocity $-v$ after it hits the floor. The coefficient of restitution between the ball and the floor (the magnitude of the ratio of the ball's velocity after it returns from the floor to its velocity before it hits the floor) is 0.5. If the ball is then dropped from height $2h$, what is its velocity after it hits the floor the second time, assuming that the coefficient of restitution is the same?

(A) ½v
(B) v
(C) $2v$
(D) $4v$

137. Two carts have the same mass. Cart A, moving to the right on a track at 6 m/s, collides elastically with cart B, moving to the left on the track at 4 m/s. What are the velocities of cart A and cart B after they collide?

(A) Cart A is moving to the left at 5 m/s, and cart B is moving to the right at 5 m/s.
(B) Cart A is moving to the left at 6 m/s, and cart B is moving to the right at 4 m/s.
(C) Cart A is moving to the left at 4 m/s, and cart B is moving to the right at 6 m/s.
(D) The two carts are moving together to the right at 5 m/s.

138. A nickel sliding on a smooth surface collides elastically and head-on with a second nickel that is stationary. What is the motion of the nickels after the collision?

(A) The first nickel stops where the second nickel had been sitting, and the second nickel moves off in a straight line with the first nickel's velocity.

(B) The first nickel bounces back and moves backward in a straight line with velocity equal to the negative of its initial velocity.

(C) Both nickels move forward along a line, with the first nickel moving more slowly than the second nickel.

(D) Both nickels move ahead along trajectories that are perpendicular to each other.

139. A nickel sliding on a smooth surface with momentum mv collides elastically and head-on with a second nickel that is stationary. Explain what happens to the nickels in terms of force.

(A) The first nickel stops where the second nickel had been sitting because the force that the second nickel exerts on the first nickel changes the momentum from mv to zero.

(B) The first nickel bounces back and moves backward in a straight line with velocity equal to the negative of its initial velocity because the force that the second nickel exerts is equal to $2mv$.

(C) Both nickels move forward along a line, with the first nickel moving more slowly than the second nickel, because the first nickel exerts more force on the second nickel, causing a large change in momentum.

(D) Both nickels move ahead along trajectories that are perpendicular to each other because the force is along the line of motion of the first nickel.

140. Two spring-loaded carts are in contact with each other, with springs loaded, on an elevated section of track, as in the illustration below. Cart A has twice the mass of cart B. When the spring is released:

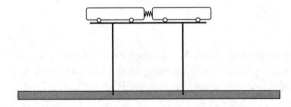

(A) cart A moves horizontally with greater velocity and hits the ground first.

(B) cart B moves horizontally with greater velocity and hits the ground first.

(C) cart B moves horizontally with less velocity and hits the ground first.

(D) cart B moves horizontally with greater velocity, and the carts hit the ground at the same time.

141. An object with a mass of 2 kg moving north at 5 m/s collides totally inelastically with an object having a mass of 4 kg that is moving west at 10 m/s. What is the result of this collision?

(A) The 4 kg object moves south at 5 m/s, and the 2 kg object moves east at 10 m/s.
(B) A 6 kg object moves southeast at 50 m/s.
(C) A 6 kg object moves southeast at about 40 m/s.
(D) A 6 kg object moves northwest at about 40 m/s.

142. In the laboratory, a 1.5 kg cart moving to the right on a track at 2 m/s collides with a 2.0 kg cart moving to the left at 2 m/s. After the collision, the 1.5 kg cart is moving to the left at 1 m/s. Determine the loss to thermal energy during this collision.

(A) 3 J
(B) 6 J
(C) 12 J
(D) 18 J

143. In the laboratory, a 1.5 kg cart moving to the right on a track at 2 m/s collides totally inelastically with a 2.0 kg cart moving to the left at 2 m/s. Determine the loss to thermal energy during this collision.

(A) 0.2 J
(B) 4.4 J
(C) 6.8 J
(D) 12 J

144. In an experiment, a small block slides down a track and hits a second, identical block at the edge of a desk 1 m above the floor. The first block is moving horizontally when it hits the stationary block, and the two collide off-center. As a result, the two blocks hit the floor moving in different directions. The first block hits the floor a distance of 0.5 m at an angle of 35° from the centerline (a line along the original trajectory of the first block), and the second block hits the floor a distance of 0.25 m at an angle of 55° from the centerline. What was the speed of the first block when it hit the second block on the track?

(A) 0.51 m/s
(B) 1.2 m/s
(C) 2.2 m/s
(D) 4.4 m/s

145. In an experiment, a small block slides down a smooth track and hits a second, identical block at the edge of a desk. The first block is moving horizontally when it hits the stationary block, and the two collide off-center. As a result, the two blocks hit the floor moving in different directions. Which of the following statements can be used to determine the speed of the moving block before the collision and the speeds of the two blocks immediately after the collision?

    (A) Linear momentum is conserved during the collision, and kinetic energy is conserved after the collision.
    (B) Both linear momentum and kinetic energy are conserved in all three dimensions.
    (C) Linear momentum is conserved during the collision and after the collision until the blocks hit the floor.
    (D) Linear momentum is conserved during the collision but is not conserved as the blocks fall to the floor.

146. A firecracker with a mass of 6 g is sitting on top of a level table. The firecracker explodes into three pieces, with masses 1 g, 2 g, and 3 g. All the pieces move in different directions at the same speed. (This won't happen often!) Which of the following illustrations shows possible velocity vectors for the three pieces?

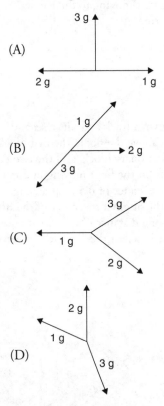

147. In which of the following situations must the net force on the object be zero?

  (A) A box is sliding down a frictionless ramp after being released at the top of the ramp.
  (B) A satellite is moving at constant speed in a circular orbit.
  (C) A box is sliding at constant speed across a level surface.
  (D) A hammer is falling to the surface of the moon after being released by an astronaut.

148. Three tension wires are attached to the top of a fence post. The tension wires are then attached to the ground so that the fence post remains stationary. Wire 1 has a tension of 1,000 N, is attached to the east side of the post, and makes a 60° angle with the ground. Wire 2 has a tension of 2,000 N, is attached to the north side of the post, and also makes a 60° angle with the ground. Which of the following equations could be used to calculate the tension in wire 3?

  (A) $T\cos 60° = \sqrt{(1,000\cos 60°)^2 + (2,000\cos 60°)^2}$

  (B) $T = \sqrt{(1,000)^2 + (2,000)^2}$

  (C) $T\cos 45° = \sqrt{(1,000\sin 60°)^2 + (2,000\cos 60°)^2}$

  (D) $T\cos 45° = \sqrt{(1,000)^2 + (2,000)^2}$

149. A box that weighs 10 N is sitting on a ramp that is angled at 30° above the horizontal. What is the friction force of the ramp on the box in newtons?

  (A) 10
  (B) 10 cos 30°
  (C) 10 sin 30°
  (D) 10 tan 30°

150. A ladder has a mass of 6 kg and is 2 m long. As shown in the illustration below, the ladder remains stable against a frictionless wall with its bottom end 1 m from the base of the wall. Rank the following: the weight of the ladder (W), the normal force of the wall on the ladder (N_w), the normal force of the floor on the ladder (N_F), and the friction force of the floor on the ladder (f).

    (A) $W > N_F > N_w > f$
    (B) $W = N_F > f = N_w$
    (C) $W > f = N_F > N_w$
    (D) $W = f > N_F = N_w$

151. An object is attached to a spring and set into oscillation. The system is in equilibrium:

    (A) at its amplitude because the instantaneous velocity is zero.
    (B) when it is moving at its greatest speed.
    (C) when its displacement is maximum.
    (D) when its instantaneous acceleration is maximum.

152. A Ping-Pong ball is dropped from the top of a building. As it falls, it will reach terminal velocity when:

    (A) the air drag force becomes greater than the weight of the ball.
    (B) the vertical forces on the ball reach equilibrium so that acceleration will be zero.
    (C) the force accelerating the ball reaches its maximum.
    (D) the final velocity of the ball is zero.

153. An oscillating pendulum is considered to be in translational equilibrium at the lowest point in its motion. Which of the following statements must be true?

(A) The tension in the pendulum string must be equal to the weight of the pendulum bob.

(B) The horizontal force accelerating the pendulum at the bottom of its swing must be equal to the air drag force on the pendulum bob.

(C) The tension in the pendulum string must be equal to mg times the sine of the angle from which the pendulum bob was released to start the motion.

(D) The tension in the pendulum string must be equal to the weight of the pendulum bob plus the centripetal force due to the pendulum's motion.

154. In order for a sled to slide at constant speed down an icy hill,

(A) the friction force backward must be equal to the inertial force propelling the sled forward.

(B) the friction force must be zero since there is no force propelling the sled forward.

(C) there must be a friction force to balance the gravitational force directed down the hill.

(D) there must be no friction force in this situation.

155. A force of 100 N is applied to a wheel, as shown in the illustration below. The radius of the wheel is 20 cm, and the radius of the axle is 5 cm. For the wheel to rotate at constant speed, determine the torque and direction of the friction force applied to the axle.

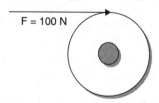

(A) 1.25 N·m clockwise

(B) 1.25 N·m counterclockwise

(C) 20 N·m clockwise

(D) 20 N·m counterclockwise

156. Several meter sticks are stacked on the edge of a table so that the top meter stick is entirely beyond the edge of the table, as shown in the illustration below. In order for this to occur:

(A) the center of the top stick must be above the stick below it.
(B) the center of each stick must be above the table.
(C) the center of mass of the entire system of sticks must be at the edge of the table.
(D) the left end of the top stick must be directly above the edge of the table.

157. When a car is driving across the pavement, which of the following statements best explains what causes the car to move forward?

(A) As the wheels roll, they exert a forward force on the pavement to cause the car to move forward.
(B) The friction force from the pavement on the tires is forward.
(C) The normal force of the pavement on the tires produces a torque that causes the tires to roll.
(D) As the wheels roll forward, they exert a forward force on the car.

158. The diameter of a car's steering wheel is about 30 cm, and the diameter of a truck's steering wheel is 40 cm. Assuming that your applied force is the same for both steering wheels, by what percentage does your applied torque increase if you are driving the truck rather than the car?

(A) 10
(B) 15
(C) 25
(D) 33

159. An acrobat performs the "trick" of walking on a loose board laid on top of a flat roof so that one-third of its length is beyond the edge of the roof. If the length of the board is 12 ft, the mass of the board is 20 kg, and the mass of the acrobat is 60 kg, how far from the edge of the roof can he stand safely?

(A) 3 ft
(B) 2.5 ft
(C) 1 ft
(D) 8 in

160. The distance of a bicycle pedal from the axle is about 18 cm. If a bicycle rider with a mass of 50 kg exerts all of his weight on the pedal, what is the torque applied at the point where the pedal is farthest forward and horizontal?

(A) 50 N·m
(B) 100 N·m
(C) 500 N·m
(D) 1,000 N·m

161. The distance from a person's elbow to his clenched fist is 30 cm. If the person slowly lifts a 5 kg object from horizontal by bending at the elbow, what is the torque exerted at the elbow?

(A) 10 N·m
(B) 15 N·m
(C) 100 N·m
(D) 150 N·m

162. In the illustration below, the rod is 1 m long and has a mass of 200 g. The pivot is 20 cm to the left of the center of the rod. The object on the left end of the rod has a mass of 1 kg, and the object on the right end has a mass of 500 g. What is the net torque on the rod?

(A) 0.9 N·m clockwise
(B) 3.5 N·m clockwise
(C) 3.5 N·m counterclockwise
(D) 20 N·m counterclockwise

163. For an object or system to be in equilibrium,

(A) the object or system must be stationary.
(B) the net force on the object or system must equal zero.
(C) the net torque on the object or system must equal zero.
(D) both the net force and the net torque on the object or system must equal zero.

Refer to the illustration below for questions 164 and 165.

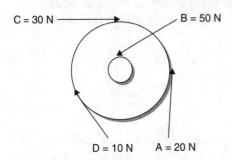

164. The illustration above shows a top view of a wheel and axle system, with forces A, B, C, and D applied at a tangent in each case. The radius of the wheel is 10 cm, and the radius of the axle is 2 cm. What is the net torque on the wheel?

   (A) 1 N·m clockwise
   (B) 1 N·m counterclockwise
   (C) 10 N·m clockwise
   (D) 10 N·m counterclockwise

165. The illustration above shows a top view of a wheel and axle system, with four forces applied to it so that the forces produce torques. Each force is assumed to be applied at a tangent to either the wheel or the axle. The wheel has a radius of 0.3 m, and the axle has a diameter of 0.1 m. If the wheel and axle system has a rotational inertia of 4 kg·m², what is the angular acceleration of the system?

   (A) 0.25 rad/s² clockwise

   (B) 0.50 rad/s² counterclockwise

   (C) 1.0 rad/s² clockwise

   (D) 2.0 rad/s² counterclockwise

166. In the illustration below, a fulcrum is placed at a point one-third the length of a rod from its left end, a 6 kg mass is attached to the left end of the rod, and a 2 kg mass is attached to the right end. To produce rotational equilibrium, a third mass (1 kg) should be attached:

(A) to the left end of the rod.
(B) halfway between the fulcrum and the right end of the rod.
(C) halfway between the fulcrum and the left end of the rod.
(D) to the right end of the rod.

167. A bridge, supported by two piers, one at each end, is 20 m long and has a mass of 20,000 kg. A 2,000 kg car is sitting on the bridge 5 m from the center. How much force is each pier exerting upward to support the bridge?

(A) 200,000 N and 20,000 N
(B) 150,000 N and 70,000 N
(C) 110,000 N and 110,000 N
(D) 105,000 N and 115,000 N

168. Two masses hang from the uniform meter stick in the illustration below: a mass of 800 g at the 15-cm mark and a mass of 350 g at the 70-cm mark. The meter stick balances horizontally on a pivot placed at the 35-cm mark. What is the mass of the meter stick?

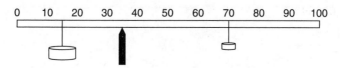

(A) 100 g
(B) 125 g
(C) 200 g
(D) 250 g

169. The meter stick in the illustration below has a mass of 0.5 kg. With a 1 kg mass hanging 0.25 m from the top end, the meter stick remains stable against a frictionless wall with its bottom end 0.50 m from the base of the wall. What is the force exerted on the stick by the floor?

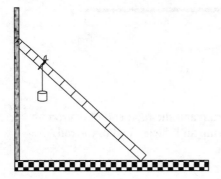

(A) 3 N
(B) 6 N
(C) 8 N
(D) 9 N

170. A screwdriver that is 12 cm long is used to pry open the lid of a paint can. The person doing this applies a downward force of 100 N at the handle end of the screwdriver and supports the screwdriver on the edge of the can 1 cm from the screwdriver's tip. What is the force required to lift open the paint can without the screwdriver?

(A) 120 N
(B) 1,100 N
(C) 2,000 N
(D) 11,000 N

171. In the illustration below, a wire with tension T helps support a horizontal wooden beam with mass M that has a sign of mass m attached to its end. The beam has a length L and is attached to the wall so that the wire makes a 40° angle. Which of the following expressions could be used to determine the tension in the wire?

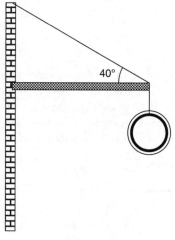

(A) $T \sin 40° = Mg + mg$
(B) $mgL + Mg(\frac{1}{2}L) = T(L \sin 40°)$
(C) $mgL + Mg(\frac{1}{2}L) = T(L \cos 40°)$
(D) $T \cos 40° = Mg + mg$

172. The ladder in the illustration below has a mass of 6 kg and is 2 m long. The ladder is stable against a frictionless wall with its bottom positioned 1 m from the base of the wall. Determine the coefficient of friction between the ladder and the floor.

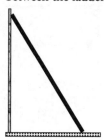

(A) 7 N
(B) 10 N
(C) 13 N
(D) 17 N

173. A meter stick with a mass of 100 g balances when a pivot is placed at the middle (on the 50 cm mark). When an unknown object is placed at the 80 cm mark, the pivot must be moved to the 60 cm mark for the system to balance. What is the mass of the unknown object?

(A) 10 g
(B) 50 g
(C) 100 g
(D) 200 g

174. A student is attempting to construct a mobile that balances various objects on sticks so that it is in equilibrium. In the illustration below, each stick is uniform, is 40 cm long, and has a mass of 10 g; the distance of an attachment from the center of the stick is noted. Determine the mass of the last object that can be attached to the mobile to make it balance.

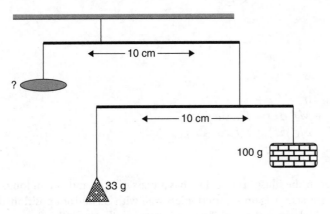

(A) 40 g
(B) 200 g
(C) 440 g
(D) 4,000 g

175. In the illustration, three objects are suspended from a horizontal rod with a pivot. Object 1 has a mass of 1 kg, object 2 has a mass of 2 kg, and object 3 has a mass of 3 kg. The distances given in the answers below are measured from the point of attachment of each object to the rod. Which of the following arrangements would result in a balanced system?

	Object 1	Object 2	Object 3
(A)	1.0 m	0.5 m	0.5 m
(B)	1.0 m	0.5 m	2.0 m
(C)	2.0 m	1.0 m	0.5 m
(D)	2.0 m	2.0 m	2.0 m

176. An object is dropped from a height of 10 m above the ground. What is the ratio of the kinetic energy of the object when it has fallen halfway to the ground to its kinetic energy just before it hits the ground?

(A) 2:1
(B) 1:1
(C) 1:2
(D) 1:4

177. An object is attached to a spring, and the system is set into motion, oscillating vertically. Which of the following statements is true regarding the motion of the object at the lowest point of its oscillation?

(A) The object's velocity and acceleration are equal to zero.
(B) The object's velocity and displacement from equilibrium are both maximum.
(C) The object's acceleration is equal to zero, and its displacement is a maximum.
(D) The object's velocity is equal to zero, and its displacement is a maximum.

CHAPTER 3

Work and Energy

178. What happens to the kinetic energy of a space vehicle moving in circular orbit around Earth when the vehicle transfers into an orbit farther from the center of Earth?

(A) Its kinetic energy increases because the vehicle now has less gravitational potential energy.

(B) Its kinetic energy increases because more work must be done by gravity to keep it in the higher orbit.

(C) Its kinetic energy decreases because the vehicle does not move as fast in its orbit when it is farther from Earth.

(D) Its kinetic energy decreases because the gravitational potential energy is less, and they must remain equal to each other.

179. A 0.5 kg rock is thrown at a speed of 5 m/s horizontally from the top of a building 20 m tall. What is the kinetic energy of the rock when it hits the ground?

(A) 6.3 J

(B) 100 J

(C) 112 J

(D) 160 J

180. An automobile with a mass of 2,000 kg accelerates from a speed of 10 m/s to a speed of 20 m/s in a time period of 6 s. What is the change in kinetic energy of the vehicle during this time period?

(A) 1,000 J
(B) 6,000 J
(C) 20,000 J
(D) 300,000 J

181. An electron is accelerated from rest to a speed of 6×10^6 m/s by an electric potential difference of 12 V. Determine the kinetic energy of the electron.

(A) 7.2×10^6 eV
(B) 12 eV
(C) 1.9×10^{-18} eV
(D) 9.6×10^6 eV

182. Which of the following is NOT a unit that could be used to measure kinetic energy?

(A) Joule
(B) Erg
(C) Electron volt
(D) Watt

183. Which of the following illustrations best represents a plot of kinetic energy versus time for an object thrown horizontally from the top of a building?

(A)

(B)

(C)

(D)

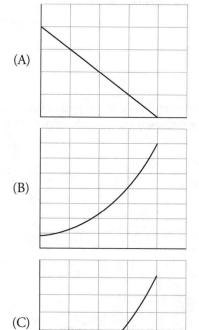

184. A block with a mass of 2 kg is moving at a speed of 3 m/s when it slides horizontally off a roof that is 4 m above the ground. The kinetic energy of the block just before it hits the ground is approximately:

(A) 9 J.
(B) 20 J.
(C) 80 J.
(D) 90 J.

185. A 2 kg ball that is dropped from a height of 4 m loses 10% of its mechanical energy to thermal energy when it hits the floor. What is the kinetic energy of the ball just after it rebounds from the floor?

(A) 48 J
(B) 64 J
(C) 72 J
(D) 88 J

186. Which of the following could be the plot of kinetic energy as a function of height above the ground for an object thrown horizontally from the top of a building?

(A)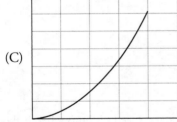

(B)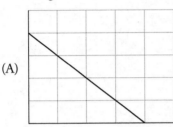

(C)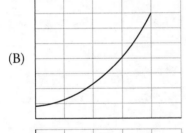

(D)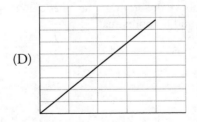

187. A rock with mass m is thrown horizontally at a speed v from the top of a building of height h. What is the kinetic energy of the rock just before it hits the ground?

(A) mgh
(B) $\frac{1}{2}mv^2$
(C) $mgh - \frac{1}{2}mv^2$
(D) $\frac{1}{2}mv^2 + mgh$

188. In the illustration below, two objects of unequal mass (20 g and 30 g) are suspended by a string over a pulley. Assuming negligible masses for the pulley and the string, determine the change in gravitational potential energy of the smaller object (with respect to Earth) after the system is released and the larger object moves downward a distance of 0.1 m.

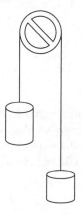

(A) 10 J
(B) 20 J
(C) 0.02 J
(D) 0.01 J

189. What is the ratio of the gravitational potential energy of an Earth-object system when the object is on the surface of Earth to the gravitational potential energy of the same system when the object is two Earth radii above the surface?

(A) 1:2
(B) 1:3
(C) 1:4
(D) 1:9

190. As Earth moves closer to the sun in its orbit (toward perihelion), the gravitational potential energy of the Earth-sun system is:

(A) greater since the two objects are closer together and gravitational forces are greater.

(B) greater since the speed of Earth is greater and both potential energy and kinetic energy increase.

(C) less since kinetic energy is greater and the sum must be constant.

(D) less since the two objects are closer and both potential energy and kinetic energy must decrease.

191. The gravitational potential energy of a system of two particles is equal to U. In a second system, the mass of each particle is twice as great, and the distance between their centers is half as great. What is the gravitational potential energy of the second system in terms of U?

(A) $\frac{1}{2}U$

(B) $2U$

(C) $4U$

(D) $8U$

192. A 40 g object is attached to a spring with spring constant $k = 200$ N/m. Compare the potential energy of the spring-object system when the spring is extended 0.01 m beyond the equilibrium position to the system's potential energy when the spring is extended twice as far, to 0.02 m beyond equilibrium.

(A) 1:1

(B) 1:2

(C) 1:4

(D) 1:16

193. A flexible plastic ruler is held securely by one end on the top of a table. The loose end of the ruler is bent horizontally a distance of 5 cm, and a 0.1 kg rock is placed against it. When the ruler is released and the rock is propelled off the edge of the table, it is determined that the rock has a speed of 2 m/s. Determine the elastic constant, k, of the ruler.

(A) 8 N/m

(B) 16 N/m

(C) 80 N/m

(D) 160 N/m

194. The graph below shows data for amplitude as a function of time for an object with a mass of 0.5 kg oscillating on a spring. At which of the following times is the spring potential energy at a maximum?

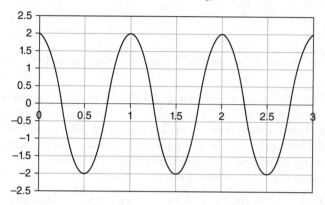

(A) $t = 0.25$ s
(B) $t = 0.50$ s
(C) $t = 1.75$ s
(D) $t = 2.75$ s

195. A spring attached to an object with a mass of 2 kg oscillates according to the equation

$$x(t) = (0.4\ m)\cos 10\ t$$

Determine the elastic constant of the spring.

(A) 10 N/m
(B) 20 N/m
(C) 100 N/m
(D) 200 N/m

196. A spring is placed on a horizontal, frictionless surface and compressed a distance of 0.1 m from its rest position with a ball of mass 0.1 kg placed at its end. When the spring is released, the ball leaves the spring traveling at 10 m/s. What is the spring constant?

(A) 50 N/m
(B) 100 N/m
(C) 500 N/m
(D) 1,000 N/m

197. If a mass oscillating on a spring is halfway between its amplitude position and its equilibrium position, how does its speed compare to the maximum speed (v_{max}) of the mass when it passes the equilibrium position?

(A) $0.25\ v_{max}$
(B) $0.5\ v_{max}$
(C) $0.7\ v_{max}$
(D) The answer can't be determined without knowing the spring constant.

198. Students place a ball at the top of a ramp and allow it to roll to the bottom. The linear speed of the ball is determined by how far from the end of the ramp the ball lands on the floor below. The calculated value for kinetic energy at the bottom of the ramp is significantly less than the gravitational potential energy change from the top to the bottom of the ramp. What is the most reasonable explanation for this discrepancy?

(A) The work done by the gravitational force on the ball reduces the amount of gravitational potential energy converted to translational kinetic energy.
(B) Some of the gravitational potential energy was converted to rotational kinetic energy.
(C) The work done by the friction force on the ball converted a significant amount of mechanical energy to thermal energy.
(D) Thermal energy was transferred to the ball from the ramp.

199. A 2 kg object slides 30 m down a snow-covered (frictionless) hill to a point that is 10 m lower on the hill. What is the work done by the gravitational force on the object?

(A) 20 J
(B) 60 J
(C) 200 J
(D) 600 J

200. The graph below displays data for a force applied to a spring. How much work is done on the spring by the applied force in extending the spring a distance of 2 m?

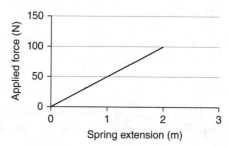

(A) 50 J
(B) 100 J
(C) 200 J
(D) The work cannot be determined without knowing the elastic constant of the spring.

201. A 1,000 kg car is moving at a constant speed of 10 m/s on a level, circular track with a radius of 50 m. How much work is done by the centripetal force on the car (in this case, the friction between the tires and the road)?

(A) 50,000 J
(B) 20,000 J
(C) 2,500 J
(D) No work is done by the centripetal force.

202. Which of the following expressions correctly describes the work done *by friction* on a box of mass m sliding a distance d across a level floor? The coefficient of kinetic friction between the box and the table is μ.

(A) μmd
(B) $-\mu mgd$
(C) μmgd
(D) $-\mu gd$

203. A box of mass m is being pushed a distance d across a level surface at constant speed. In which of the following cases would the most work be done by a force F on the box?

(A) The force F is horizontal and parallel to the floor.
(B) The force F is at a 30° angle to the floor.
(C) The force F is at a 45° angle to the floor.
(D) The force F is at a 60° angle to the floor.

204. On a curved, level roadway with a radius of 100 m, the suggested speed limit is 25 mph (approximately 10 m/s). To safely negotiate the curve at the posted speed, what must the coefficient of friction be between a car's tires and the road?

(A) 0.1
(B) 0.2
(C) 0.3
(D) 0.4

205. An arrow moving at 10 m/s is stopped by a target. If the arrow has a mass of 250 g and penetrates 4 cm into the target, what is the force exerted by the arrow on the target?

(A) 1,250 N
(B) 425 N
(C) 310 N
(D) 25 N

206. A ball with a mass of 250 g is thrown horizontally at a speed of 4 m/s from the top of a platform that is 10 m high. What is the speed of the ball when it hits the ground?

(A) 4 m/s
(B) 8 m/s
(C) 11 m/s
(D) 15 m/s

207. A box with a mass of 6 kg and initially moving at 2 m/s slides a distance of 1 m across a rough floor to a stop. Which of the following values best estimates the coefficient of friction between the box and the floor?

(A) 0.05
(B) 0.1
(C) 0.2
(D) 0.4

208. Students set up a box race in which two boxes are allowed to slide down a ramp so that they are moving at the same speed when they reach the floor. The boxes are identical, except that box A contains one book and box B is filled with books so that its mass is 10 times the mass of box A. The distance each box travels across the floor after leaving the ramp is compared, and the box that travels farther is declared the winner. Which box will win the competition?

(A) Box A.
(B) Box B.
(C) It will be a tie; that is, the boxes will travel the same distance across the floor.
(D) The outcome cannot be determined without knowing the density of the contents of each box.

209. The graph below shows data for amplitude as a function of time for an object with a mass of 0.5 kg oscillating on a spring. During which of the following time intervals does the spring do the largest magnitude of net work on the object attached to it?

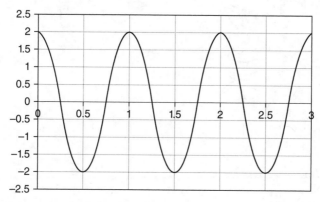

(A) $t = 0$ to $t = 0.5$ s
(B) $t = 0$ to $t = 1.0$ s
(C) $t = 2.5$ to $t = 2.75$ s
(D) $t = 1.0$ to $t = 1.5$ s

210. A horizontal spring with a spring constant of 200 N/m is placed on a horizontal surface and attached at one end to a wall. A block with a mass of 0.5 kg is used to compress the spring a distance of 5 cm. If the mass of the spring is negligible and the coefficient of friction between the block and the surface is 0.02, determine the speed of the block at the moment it loses contact with the spring.

(A) 1 m/s
(B) 0.5 m/s
(C) 0.1 m/s
(D) 0.02 m/s

211. Students want to determine the spring constant of a spring in a small pop-up toy, as shown in the illustration below. They assume that the mass of the small plastic top of the toy is negligible. When the students put a 20 g glob of putty on the toy, then push the toy down 1 cm and release it, the spring causes the toy to move an upward distance of 8 cm. This is just one trial in a larger set of trials using varying amounts of putty. Using a preliminary calculation from this trial, what would the students predict for the spring constant?

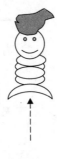

(A) 80 N/m
(B) 160 N/m
(C) 320 N/m
(D) 480 N/m

212. What is the work done in placing a satellite of mass m in orbit at a distance R from Earth's center?

(A) The work is equal to the weight of the satellite plus the kinetic energy of the satellite.
(B) The work is equal to the gravitational potential energy of the satellite at that altitude above Earth's surface.
(C) The work is equal to the gravitational potential energy of the satellite plus the centripetal force necessary to keep the satellite in orbit at that altitude.
(D) The work is equal to the change in gravitational potential energy of the satellite from the surface to that altitude plus the change in kinetic energy of the satellite.

213. In which of the following cases has a person done the most work on the system described?

(A) Moving a 20 kg box at constant speed across a surface with a coefficient of friction of 0.05, using a force of 10 N for a distance of 10 m
(B) Lifting a 20 kg box onto a shelf that is 2 m high
(C) Holding a 20 kg box 2 m above the floor for 10 minutes
(D) Pushing a 20 kg box across a frictionless surface to accelerate it from rest to 5 m/s

214. An 11 lb bowling ball (with a mass of about 5 kg) is dropped from a height of 1 m onto a floor. If the dent the ball makes in the floor is about 1 cm deep, estimate the average force the ball exerted on the floor.

(A) 50 N
(B) 250 N
(C) 2,500 N
(D) 5,000 N

215. A 2,000 kg automobile accelerates from rest to a speed of 40 m/s in 20 s. What is the average power, in kilowatts, produced by the automobile during this time interval?

(A) 10 kW
(B) 20 kW
(C) 40 kW
(D) 80 kW

216. If a lightbulb uses 40 W of power for an hour, what is the energy used by the bulb?

(A) 40 J
(B) 240 J
(C) 3,600 J
(D) 144,000 J

217. An average force of 0.2 N is exerted on a 2 kg object to accelerate it from a speed of 2 m/s to 3 m/s in a time interval of 10 s. Determine the average power generated.

(A) 0.5 W
(B) 2.0 W
(C) 5.0 W
(D) 20.0 W

218. Experimental data in the chart below show the total energy used by a device as a function of time. What is the average power consumption of this device from $t = 0$ to $t = 10$ s?

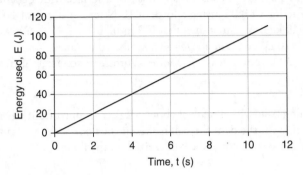

(A) 0.5 W
(B) 10 W
(C) 500 W
(D) 1,000 W

219. A small metal cube with a temperature of 308 K is placed in contact with a much larger cube of the same metal with a temperature of 290 K. Assuming no loss of energy to the environment around the cubes, which of the following statements is true regarding the transfer of energy that takes place?

(A) The smaller cube will undergo a greater change in temperature than the larger cube.
(B) After a long time, the final temperature of both cubes will be 299 K.
(C) The smaller cube will contain more internal energy than the larger cube after the two cubes reach an equilibrium temperature.
(D) The smaller cube will actually transfer more heat to the larger cube than the larger cube transfers to the smaller one.

220. A 1 kg block of metal at 200 K is brought into contact with a 3 kg block of a different metal at 300 K. Assuming no loss of energy to the environment around the blocks, which of the following statements is true regarding the temperatures of the blocks after a long time has passed?

(A) The final temperature of each block will be 250 K because the blocks will reach thermal equilibrium.
(B) The temperatures of the two blocks will be the same, so all molecules will have the same average speed.
(C) The temperatures of the two blocks will be the same, so the molecules in both will have the same average kinetic energy.
(D) The final temperatures of the blocks can be the same only if the two blocks are made of the same materials.

221. A thermodynamic cycle for one mole of an ideal gas is described by the pressure versus volume graph below. Determine the net thermal energy lost or gained by the system during one complete cycle, A-B-C.

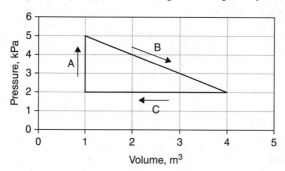

(A) 12,000 J added to the gas
(B) 6,000 J added to the gas
(C) 4,500 J added to the gas
(D) 20,000 J lost by the gas

222. The pressure versus volume graph describes a cycle for a thermodynamic process A-B-C-A for an ideal gas. Pressure is measured in kilopascals and volume in cubic meters. In step AB of the process, 78 kJ of energy are added while volume is held constant. In step BC, the gas remains at constant temperature, and 50 kJ of energy are removed from the system. In step CA, 20 kJ of energy are removed. How much work is done by the gas in step BC?

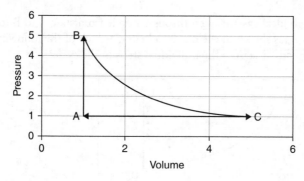

(A) 48 kJ
(B) 24 kJ
(C) 12 kJ
(D) 8 kJ

223. The diagram illustrates the pressure and volume changes for two moles of an ideal gas as it is taken through a cycle from state A to B to C and back to A. Which of the following most closely estimates the amount of work done on the gas during the cycle?

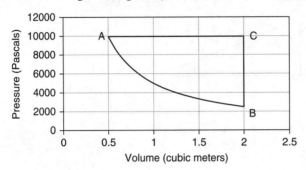

(A) 10,000 J
(B) 6,000 J
(C) 2,000 J
(D) No work is done on the gas during the cycle shown.

224. During an isothermal process involving an ideal gas, the pressure of the gas is doubled. Which of the following statements is true?

(A) The volume remains constant.
(B) The temperature also doubles.
(C) The volume and temperature of the gas also double.
(D) The temperature remains constant.

225. Two moles of an ideal gas are taken through a cycle from state A to B to C and back to A, as shown in the diagram below. Which of the following statements correctly describes the individual steps in the cycle?

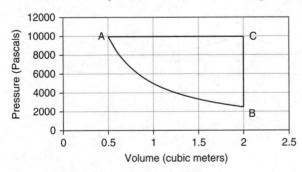

(A) AB is isothermal, and BC is isovolumetric.
(B) CA is isothermal, and BC is isobaric.
(C) AB is adiabatic, and CA is isobaric.
(D) AB is isothermal, and BC is isobaric.

226. The pressure versus volume graph below describes a thermodynamic process A-B-C-A for an ideal gas in which step BC is isothermal. The term *adiabatic* describes a process in which no heat is transferred into or out of a system. Which of the steps in the process could be adiabatic?

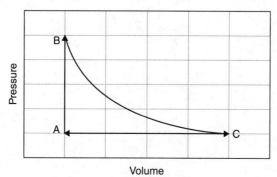

(A) AB because no work is done on or by the gas.
(B) BC because temperature remains constant.
(C) CA because there is no pressure change and thus no work is done on or by the gas.
(D) None of these processes could be adiabatic.

Importance of Fluids for the Circulation of Blood, Gas Movement, and Gas Exchange

CHAPTER 4

Fluids

227. Since blood is not an ideal fluid, as it flows through arteries:

   (A) it flows with nearly constant speed throughout the cross section of a blood vessel.

   (B) its viscosity causes it to move with a slower speed near the center of a blood vessel.

   (C) its viscosity causes it to move with a slower speed near the walls of a blood vessel.

   (D) the viscosity of the blood does not affect its speed of flow.

228. As blood flows in a typical arteriole in the body, its speed may be on the order of 1 cm/s. When the arteriole branches into several hundred capillaries, each with smaller diameter:

   (A) the speed of blood in the capillaries increases since the capillaries are smaller in diameter, increasing gas exchange with the surroundings.

   (B) the speed of blood in the capillaries decreases since the capillaries have a total diameter that is less, increasing gas exchange with the surroundings.

   (C) the speed of blood in the capillaries increases since the capillaries are smaller in diameter, decreasing gas exchange with the surroundings.

   (D) the speed of blood in the capillaries decreases since the capillaries have a total diameter that is less, decreasing gas exchange with the surroundings.

229. An irregularly shaped piece of halite (salt) has a mass of 220 g. In order to find its volume without dissolving it, it is submerged in oil, which has a density of 0.80 g/cm^3. The sample displaces 100 ml of oil. What is the density of the sample?

(A) 2.8 g/cm^3
(B) 2.2 g/cm^3
(C) 1.8 g/cm^3
(D) 0.45 g/cm^3

230. A block of wood is placed in water and floats 60% submerged (and thus 40% above water). When the block is placed in an alcohol that is 90% as dense as water, the block:

(A) floats 90% under the surface of the alcohol.
(B) floats 67% under the surface of the alcohol.
(C) floats 54% under the surface of the alcohol.
(D) sinks in the alcohol.

231. An object with volume V floats in a fluid with density ρ so that the object is 75% submerged in the fluid. Which of the following correctly expresses the density of the object?

(A) $\dfrac{4\rho}{3}$

(B) $\dfrac{3\rho}{4}$

(C) $\dfrac{\rho}{3}$

(D) $\dfrac{\rho}{4}$

232. A solution is made up of two liquids that are immiscible; that is, they do not dissolve in each other to produce a reduction in total volume. The solution is made of 60 ml of liquid A, which has a specific gravity of 0.5, and 40 ml of liquid B, which has a specific gravity of 0.7. What is the specific gravity of the solution?

(A) 0.58
(B) 0.67
(C) 0.75
(D) 1.2

233. A ball floats half submerged in a liquid. Which of the following statements is true?

(A) The ball's density is the same as the liquid's density.
(B) The buoyant force on the ball is greater than the weight of the ball.
(C) The buoyant force on the ball is less than the weight of the ball.
(D) The ball's weight is equal to the weight of the fluid displaced.

234. A block of a certain material that is insoluble in water sinks when it is placed in a container of distilled water, then eventually rises to the surface. The block is removed and placed in a second container of distilled water, where the block floats and then eventually sinks. Which of the following is the best explanation for this?

(A) The block has a greater density than distilled water at room temperature.
(B) The first container was filled with hot water.
(C) The first container was filled with cold water.
(D) Both containers initially contain water at room temperature.

235. In the illustration below, a bar of metal is suspended underwater by two cords. If T is the tension in each cord, W is the weight of the bar in air, and F is the buoyant force of the water on the bar, which of the following equations correctly expresses the forces on the bar of metal?

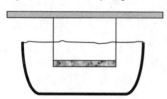

(A) $F = 2T - W$
(B) $2T + F = W$
(C) $W > 2T - F$
(D) $2T = W$

236. A rock is tied to a spring scale and lowered into water in a graduated cylinder so that the rock is submerged and the spring scale reads 0.80 N. When the rock goes underwater, the water level in the cylinder rises from the 35 ml mark to the 45 ml mark. What is the mass of the rock?

(A) 40 g
(B) 50 g
(C) 80 g
(D) 90 g

237. A ball floats 60% below the surface when it is placed in water and 70% below the surface when it is placed in a second liquid. The density of water is 1,000 kg/m³. Which of the following most closely approximates the density of the second liquid?

(A) 550 kg/m³
(B) 600 kg/m³
(C) 860 kg/m³
(D) 1,100 kg/m³

238. A ball with a radius of 2 cm and a mass of 20 g floats in water. What is the buoyant force on the ball?

(A) 0.1 N
(B) 0.2 N
(C) 0.3 N
(D) 0.4 N

239. Water is poured into a U-shaped tube. Oil is poured into one side of the tube, and the liquid levels are allowed to come to equilibrium. Using the information given in the illustration below, determine the density of the oil.

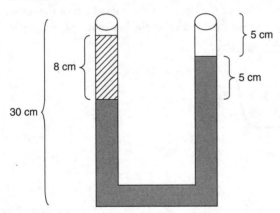

(A) 600 kg/m³
(B) 700 kg/m³
(C) 800 kg/m³
(D) 900 kg/m³

240. The density of freshwater is 1,000 kg/m³, and standard atmospheric pressure is 101 kPa. Determine the absolute pressure at the bottom of a freshwater lake that has a depth of 20 m and a surface area of 21,000 m².

(A) 100 kPa
(B) 200 kPa
(C) 300 kPa
(D) 400 kPa

241. Freshwater lake A has a surface area of 800 m² and a depth of 40 m, and freshwater lake B has a surface area of 1,000 m² and a depth of 20 m. Compare the total pressure at the bottom of lake A with that at the bottom of lake B.

(A) Lake A has greater pressure at the bottom because it has a greater depth.
(B) Lake A has greater pressure at the bottom because it has a greater volume of water.
(C) Lake B has greater pressure at the bottom because it has a greater surface area.
(D) The two lakes have equal pressure at the bottom.

242. A tank is 8 m tall and has a bottom area of 50 m². It is filled to a depth of 6 m with freshwater. Calculate the absolute pressure at the bottom of the tank.

(A) 81,000 Pa
(B) 101,000 Pa
(C) 161,000 Pa
(D) 181,000 Pa

243. A pitot tube is a device that:

(A) uses measurements of fluid pressure to measure the depth of a fluid (such as in the ocean).
(B) uses measurements of changes in velocity to measure fluid quantity (such as on nozzles).
(C) uses measurements of fluid depth to measure pressure (such as in a gasoline tank).
(D) uses difference in fluid flow pressure to determine speed (such as an airplane).

244. A sudden increase in blood flow in the heart can cause the mitral valve to malfunction, causing heart failure (called hypertrophic obstructive cardio-myopathy). Which is the most accurate description of the fluid physics for this phenomenon?

(A) Blood flows through a constricted vessel, causing velocity to increase and pressure to decrease in that vessel, pulling on the valve.

(B) Blood flows through a constricted vessel, causing velocity to increase and pressure to increase in that vessel, pulling on the valve.

(C) Blood flows through a widened region in a vessel, causing velocity to increase and pressure to increase in that vessel, pulling on the valve.

(D) Blood flows through a widened region in a vessel, causing velocity to increase and pressure to decrease in that vessel, pulling on the valve.

245. A tank is 8 m tall and has a bottom area of 50 m². It is filled to a depth of 6 m with freshwater. Calculate the fluid force on the bottom of the tank.

(A) 1×10^5 N
(B) 8×10^5 N
(C) 4×10^6 N
(D) 8×10^6 N

246. The average density of seawater is 1,025 kg/m³. Calculate the force, in newtons, on the top of a 1 m² section of a sunken ship at a depth of 4,000 m.

(A) 1×10^5 N
(B) 4×10^6 N
(C) 4×10^7 N
(D) 1×10^8 N

247. The total fluid pressure on a scuba diver at the bottom of a lake does NOT depend on which of the following factors?

(A) Atmospheric pressure
(B) The density of the water
(C) Water depth
(D) The surface area of the lake

248. An air bubble with a volume of 0.001 m³ is released at a depth of 21 m in a freshwater lake. The volume of the bubble when it reaches the surface is nearest to:

(A) 0.001 m³.
(B) 0.002 m³.
(C) 0.003 m³.
(D) 0.004 m³.

249. A balloon filled with helium gas will float to the ceiling of a room on Earth. What will happen to the same balloon when it is released on the surface of the moon?

(A) The gravitational force on the moon is less, so the balloon has less weight and will rise even faster.

(B) Since there is no atmosphere on the moon, the balloon will expand to a larger volume and float more easily than on Earth.

(C) Since there is no air on the moon to provide a buoyant force on the balloon, it will sink to the surface.

(D) Since the surface of the moon is so cold, the balloon will shrink and thus have a lower density.

250. A certain pipe carries water at 20°C, delivering 10 m³ per minute. The water is then cooled to 15°C. How does the volume rate of flow compare, and what is the best explanation?

(A) The flow rate will stay the same because rate of flow does not depend on temperature.

(B) The flow rate will increase because viscosity increases when temperature is lower.

(C) The flow rate will decrease because the decrease in viscosity will decrease speed.

(D) The flow rate will decrease because viscosity increases.

251. Students are performing an experiment to determine the viscosities of various liquids by dropping a small metal sphere into graduated cylinders filled with the liquids, taking measurements, and then using the following equation to determine the viscosity of each liquid,

$$\eta = \frac{2(\Delta\rho)^2 gr^2}{9v}$$

where η is viscosity, $\Delta\rho$ is the difference in densities between the sphere and the liquid, g is 9.8 m/s², r is the radius of the sphere, and v is the speed of the sphere as it falls through the liquid. Water has a viscosity of 0.001 Pa·s and a density of 1,000 kg/m³, and olive oil has a viscosity of 0.1 Pa·s and a density of 900 kg/m³. The metal sphere has a radius of 1 cm and a density of 7,500 kg/m³. How would the ball's speed falling through water compare to its speed falling through olive oil?

(A) The speed is about the same for each liquid.

(B) The ball will fall about 10 times faster through water than through olive oil.

(C) The ball will fall about 100 times faster through water than through olive oil.

(D) The ball will fall about 500 times faster through water than through olive oil.

252. Water flows horizontally from a larger pipe with a diameter of 20 cm to a smaller pipe with a diameter from 5 cm to 10 cm. The smaller pipe then curves upward, and the water flows at a level 2 m higher, as in the illustration below. If the speed of the water is 4 m/s in the larger pipe, what is the speed of the water in the smaller pipe as it flows at the higher level?

v = 4 m/s   2 m

(A) 8 m/s
(B) 10 m/s
(C) 12 m/s
(D) 16 m/s

253. If you place your thumb over the end of a garden hose of running water, what is the effect on the speed of the water flow and the amount of water leaving the hose each second?

(A) Both the speed of flow and the amount of water flow increase.
(B) The speed of flow increases, and the amount of water flow decreases.
(C) The speed of flow increases, and the amount of water flow stays the same.
(D) The speed of flow decreases, and the amount of water flow increases.

254. A trough with a semicircular cross section is level-full, with water flowing at a speed of 3 m/s. If the depth of the water at the center of the trough is 0.20 m, what is the approximate volume of water flowing past a given point per hour?

(A) 120 m^3
(B) 680 m^3
(C) 1,400 m^3
(D) 2,200 m^3

255. An increase in which of the following properties of a moving fluid will NOT produce an increase in the turbulence of the fluid flow?

(A) The density of the fluid
(B) The diameter of the obstacle encountered in the fluid flow path
(C) The velocity of the fluid flow
(D) The viscosity of the fluid

256. In which of the following situations is blood flow in a vessel most likely to become turbulent?

(A) The blood flows from a vessel of small diameter to a vessel of larger diameter.
(B) The blood flows from a vessel of large diameter to a vessel of smaller diameter.
(C) The blood becomes less dense due to hydration.
(D) The blood becomes more viscous.

257. Which of the following properties of real fluids are not found in "ideal fluids"?

(A) Density and viscosity
(B) Viscosity and surface tension
(C) Surface tension and density
(D) None of the above

258. Which of the following actions would NOT be effective in reducing surface tension in water?

(A) Heating
(B) Adding an inorganic salt
(C) Adding sugar
(D) Adding a surfactant

259. The illustration below shows an open container of water with a spout 60 cm from the bottom that allows a stream of water to flow out of the container. When the height of water above the spout is 45 cm, what is the speed of the water flowing out of the spout?

(A) 3.0 m/s
(B) 5.0 m/s
(C) 6.0 m/s
(D) 7.5 m/s

260. The speed of air moving over the top of a thin airfoil, such as an airplane wing, is 50 m/s, and the speed of air moving under the airfoil is 40 m/s. If the area of the surface is approximately 30 m^2, what is the lift force on the airfoil due to the moving air?

(A) 580 N
(B) 1,000 N
(C) 10,200 N
(D) 17,400 N

261. A student wants to determine the speed of water flowing from a garden hose. The student turns the water flow on to maximum and directs the hose straight upward. The water stream travels to a maximum height of 2 m above the spout of the hose. What is the approximate speed of the water?

(A) 2 m/s
(B) 4 m/s
(C) 6 m/s
(D) 8 m/s

262. Bernoulli's equation is a statement of which physics principle?

(A) Conservation of mass in fluid flow
(B) Conservation of linear momentum in fluid flow
(C) Conservation of energy in fluid flow
(D) The property of laminar flow of fluids

263. Air is moving horizontally from a wide pipe of diameter 1 cm at a speed of 2 m/s to a narrow pipe of diameter 0.5 cm. Assume that the density of air is 1.29 kg/m^3 and neglect any change in density due to compression. What is the change in the internal pressure of the air?

(A) 10 Pa
(B) 20 Pa
(C) 30 Pa
(D) 40 Pa

264. Blood flowing in an artery must have a net pressure exerted on the blood to cause it to continue flowing, which is not necessary for an ideal fluid. The viscosity of blood causes the speed of the blood to be greatest near the center of the artery and almost zero near the walls of the artery. For proper flow in the artery, which must be true about the blood pressure?

(A) The pressure difference between the two ends must be inversely proportional to artery length and inversely proportional to the diameter.

(B) The pressure difference between the two ends must be directly proportional to artery length and to the speed of blood flow.

(C) The pressure difference must be inversely proportional to blood viscosity and directly proportional to artery length.

(D) The pressure difference must be directly proportional to blood viscosity and inversely proportional to speed of blood flow.

265. When you're at rest, your heart pumps about 5 liters per minute. The density of blood is 1.06 kg/l. About what mass of blood does your heart pump in a day?

(A) 120 kg
(B) 760 kg
(C) 318 kg
(D) 7,600 kg

CHAPTER 5

Kinetic Theory of Gases

266. By what mechanism can gas molecules exert pressure on the walls of their container?

(A) As the molecules strike the wall, they exert a force that causes a pressure equal to the force divided by area of the wall.

(B) As the molecules strike the wall, the wall exerts a force on each molecule that changes its momentum.

(C) Each collision of a molecule with the container wall causes a force on the wall that is greater than the force the wall can exert on the molecule.

(D) During each collision with the wall, a molecule rebounds with more energy than before the collision.

267. A group of students wants to perform an experiment to investigate the ideal gas law. They decide to use air as the gas to investigate changes in pressure, volume, and temperature. Which property of air is likely to cause the most uncertainty in their experiments?

(A) The polarity of nitrogen molecules will cause interactive forces between molecules.

(B) The polarity of oxygen molecules will cause interactive forces between molecules.

(C) The diatomic nitrogen molecules will have extra rotational or bond energy.

(D) The students would not have enough molecules in a reasonable space to produce statistically significant results.

268. An ideal gas is taken through one step of a thermodynamic cycle. During that step, which of the following would not change the average kinetic energy of the gas molecules?

(A) An isothermal decrease in volume
(B) An increase in pressure at constant volume
(C) An adiabatic expansion at constant volume
(D) An isobaric expansion

269. If the temperature of an ideal gas is doubled, what is the change in the average velocity of gas molecules?

(A) The average velocity of gas molecules will not change.
(B) The average velocity will be doubled.
(C) The average velocity will be four times as much.
(D) The average velocity of the molecules will be multiplied by the square root of two.

270. A container of ideal gas consists of a cylinder with a movable piston that does not allow gas molecules to enter or leave as the piston is moved. The pressure in the container is P, and the volume is V before the piston is moved. The piston is then moved slowly so that the temperature does not change as the volume is reduced to $V/2$. What is the best explanation for what happens to the gas pressure in terms of molecular motion?

(A) The average speed of the molecules is greater, so they exert more force on the walls of the container.
(B) The average speed of the molecules stays the same, but they collide with the walls of the container more often, increasing pressure.
(C) The average speed of the molecules is less, but they collide with the walls of the smaller container more often.
(D) The average speed of the molecules does not change, but the larger volume means that collisions with the walls are less frequent, so the pressure inside the container decreases.

271. A rigid container of an ideal gas is heated so that the absolute temperature of the gas doubles while the volume remains constant. The molecules of the gas:

(A) increase in pressure, so they do more work on the walls of the container.
(B) have twice as much internal energy.
(C) must give off energy since they cannot expand.
(D) have twice the average speed that they had before.

272. What is the effect on the average kinetic energy of the molecules of an ideal gas when the absolute temperature of the gas is doubled?

(A) The average kinetic energy is not changed.
(B) The average kinetic energy is also doubled.
(C) The average kinetic energy is quadrupled.
(D) The average kinetic energy is multiplied by the square root of two.

273. An ideal gas is one that behaves according to a set of relationships and equations, such as the ideal gas law, $PV = nRT$. Which of the following statements does NOT necessarily define an ideal gas?

(A) All collisions of molecules within an ideal gas are elastic.
(B) A system of an ideal gas consists of a large number of molecules.
(C) Ideal gas molecules are point particles.
(D) Ideal gas molecules always expand isothermally when pressure is decreased

274. In the laboratory, a barometer is sealed into a container of an ideal gas as the gas undergoes a series of thermodynamic changes. During which of the following processes would the barometer reading have to remain constant?

(A) An isothermal process during which no work is done on or by the gas
(B) An adiabatic process
(C) An isovolumetric process during which the internal energy of the gas increases
(D) A process during which volume increases and temperature decreases

275. The diagram below shows a solid curve (B) representing a distribution of the number of molecules as a function of molecular speed at a given temperature. Which dashed line best represents the predicted distribution for the same gas at a higher absolute temperature?

(A) Curve A
(B) Curve B
(C) Curve C
(D) Curve D

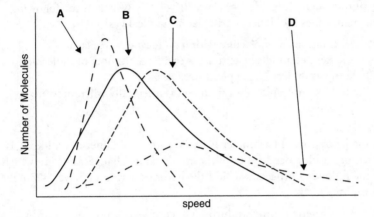

PART 3

Electrical Circuits and Their Elements

CHAPTER 6

Electrostatics

276. Four solid metallic spheres 1, 2, 3, and 4 have diameters of D, 2D, 3D, and 4D, respectively. The same amount of negative charge is transferred to each sphere. Which choice correctly ranks the electric potential at the surface ofeach sphere?

(A) $1 > 2 > 3 > 4$
(B) $4 > 3 > 2 > 1$
(C) All of the spheres have the same nonzero electric potential.
(D) The electric potential for all four spheres is zero.

277. Four solid metallic spheres 1, 2, 3, and 4 have diameters of D, 2D, 3D, and 4D, respectively. The same amount of negative charge is transferred to each sphere. Which choice correctly ranks the electric field strength just inside the surface of each sphere?

(A) $1 > 2 > 3 > 4$
(B) $4 > 3 > 2 > 1$
(C) All of the spheres have the same nonzero electric field inside.
(D) All of the spheres have zero electric field inside.

278. Four solid metallic spheres 1, 2, 3, and 4 have diameters of D, 2D, 3D, and 4D, respectively. The same amount of negative charge is transferred to each sphere. Which choice correctly ranks the electric field strength on the exterior surface of each sphere?

(A) $1 > 2 > 3 > 4$
(B) $4 > 3 > 2 > 1$
(C) All of the spheres have the same nonzero electric field on the exterior surface.
(D) All of the spheres have zero electric field on their exterior surfaces.

279. How many electrons are transferred in the process of charging a latex balloon to 1.6×10^{-8} C?

(A) 1×10^{11}
(B) 2.56×10^{-27}
(C) 1×10^{27}
(D) 1×10^{-25}

280. A metal sphere with a charge of $+2Q$ comes into contact with a metal sphere of identical size that has a charge of $-4Q$. The spheres are then separated. What are the charges on the spheres after they are separated?

(A) Both spheres have zero net charge.
(B) Each sphere has a charge of $-2Q$.
(C) Each sphere has a charge of $-Q$.
(D) Each sphere retains its original charge.

281. A negatively charged rod is brought near a second rod that is neutral and suspended by a nonconducting string. The second rod begins to move toward the negative rod, showing attraction of the two rods. After the first rod is removed without touching the second rod, the second rod:

(A) has no net charge.
(B) has a positive net charge.
(C) has a negative net charge.
(D) is polarized, with one end negative and one end positive.

282. A negatively charged rod is brought near (but not touching) a second rod that is neutral and suspended by a nonconducting string. A wire is connected from the second rod to the ground. With the first rod held in place, the ground wire is cut and the first rod is removed. After the first rod is removed, the second rod:

(A) has no net charge.
(B) has a positive net charge.
(C) has a negative net charge.
(D) is polarized, with one end negative and one end positive.

283. An isolated solid metal sphere that sits on an insulating stand is given a net charge of −10 μC. Which of the following statements best describes the charged sphere?

(A) The net charge will be distributed evenly throughout the volume of the sphere.

(B) The net charge will be distributed evenly over the surface of the sphere.

(C) The net charge will concentrate on the side of the sphere near the insulating stand.

(D) The net charge will be distributed evenly, with half the charge on the outside of the sphere and half the charge on the inside of the sphere.

284. An isolated nonconducting sphere is given a net charge of −10 μC by touching it with a negatively charged rod. Which of the following statements best describes the charged sphere?

(A) The net charge will be distributed evenly throughout the volume of the sphere.

(B) The net charge will be distributed evenly over the surface of the sphere.

(C) The net charge will concentrate on the side of the sphere where the rod touched it.

(D) The net charge will be distributed evenly, with half the charge on the outside of the sphere and half the charge on the inside of the sphere.

285. The electric force between two charged objects is 0.02 N. If each object is given twice its original charge and the objects are located at their original distance from each other, what is the new force?

(A) 0.01 N
(B) 0.02 N
(C) 0.04 N
(D) 0.08 N

286. The electric force between two charged objects is 0.02 N. If the objects are moved four times as far apart, what is the new force?

(A) 0.0012 N
(B) 0.0025 N
(C) 0.0050 N
(D) 0.01 N

287. Four equally charged positive particles are held in position in a square arrangement so that each side of the square has a length R. What is the net electrical force exerted by the four positive particles on an electron placed in the center of the square?

(A) $F = \dfrac{3kq^2}{R^2}$

(B) $F = \dfrac{4kq^2}{R^2}$

(C) $F = \dfrac{\sqrt{2}kq^2}{R^2}$

(D) 0

288. The illustration below shows three charged particles held in position along a line. What is the net electric force on the particle with charge q_2 due to the other two charges? Let $k = 1/(4\pi\varepsilon_o)$.

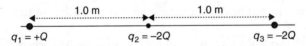

(A) $6kQ^2$ to the left
(B) $6kQ^2$ to the right
(C) $3kQ^2$ to the left
(D) $3kQ^2$ to the right

289. In a laboratory, an oil droplet carrying a two-electron charge is observed to hover between electrically charged plates so that the electric force exerted upward on the droplet is equal to the gravitational force downward on the droplet. Which of the following expressions can be used to determine the mass of the oil droplet?

(A) $m = \dfrac{gE}{2e}$

(B) $m = \dfrac{2eE}{g}$

(C) $m = \dfrac{eE}{g}$

(D) $m = \dfrac{gE}{e}$

290. Two particles, each carrying a net charge of +6 μC, are placed on the x axis at $x = -3$ m and $x = +3$ m, as shown in the illustration. What is the electric force due to the two charges on a particle with a charge of +6 μC placed at point P, which is located at position (0, +3 m)?

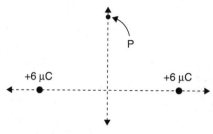

+6 μC   +6 μC

(A) 0.002 N
(B) 0.025 N
(C) 4,200 N
(D) 8,400 N

291. The theoretical distance of an electron (in its ground state) from the proton nucleus of a hydrogen atom, which is called the Bohr radius, is approximately 5.29×10^{-11} m. What is the electric force of the proton on the electron at this distance?

(A) 1.5×10^{-17} N
(B) 1.5×10^{-10} N
(C) 8.2×10^{-7} N
(D) 8.2×10^{-8} N

292. The atomic radius of a carbon atom is about 70 pm, or about 70×10^{-12} m. What is the force of the nucleus of a carbon atom (atomic number = 12) on an outer-shell electron at that radial distance?

(A) 1.5×10^{-17} N
(B) 1.5×10^{-10} N
(C) 4.7×10^{-8} N
(D) 5.6×10^{-7} N

293. Two particles, each carrying a net charge of +6 μC, are placed on the x axis at $x = -3$ m and $x = +3$ m, as shown in the illustration below. What is the electric field due to the two charges at point P, which is located at position $(0, +3$ m$)$?

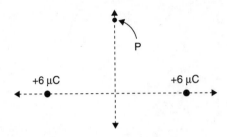

(A) 12 N/C

(B) $6\sqrt{2}$ N/C

(C) 4,200 N/C

(D) 8,400 N/C

294. Determine the electric field at a distance of 2 cm from the center of an object with a charge of 2 nC.

(A) 4,500 N/C

(B) 9,000 N/C

(C) 45,000 N/C

(D) 90,000 N/C

295. Four equally charged positive particles are held in position in a square arrangement so that each side of the square has a length R. What is the net electric field at the center of the square due to the four charges?

(A) $E = \dfrac{4kq}{(\sqrt{2}R/2)^2}$

(B) $E = \dfrac{4kq}{R^2}$

(C) $E = \dfrac{\sqrt{2}kq}{R^2}$

(D) 0

296. Four charged particles—two of charge $+q$ and two of charge $-q$—are held in position in a square arrangement so that each side of the square has a length R. The two positive charges are held at opposite corners, and the two negative charges are held at opposite corners. What is the net electric field at the center of the square due to the four charges?

(A) $E = \dfrac{4kq}{(\sqrt{2}R/2)^2}$

(B) $E = \dfrac{4kq}{R^2}$

(C) $E = \dfrac{\sqrt{2}kq}{R^2}$

(D) 0

297. An isolated hollow metal sphere has a net positive charge transferred to it. Where is the electric field strongest?

(A) At the exact center of the sphere
(B) Just inside the outer surface of the sphere
(C) Just outside the outer surface of the sphere
(D) At all points halfway from the outer surface to the center of the sphere

Refer to the illustration below for questions 298 and 299.

298. An uncharged solid metal sphere is placed in a uniform electric field directed to the right, as shown in the illustration above. Which of the following statements best describes what will happen to the sphere?

(A) Since the sphere is uncharged, nothing will happen to it in the field.
(B) Charges in the sphere will separate, with the right side of the sphere becoming more positive.
(C) Charges in the sphere will separate, with the right side of the sphere becoming more negative.
(D) The field will exert a force on the electrons, causing them to move away to the right and leaving the sphere with a net positive charge.

299. An uncharged metal sphere is placed in a uniform electric field, as shown in the illustration above. Which of the following illustrations best represents the electric field in the region of the sphere after the sphere is placed in the field?

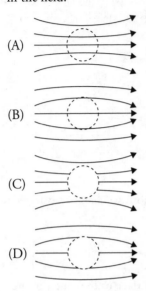

300. The illustration below shows two parallel charged metal plates. Which of the following statements is NOT true regarding the situation shown?

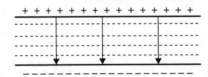

(A) The arrows represent the direction of the electric field between the plates.

(B) The horizontal dashed lines represent equipotential surfaces.

(C) The top plate is at a higher electric potential than the bottom plate.

(D) The electric field increases in magnitude moving upward in the diagram.

301. The illustration below shows three charged particles held in position along a line. What is the net electric field at point P due to the two charges? Let $k = 1/(4\pi\varepsilon_o)$.

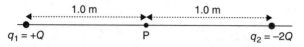

(A) kQ to the left
(B) kQ to the right
(C) $3kQ$ to the left
(D) $3kQ$ to the right

302. Assuming that all the charges in the illustration below have the same magnitude, which of the following combinations of charges would require the greatest amount of work to assemble in the triangular arrangement shown?

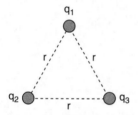

(A) Three positive charges
(B) Three negative charges
(C) Two positive charges and one negative charge
(D) Either case in which all three charges have the same sign

303. As the distance from a charge doubles:

(A) the electric field reduces to one-half, and the electric potential reduces to one-half.
(B) the electric field remains constant, and the electric potential reduces to one-half.
(C) the electric field reduces to one-quarter, and the electric potential reduces to one-half.
(D) the electric field reduces to one-quarter, and the electric potential reduces to one-quarter.

304. The two charges in the illustration below are held in position on the x axis, with the $+2q$ charge at $x = 3$ and the $-4q$ charge at $x = 6$. At what point on the line between the two charges is the absolute electric potential equal to zero?

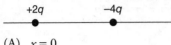

(A) $x = 0$
(B) $x = 4$
(C) $x = 4.5$
(D) $x = 5$

305. In the illustration below, the arrows represent a uniform electric field of magnitude 100 N/C. A charged particle is moved a distance of 0.02 m from point X to point Y along a path. What is the magnitude of the change in electric potential of the particle, in volts, when it moves from point X to point Y?

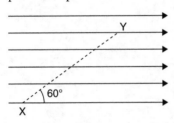

(A) $(100)(0.02)$
(B) $(100)(0.02) \sin 60°$
(C) $(100)(0.02) \cos 60°$
(D) $100/0.02$

306. In the illustration below, three charges of equal magnitude are held in position in a triangular arrangement. Where could a line be drawn so that every point on the line has the same electric potential due to the three charges?

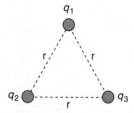

(A) Along a line from charge q_1 to charge q_2
(B) Along a line from charge q_1 straight down, perpendicular to the line between q_2 and q_3
(C) Along a line from the center of the triangle straight outward, perpendicular to the page
(D) Along a line through charge q_1, left to right, parallel to the line between q_2 and q_3

307. In the illustration below, two particles carry the same amount of positive charge. Which of the dashed lines could be an electric equipotential line for the two charged particles?

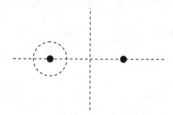

(A) The vertical line that is located halfway between the two charged particles, with every point on the line equidistant from the two particles.
(B) The circle around one charged particle, with every point on the circle equidistant from the center of the charged particle.
(C) The horizontal line that runs directly through the center of each charge.
(D) None of the three lines could be an equipotential line for both charges.

308. Estimate the potential energy of a 3×10^{-6} C charge when it is placed at a distance of 0.01 m from another 3×10^{-6} C charge. (Use 9×10^9 N·m²/C² for $1/(4\pi\varepsilon_o)$, or Coulomb's constant.)

(A) 8.1 J
(B) 81 J
(C) 810 J
(D) 2.7 MJ

CHAPTER 7

Circuits

309. When a net charge of 3.6 μC moves past a given point in 10 ms, what is the electric current?

(A) 0.36 mA
(B) 0.36 A
(C) 3.6 A
(D) 36 A

310. Which of the following quantities is equivalent to one ampere (A)?

(A) 1 C/s
(B) 1 J·s/C
(C) 1 V·J
(D) 1 V/s

311.   ++++++++++++++++++++++++
‾‾‾‾‾‾‾‾‾‾‾‾‾‾‾‾‾‾‾‾‾‾‾‾‾‾

‾‾‾‾‾‾‾‾‾‾‾‾‾‾‾‾‾‾‾‾‾‾‾‾
- - - - - - - - - - - - - - - - - - - -

Two parallel metal plates are charged, with $+Q$ on the top plate and $-Q$ on the bottom plate. What are the directions between the plates of the electric field, the increase in electric potential, and the electric force on a proton?

(A) Upward, upward, downward
(B) Upward, downward, upward
(C) Downward, upward, downward
(D) Downward, downward, downward

Questions 312 and 313 refer to the diagram below.

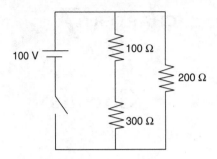

312. Determine the total resistance of the three resistors connected as shown.

    (A) 600 Ω
    (B) 520 Ω
    (C) 133 Ω
    (D) 55 Ω

313. Rank the resistors in order of the amount of current flowing through each.

    (A) 100 Ω > 200 Ω > 300 Ω
    (B) 300 Ω > 200 Ω > 100 Ω
    (C) 100 Ω = 300 Ω > 200 Ω
    (D) 100 Ω = 300 Ω < 200 Ω

314. Four resistors have the relative lengths and cross-sectional areas indicated and are made of material with the same resistivity. Which has the greatest resistance?

    (A) Length $2L$ and area A
    (B) Length L and area $2A$
    (C) Length $4L$ and area $4A$
    (D) Length $4L$ and area A

315.

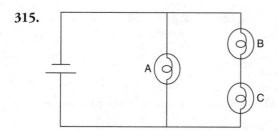

In the circuit above, three identical lightbulbs are connected as shown. Which is a true statement regarding the currents through the bulbs and the potential differences across the bulbs?

(A) The current in bulb A is the greatest, and the potential difference across bulb A is less than that across either bulb B or bulb C.

(B) The current in bulb B is greater than that in bulb A, and the potential difference across bulb B is greater than the potential difference across bulb A.

(C) The current and potential difference in bulb B are both greater than those in bulb C.

(D) The potential difference across bulb A is equal to the sum of the potential differences across bulbs B and C.

Questions 316 and 317 refer to the circuit diagram below.

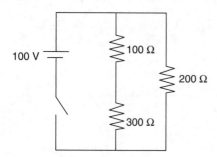

316. After the switch is closed, which resistor in the diagram above will have a potential difference across it of 100 V?

(A) Only the 100 Ω resistor

(B) Only the 200 Ω resistor

(C) Only the 300 Ω resistor

(D) The 100 Ω and 300 Ω resistors will each have a potential difference of 100 V.

317. When the switch is closed in the circuit above, the current through the battery is 0.75 A. Which resistor will have a current of 0.5 A through it?

(A) Only the 100 Ω resistor
(B) Only the 200 Ω resistor
(C) Only the 300 Ω resistor
(D) The 100 Ω and 300 Ω resistors will each have a current of 0.5 A.

318. A lightbulb labeled 40 W is connected to 120 V. How much electrical energy does the bulb use in 1 hour?

(A) 30 J
(B) 90 J
(C) 2,400 J
(D) 144,000 J

319. In the circuit diagram below, the resistors are connected to an emf of 20 V. Assuming negligible resistance in the wires and in the battery, determine the current in the 3 Ω resistor when the switch is closed.

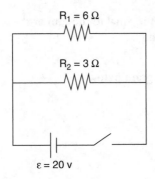

$R_1 = 6\ \Omega$

$R_2 = 3\ \Omega$

$\varepsilon = 20\ v$

(A) 10 A
(B) 6.7 A
(C) 3.3 A
(D) 2.0 A

320. In the diagram below, three identical resistors, each with resistance R, are connected to a battery with potential difference V. When the switch is closed, the current in the resistor on the far right in the diagram could be determined by using which of the following formulas?

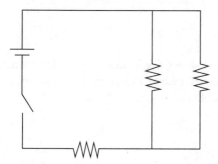

(A) $\dfrac{2V}{3R}$

(B) $\dfrac{V}{3R}$

(C) $\dfrac{4V}{3R}$

(D) $\dfrac{V}{4R}$

321. In a circuit, a 20 Ω resistor and a 30 Ω resistor are connected in series to a 10 V battery. After the switch is closed, what is the electric potential difference in the 20 Ω resistor?

(A) 10 V
(B) 6 V
(C) 5 V
(D) 4 V

322. A lead-acid battery with an emf of 12 V has an internal resistance of 2 Ω. What is the current through the battery when it is connected to an external resistance of 16 Ω?

(A) 0.50 A
(B) 0.67 A
(C) 1.5 A
(D) 2.0 A

323. A battery with an emf of 12 V delivers 10 V to an external circuit when the current in the circuit is 1 A. What is the internal resistance of the battery?

(A) Negligible
(B) 0.5 Ω
(C) 1 Ω
(D) 2 Ω

324. The circuit in the diagram below shows five identical lightbulbs connected to a battery. If each bulb has a resistance of 100 Ω, find the equivalent (total) resistance of the five bulbs.

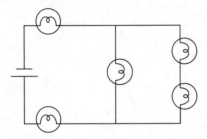

(A) 500 Ω
(B) 270 Ω
(C) 80 Ω
(D) 50 Ω

325. In the diagram below, three 100 Ω resistors are connected in a circuit. What is the equivalent resistance of the three resistors?

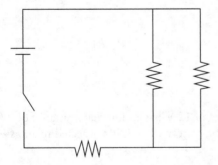

(A) 300 Ω
(B) 200 Ω
(C) 150 Ω
(D) 100 Ω

326. In the diagram below, four resistors are connected in a circuit. What is the equivalent resistance of the four resistors?

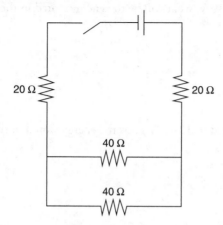

(A) 120 Ω
(B) 100 Ω
(C) 80 Ω
(D) 60 Ω

327. Which of the following statements is true of all combinations of resistors arranged in parallel?

(A) The current splits so that each resistor has the same current.
(B) The potential difference across each branch of the combination is the same.
(C) Both the current and the potential difference are the same in each branch.
(D) The total resistance increases as more resistors are added in parallel.

328. Which of the following formulas correctly expresses the resistivity of a resistor that has resistance R, length L, and cross-sectional area A?

(A) $\rho = \dfrac{RL}{A}$

(B) $\rho = \dfrac{RA}{L}$

(C) $\rho = \dfrac{AL}{R}$

(D) $\rho = \dfrac{R^2 L}{A}$

329. A parallel plate capacitor stores 100 μJ of energy when charged to an electric potential difference of 20 V. If the same capacitor is charged again to a potential difference of only 10 V, what will be the energy stored in the capacitor?

(A) 200 μJ
(B) 100 μJ
(C) 50 μJ
(D) 25 μJ

330. A 2,000 μF capacitor is charged to 10 V. What is the energy stored in the capacitor?

(A) 0.2 J
(B) 0.1 J
(C) 200,000 J
(D) 100,000 J

331. A 2,000 μF capacitor is charged to 10 V. Without removing any of the charges or changing the plate area or dielectric, the plates are moved apart so that there is twice the distance between them as before. What happens to the energy stored in the capacitor?

(A) Positive work is done in moving the plates apart, so the energy stored in the capacitor increases.
(B) The capacitance increases when the distance between plates increases, so the potential difference between the plates also increases and the energy in the capacitor increases.
(C) Negative work is done in moving the plates apart, so the energy stored in the capacitor decreases.
(D) The capacitance decreases when the distance between the plates increases, so the energy stored in the capacitor stays the same.

332. A capacitor is charged to a potential difference of 10 V. Compare the energy stored in the same capacitor if it is charged to 20 V.

(A) The energy is the same in both cases.
(B) There is one-half as much energy at 20 V.
(C) There is twice as much energy at 20 V.
(D) There is four times as much energy at 20 V.

333. In the circuit diagram below, two capacitors are connected to a 10 V battery. After the capacitors are charged, what are the properties of charge and potential difference for each capacitor?

20 µF   40 µF

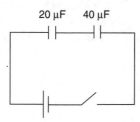

(A) Both capacitors have the same charge, but the smaller capacitor has twice the voltage.

(B) Both capacitors have the same voltage, but the smaller capacitor has half as much charge.

(C) The smaller capacitor has half as much charge and twice the voltage.

(D) Both capacitors have the same charge, but the smaller capacitor has half as much voltage.

334. A 2,000 µF capacitor and a 4,000 µF capacitor are connected in series in a circuit with a 100 V battery. What is the equivalent capacitance of the two capacitors?

(A) 1,300 µF

(B) 2,000 µF

(C) 3,000 µF

(D) 6,000 µF

335. A 2,000 µF capacitor and a 4,000 µF capacitor are connected in parallel in a circuit with a 100 V battery. What is the equivalent capacitance of the two capacitors?

(A) 6,000 µF

(B) 3,000 µF

(C) 2,000 µF

(D) 1,300 µF

336. A parallel plate capacitor with plate area A and plate separation d and containing a dielectric with dielectric constant κ is charged to a potential difference of 20 V. The capacitor is discharged, and the dielectric is replaced with a material that has a dielectric constant of $\frac{1}{2}\kappa$, without changing A or d. The modified capacitor is then charged again to 20 V. Compare the charge Q_2 stored on the modified capacitor to the charge Q_1 stored on the original capacitor.

    (A) $Q_2 = Q_1$
    (B) $Q_2 = 2Q_1$
    (C) $Q_2 = 4Q_1$
    (D) $Q_2 = \frac{1}{2}Q_1$

337. The circuit in the diagram below consists of a 1 MΩ resistor, a battery with an emf of 20 V, and a 1,000 μF capacitor. The switch is closed, and the capacitor is charged for a very long time. What is the charge on the capacitor?

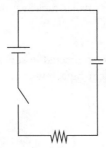

    (A) 100 μC
    (B) 10,000 μC
    (C) 2,000 μC
    (D) 20,000 μC

338. The circuit shown below consists of two identical 50 Ω resistors, a 100 μF capacitor, and a battery with a potential difference of 10 V. The switch is closed, and the capacitor is charged for a very long time. What is the potential difference across the plates of the capacitor?

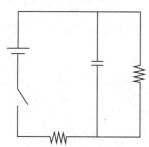

(A) 10 V
(B) 9 V
(C) 5 V
(D) 1 V

339. Which of the following statements is true regarding the electrical conductivity of a wire?

(A) When an electric potential difference is applied across the metal, the resulting electric field causes electrons to move from one end of the wire to the other.
(B) The electrical conductivity of a wire is proportional to the length of the wire.
(C) Increasing the cross-sectional area of a wire increases the resistance to movement of the electrons in the wire, so the conductivity decreases.
(D) All of the above.

340. During which of the following actions is the most average power required?

(A) Lifting a 5 kg block to a height of 2 m in 2 s
(B) Pushing a block across a level surface with a net force of 10 N at a velocity of 3 m/s
(C) Changing the kinetic energy of a rolling wheel from 15 J to 55 J in 20 s
(D) Burning a lightbulb that has a resistance of 10 Ω using 2 A

341. A 12 V battery is connected to a 4 Ω resistor in a circuit. What is the power dissipated as heat by the resistor?

(A) 48 W
(B) 36 W
(C) 24 W
(D) 12 W

342. In the diagram below, what is the total power output of the battery in the circuit?

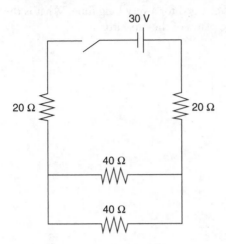

(A) 90 W
(B) 60 W
(C) 45 W
(D) 15 W

343. Which is a correct statement about electric meters?

(A) A voltmeter has very high internal resistance and should be connected in series with the electrical component on which it is taking a measurement.
(B) A voltmeter has very low internal resistance and should be connected in parallel with the component on which it is taking a measurement.
(C) A voltmeter has very high internal resistance and should be connected in parallel with the component on which it is taking a measurement.
(D) A voltmeter has very low internal resistance and should be connected in series with the component on which it is taking a measurement.

344. Which is a correct statement about electric meters?

(A) An ammeter has very high internal resistance and should be connected in series with the electrical component on which it is taking a measurement.
(B) An ammeter has very low internal resistance and should be connected in parallel with the component on which it is taking a measurement.
(C) An ammeter has very high internal resistance and should be connected in parallel with the component on which it is taking a measurement.
(D) An ammeter has very low internal resistance and should be connected in series with the component on which it is taking a measurement.

PART 4

How Light and Sound Interact with Matter

CHAPTER 8

Sound

345. A certain wave is produced by the oscillations of particles of a medium in the +y and –y direction, as the wave pulses travel in the +x direction. What type of wave is this?

(A) Transverse
(B) Longitudinal
(C) Compressional
(D) Spherical

346. Sound waves produced in one end of a cardboard tube (point A) move to the ear of a listener at the other end of the tube (point B). As the waves move from A to B inside the tube, which of the following occurs?

(A) Energy is transferred from A to B.
(B) Air molecules are transferred from A to B.
(C) Oscillations of molecules occur perpendicular to a line from A to B.
(D) The frequency of oscillations decreases as the waves move in the tube from A to B.

347. As a musician "warms up" a wind instrument to play, the temperature of the air in the instrument increases. What is the result of this change in the fundamental for the instrument?

(A) An increase in frequency and wavelength
(B) An increase in frequency and a decrease in wavelength
(C) An increase in wave speed and frequency
(D) An increase in wave speed and a decrease in frequency

348. The graph below records position as a function of time for two different sound sources; the solid line is source A, and the dashed line is source B. Which of the following statements correctly compares the two waves?

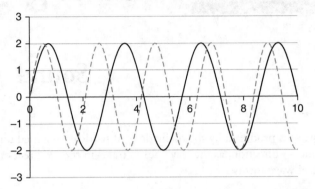

(A) Sound wave A has a higher frequency than sound wave B.
(B) Sound wave A has a higher amplitude than sound wave B.
(C) The two waves undergo constructive interference at about 8.0 s.
(D) The two waves undergo destructive interference at about 4.2 s.

349. In the illustration below, there are two small openings on the left spaced 1 mm apart. Waves coming from the left go through the openings in the same phase and produce an interference pattern with a central maximum at point B and a first-order maximum at point A. Assuming that point P is the midpoint between the openings, line PB is 10 cm from the opening, and point A is 2 mm from point B, what is a possible wavelength of the waves?

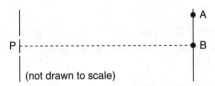

(not drawn to scale)

(A) 0.02 mm
(B) 1 mm
(C) 200 mm
(D) 10 cm

350. The wave diagram below of amplitude (m) as a function of time (s) represents two oscillators of the same amplitude but with different frequency. The wave for oscillation A is indicated with a solid line, and the wave for oscillation B is indicated with a dashed line. The period of wave A is 2.9 s, and the period of wave B is 2.1 s. At what times would the waves come closest to being in the same phase?

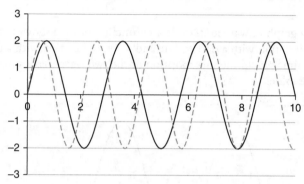

(A) Wave A at $t = 0$ and wave B at $t = 1$
(B) Wave A at $t = 0.7$ and wave B at $t = 3.7$
(C) Wave A at $t = 2.2$ and wave B at $t = 3.7$
(D) Wave A at $t = 6.5$ and wave B at $t = 8.3$

351. A speaker is moved twice as far away from you, but the volume is turned up so that the intensity at the source doubles. What is the resultant intensity of the sound where you sit compared to what it was before the speaker was moved and the volume adjusted?

(A) Half the intensity
(B) One-fourth the intensity
(C) Twice the intensity
(D) Four times the intensity

352. The equation to calculate the decibel level for sound is $\beta = 10 \log(I/I_o)$, where I_o is the intensity of the lowest limit of human hearing, 1×10^{-12} W/m². What is the corresponding decibel level of a sound that has an intensity of 1×10^{-10} W/m²?

(A) 2 dB
(B) 10 dB
(C) 20 dB
(D) 40 dB

353. If the sound level in a room increases from 50 dB to 60 dB, by what factor has the actual intensity increased?

(A) 2 times greater
(B) 6 times greater
(C) 10 times greater
(D) 100 times greater

354. The following graph of wave amplitude as a function of time shows two waves: a sine function with a dashed line and a cosine function with a solid line. At what time would the superposition of the two waves have a maximum positive value?

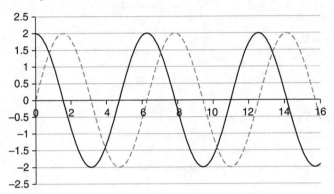

(A) $t = 0$
(B) $t = 7$
(C) $t = 9$
(D) $t = 12$

355. The graph below shows two wave pulses, each traveling at a speed of 5 m/s in the direction shown along the x axis. The y axis is amplitude in meters, and the x axis is position in meters. After what time would the superposition of the two waves equal zero?

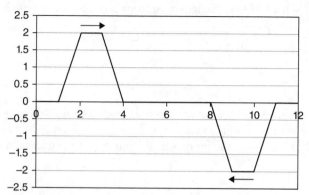

(A) $t = 0.1$ s
(B) $t = 0.2$ s
(C) $t = 0.5$ s
(D) $t = 0.7$ s

356. Two mechanical wave pulses are moving along the x axis toward each other at the same speed. If the pulses are traveling at 2 m/s, at what time after the "snapshot" below will the waves superimpose to produce a wave of the greatest amplitude?

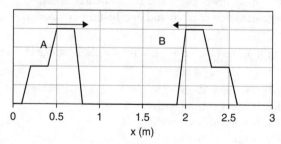

(A) 0.25 s
(B) 0.38 s
(C) 0.75 s
(D) 1.0 s

357. Two speakers output the same tone in the same phase. A person sitting in a chair across the room at the same distance from both speakers hears the tone very well. However, when the person moves the chair to the right so that he is one-half meter closer to one speaker than to the other, he is not able to hear the tone well. What is the wavelength of the tone produced by the speakers?

(A) ¼ m
(B) ½ m
(C) 1 m
(D) 1½ m

358. Blowing across a tube that is open at both ends produces a musical note. Assuming that the length of the tube is L and the speed of sound in the air inside the tube is v, what is the fundamental frequency of the musical note?

(A) $2L/v$
(B) $4L/v$
(C) $v/4L$
(D) $v/2L$

359. Blowing across a tube that is open at both ends produces a musical note. If you place your finger over the open end of the tube at the bottom and blow across the top of the tube, a second note is produced. Compare the pitch and frequency of the second note to the pitch and frequency of the original note.

(A) The second note has a higher pitch and twice the frequency.
(B) The second note has a higher pitch and one-half the frequency.
(C) The second note has a lower pitch and twice the frequency.
(D) The second note has a lower pitch and one-half the frequency.

360. A tube that is 20 cm long and closed at one end should produce the same fundamental note as a:

(A) 10 cm tube that is open at both ends.
(B) 20 cm tube that is open at both ends.
(C) 30 cm tube that is open at both ends.
(D) 40 cm tube that is open at both ends.

361. A guitar string that is attached at both ends is 40 cm long and produces a fundamental note of frequency 200 Hz when it is plucked. What are the frequencies of the first and second overtones of this string?

(A) 200 and 300 Hz
(B) 100 and 200 Hz
(C) 200 and 400 Hz
(D) 400 and 600 Hz

362. The air column in a tube that is open at one end and closed at the other end is 0.8 m long and produces a fundamental note of frequency 100 Hz when the tube is struck to set up a standing wave. What are the frequencies of the first two overtones of this tube?

(A) 200 and 300 Hz
(B) 100 and 300 Hz
(C) 200 and 400 Hz
(D) 300 and 500 Hz

363. The mixture of fundamental frequencies and overtones that produces the sound unique to a musical instrument is called:

(A) pitch.
(B) harmony.
(C) quality.
(D) synchrony.

364. A tube that is open at both ends and a tube that is open at one end and closed at the other end both resonate at a fundamental frequency f. What is the next higher frequency at which each tube will resonate?

	Open Tube	Closed Tube
(A)	f	$2f$
(B)	$2f$	$2f$
(C)	$2f$	$3f$
(D)	$2f$	$4f$

365. A tube with a length l that is open at one end and closed at the other end produces a standing wave with a fundamental frequency f. If the tube is cut in half, what is the fundamental frequency of the shorter tube?

(A) $f/4$
(B) $f/2$
(C) $2f$
(D) $4f$

366. A string is stretched between two fixed points, and a standing wave of two complete loops is produced on the string using a frequency generator. Which of the following actions will produce a standing wave of three complete loops on the string?

(A) Decrease the frequency setting on the generator, keeping all other conditions the same.
(B) Replace the string with a thinner string of the same length and tension.
(C) Loosen the string to decrease the tension.
(D) Move the supports apart to increase the distance between the fixed points.

367. Two tuning forks, with frequencies of 256 and 260 Hz, respectively, are struck at the same time. An observer hears four beats per second. What causes this?

(A) Constructive and destructive interference of superimposed waves
(B) Refraction of the overlapping waves
(C) Diffraction of waves through the tuning forks
(D) Attenuation and damping of the superimposed waves

368. Three tuning forks have the same frequency. A piece of clay is attached to the top of one tuning fork, which is labeled Y. A second tuning fork is left unchanged and is labeled X. A third tuning fork has a different piece of clay attached to the top and is labeled Z. When X and Y are struck simultaneously, 5 beats per second are produced. When Y and Z are struck simultaneously, 3 beats per second are produced. How does the frequency of tuning fork Z compare to the frequency of tuning fork X?

(A) Tuning fork Z is 3 Hz less than tuning fork X.
(B) Tuning fork Z is 8 Hz less than tuning fork X.
(C) Tuning fork Z is either 8 Hz or 2 Hz less than tuning fork X.
(D) Tuning fork Z is 5 Hz greater than tuning fork X.

369. On a street corner, you are playing middle A (440 Hz) on a saxophone. In the open bed of an approaching pickup truck, a trombone is also playing middle A. You hear a beat frequency of 4 Hz. What frequency do you hear from the trombone, and what property of sound waves is being demonstrated in this problem?

	Frequency	**Property**
(A)	444 Hz	Doppler effect
(B)	444 Hz	Fundamental frequency
(C)	436 Hz	Doppler effect
(D)	436 Hz	Harmonics

370. Two open plastic pipes produce the same 260 Hz frequency when they are struck. One pipe is sanded so that it is slightly shorter, and the pipes then produce 4 beats per second when they are struck at the same time. What is the frequency of the shorter pipe?

(A) 65 Hz
(B) 256 Hz
(C) 264 Hz
(D) 1,040 Hz

371. A clarinet is tuned to play middle C. Which property of the note does NOT change as the clarinet is played and the air inside the instrument becomes warmer?

(A) Wavelength
(B) Speed
(C) Frequency
(D) Pitch

372. As sound waves travel in a fluid from a region of higher density to a region of lower density, the waves may change direction. What is the best explanation for this?

(A) Diffraction
(B) Attenuation
(C) Reflection
(D) Refraction

373. As sound travels through a medium, its amplitude decreases or is attenuated by scattering and absorption. Attenuation of sound in fluids directly increases with:

(A) the density of the medium and the frequency of the sound.
(B) the frequency of the sound and the viscosity of the medium.
(C) the density of the medium and the speed of sound in the medium.
(D) the speed and frequency of the sound.

374. Generally speaking, the speed of sound will be highest in air that is:

(A) more dense and less elastic.
(B) less dense and less elastic.
(C) more dense and more elastic.
(D) less dense and more elastic.

375. Which of the following is an example of sound diffraction?

(A) A car horn sounds less loud as it moves away from you.
(B) You are able to hear a sound from an invisible car horn around the corner of a building.
(C) A fire truck siren sounds higher in pitch when it is moving toward you than when the truck stops.
(D) On a cold night at the ballpark, you see the batter hit a ball and then hear the sound.

376. Ultrasonic sound waves can be transmitted into and reflected from different media, such as human tissue, to identify the structure based on how strongly the transmitted sound amplitude decreases as a function of distance and frequency. Which of the following is the constant that quantifies this decrease in amplitude in a given material?

(A) The elastic constant
(B) The attenuation coefficient
(C) The coefficient of restitution
(D) The coefficient of linear expansion

377. Which of the following situations will produce the greatest Doppler shift of frequency for the frequency of a siren heard by an observer?

(A) The observer is sitting at an intersection as the siren approaches the intersection from the east at a speed of 30 m/s.
(B) The siren is located at an intersection as the observer is moving away from the intersection toward the west at 30 m/s.
(C) The observer is in a car moving north at 30 m/s toward an intersection as the siren is moving toward the same intersection from the east at a speed of 30 m/s.
(D) The observer is in a car moving north at 30 m/s away from an intersection as the siren is moving toward the same intersection from the south at a speed of 30 m/s.

378. You are driving on a divided highway at 30 m/s, and you encounter an emergency vehicle with a siren that is emitting a constant frequency. In which of the following situations will you hear the highest frequency from the siren?

(A) The emergency vehicle is behind you, moving in your direction at 40 m/s.
(B) The emergency vehicle is ahead of you, moving away from you at 40 m/s.
(C) The emergency vehicle is ahead of you, moving toward you from the other direction at 40 m/s.
(D) The emergency vehicle is in the lane next to you, moving in the same direction at 30 m/s.

379. Ultrasound can be used to speed up chemical reactions because the ultrasonic signal:

(A) can interact directly with molecules to give them the energy to react.
(B) produces local extremes in temperature and pressure, thereby increasing the reaction rate.
(C) breaks up solids in solutions, thereby increasing the reaction rate.
(D) Both B and C are possibilities.

380. Which of the following best describes ultrasonic?

(A) Sound pressure with a frequency higher than 20,000 Hz
(B) Cyclic pressure in a medium with a frequency lower than 20 Hz
(C) Supersonic pressure oscillations in a medium
(D) Sound that cannot be perceived by humans due to differences in physical properties

CHAPTER 9

Electromagnetic Radiation and Optics

381. Which of the following statements is NOT true regarding electromagnetic waves?

(A) They all travel at the same speed in a vacuum.
(B) They can be polarized.
(C) Their frequency is directly proportional to their wavelength.
(D) They are formed from oscillating electric and magnetic fields.

382. Which of the following correctly ranks radiations from lowest frequency to highest frequency?

(A) Red, green, infrared, gamma
(B) Infrared, blue, ultraviolet, X-ray
(C) Yellow, red, infrared, radio
(D) Ultraviolet, green, red, infrared

383. Which of the following wavelength ranges falls within the range of ultraviolet light?

(A) 530–600 nm
(B) 250–300 nm
(C) 450–550 nm
(D) 600–700 nm

384. Interference of light as it passes through a double slit produces a pattern of light and dark bands. What property of light is this type of interference evidence of?

(A) Light has a particle nature such that the momentum of photons causes them to cancel their motions when they collide.

(B) Light is attenuated, or absorbed, by the region around the double slits, leaving only certain beams of light and producing a pattern of light and dark.

(C) Light has a wave nature so that it cannot pass efficiently through the double slits, leaving only certain rays of light to produce a pattern on a screen.

(D) Light has a wave nature so that the wave patterns produced by the two slits interfere constructively and destructively to produce a pattern.

385. An interference pattern is produced by light from a monochromatic source passing through a double slit. The amplitude of the pattern at the very center is a maximum because the path length difference from each slit to the center of the screen is:

(A) zero.

(B) maximum.

(C) one wavelength.

(D) one-half wavelength.

386. A thin film with an index of refraction of 1.3 is layered on top of glass so that there is air above the film and glass below the film. In order for green light to be reflected from the film so that the film appears green in full sunlight, the minimum thickness of the film must be:

(A) one-half the wavelength of green light in air.

(B) one-fourth the wavelength of green light in the film.

(C) one-half the wavelength of green light in the film.

(D) one-fourth the wavelength of green light in air.

387. When a large soap bubble is viewed in white light, it produces many colors. Which of the following statements best explains this phenomenon?

(A) Different thicknesses in the bubble reflect different colors.

(B) The bubble acts as a prism and separates the light into a spectrum of colors.

(C) White light is made up of all the colors of the rainbow.

(D) You can view the bubble from any angle, so you see all the colors.

388. As a wave passes through an opening that is approximately equal to its wavelength, the wave will bend or change direction, leading to interference of waves from each side of the opening. This is a demonstration of:

(A) diffraction.
(B) reflection.
(C) refraction.
(D) dispersion.

389. Using the equation $m\lambda = d \sin \theta$, which of the following conditions is NOT included for fringes produced by single-slit diffraction?

(A) The central maximum is of double width.
(B) The width of the single slit is d.
(C) Bright fringes occur at $m = 1, 2, 3$, etc.
(D) Dark fringes occur at $m = 1, 2, 3$, etc.

390. As the wavelength of light shining through a single-slit aperture increases, what happens to the interference pattern formed?

(A) Nothing changes in the pattern.
(B) The pattern becomes more spread out.
(C) The pattern moves closer together.
(D) Single slits don't produce interference patterns.

391. In a classroom demonstration, a red laser is shone through a diffraction grating, producing a pattern of bright spots on the wall. Maintaining all other conditions, the red laser is replaced with a green laser. The pattern of bright spots will:

(A) move closer together.
(B) move farther apart.
(C) remain the same, but the central maximum will be much wider.
(D) remain the same, but the entire pattern will shift to either the right or the left.

392. In a diffraction experiment performed on a scale where the slit width is fairly large, the angle θ between bright lines for any set of bright lines becomes very small. In this situation, the diffraction equation, $m\lambda = d \sin\theta$, can take on a simpler form. What is that form, and what is the reason that it can be simplified?

(A) $\theta = \dfrac{m\lambda}{d}$ because $\sin\theta$ is almost equal to θ for very small angles.

(B) $\theta = \dfrac{md}{\lambda}$ because the ratio of d to λ is very close to 1.

(C) $\tan\theta = \dfrac{m\lambda}{d}$ because sin and tan are almost equal for very small angles.

(D) $\sin\theta = \dfrac{\lambda}{d}$ because when the angle is small, the functions are the same for all values of m.

393. Which of the following will not result in polarization of waves?
(A) Visible light passing through a vacuum
(B) Radio waves passing through air
(C) Gamma rays passing through a vacuum
(D) Sound waves passing through air

394. Which of the following statements is true regarding the polarization of light?
(A) The intensity of polarized light is not changed when it passes through a polarizer.
(B) The amount by which the intensity of unpolarized light is reduced depends on the incident angle as it reaches the polarizer.
(C) The intensity of polarized light is reduced by half when it passes through a polarizer.
(D) The intensity of polarized light is not affected by the incident angle as it reaches a polarizer.

395. Which of the following statements best describes the polarization of light by reflection?
(A) Light reflected from metallic surfaces is usually polarized.
(B) Light reflected from a horizontal surface is generally polarized in the vertical direction.
(C) Reflected light is completely polarized when the reflected beam is perpendicular to the refracted beam.
(D) Polarization is most complete when the light is incident to the surface along the normal.

396. What is meant by the "red shift" of distant objects in the universe?

(A) An observed increase in the frequency of light emitted by objects moving away from Earth

(B) An observed decrease in the frequency of light emitted by objects moving away from Earth

(C) An observed increase in the frequency of light emitted by objects moving toward Earth

(D) An observed decrease in the frequency of light emitted by objects moving toward Earth

397. White light enters a right-angle glass prism from the left, as shown. Which is the most likely possibility for the refracted rays?

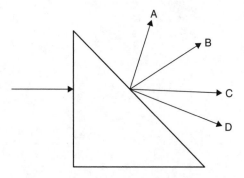

(A) Ray A is red light, and ray B is violet light.

(B) Ray A is violet light, and ray B is red light.

(C) Ray C is violet light, and ray D is red light.

(D) Ray C is red light, and ray D is violet light.

398. A light wave propagates in the positive x direction, with the electric field oscillation in the y direction. In what direction is the magnetic field oscillation?

(A) The negative x direction

(B) The y direction

(C) The z direction

(D) It cannot be determined from this information.

399. Mixing light in proportions of which of these three combinations could NOT produce white light?

(A) Red, blue, and magenta

(B) Green, yellow, and cyan

(C) Red, yellow, and blue

(D) Blue, green, and yellow

400. In which of the following cases will light change phase?

(A) Refraction from a medium of lower index of refraction to a medium of higher index of refraction

(B) Refraction from a medium of higher index of refraction to a medium of lower index of refraction

(C) Reflection from a medium of lower index of refraction to a medium of higher index of refraction

(D) Reflection from a medium of higher index of refraction to a medium of lower index of refraction

CHAPTER 10

Absorption Spectra

401. The energy level diagram below shows the first four energy states and possible transitions for an electron in an atom. Which transition would emit a photon with the highest frequency?

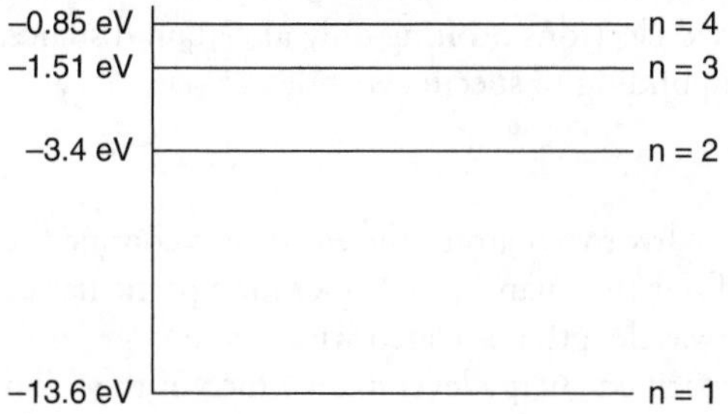

−0.85 eV	n = 4
−1.51 eV	n = 3
−3.4 eV	n = 2
−13.6 eV	n = 1

(A) $n = 4$ to $n = 2$
(B) $n = 1$ to $n = 3$
(C) $n = 3$ to $n = 1$
(D) $n = 1$ to $n = 4$

402. In the Bohr model of the atom, if the energy of an electron in the lowest energy state (ground state) is E, what is the energy of an electron in energy state n?

(A) nE
(B) E/n
(C) n^2E
(D) E/n^2

403. In the Bohr model of the atom, if R is the orbital radius of an electron in the lowest energy state, what would the radius of an electron in the third energy level be?

(A) $2R$
(B) $3R$
(C) $6R$
(D) $9R$

404. Which of the following statements is true regarding the development of the Bohr model of the atom?

(A) Compared to the previous Rutherford model, the Bohr model emphasized the structure of the nucleus.
(B) The Bohr model was a planetary model for the electrons, with the electrons orbiting the nucleus in a circular path around the nucleus.
(C) The Bohr model had electrons orbiting only at certain distances from the nucleus, corresponding to specific energies.
(D) All of the above.

405. In the Bohr model of the hydrogen atom, the electron is confined to specific energy states. If n is the quantum number for a particular energy level, λ_n is the electron wavelength associated with that energy level, and R is the radius for the specified energy level, then which of the following equations must be correct?

(A) $2\pi R = n\lambda$
(B) $2\pi\lambda = nR$
(C) $\pi R = n\lambda$
(D) $R^2 = n\lambda$

406. Determine the wavelength for an electron in the Bohr model of the hydrogen atom if the electron is in energy state $n = 1$ with an energy E.

(A) $\lambda = \dfrac{hc}{E}$

(B) $\lambda = \dfrac{E}{h}$

(C) $\lambda = \dfrac{h}{E}$

(D) $\lambda = \dfrac{hf}{E}$

Refer to the diagram below to answer questions 407 and 408.

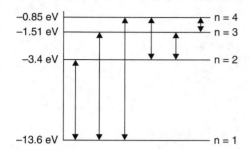

407. The energy diagram shows the absorption/emission spectrum for hydrogen. What is the smallest energy possible for an emitted photon from hydrogen?

(A) 13.6 eV
(B) 3.4 eV
(C) 0.85 eV
(D) 0.66 eV

408. The energy diagram shows the absorption/emission spectrum for hydrogen. What energy transition would emit a photon with the shortest wavelength?

(A) $n = 2$ to $n = 1$
(B) $n = 3$ to $n = 2$
(C) $n = 4$ to $n = 1$
(D) $n = 4$ to $n = 3$

409. An electron changes energy states from higher energy E_2 to lower energy E_1. Which of the following correctly expresses the wavelength of light emitted in this transition?

(A) $\dfrac{hf}{E_2 - E_1}$

(B) $\dfrac{hc}{E_2 - E_1}$

(C) $\dfrac{f}{E_2 - E_1}$

(D) $\dfrac{E_2 - E_1}{hc}$

410. The illustration below shows a beam of protons entering a magnetic field at angle *x*. What will be the initial change in direction of the motion of the protons as they enter the field?

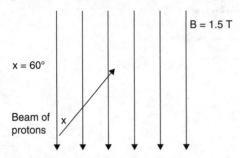

(A) Upward on the page
(B) Downward on the page
(C) Into the page
(D) Out of the page

411. The mass of a charged particle can be determined by analyzing its motion as it moves into a magnetic field in a synchrotron. Assume that a particle with a charge of +2e is moving at velocity *v* into a magnetic field of strength *B*, perpendicular to the direction of the field. The particle moves in a circular path with a radius *R*. Which of the following equations can be used to calculate the mass of the particle?

(A) $m = \dfrac{eB}{vR}$

(B) $m = \dfrac{2eB}{vR}$

(C) $m = \dfrac{2eBR}{v}$

(D) $m = \dfrac{eB}{2vR}$

412. In the illustration below, a charged particle is propelled from the left, in the +x direction, into a magnetic field. As the particle enters the field, it curves downward on the page, in the –y direction. In what direction would an electric field be added to the magnetic region so that the same charged particle would continue straight through the magnetic field in the +x direction without changing direction?

(A) The electric field would be directed in the +x direction.
(B) The electric field would be directed in the +y direction.
(C) The electric field would be directed in the –y direction.
(D) The electric field would be directed in the +z direction.

413. In the illustration below, an electron moves into a region with a uniform magnetic field directed out of the page. In what direction would an electric field be added to the magnetic region so that the electron moves in a straight line across the region from left to right?

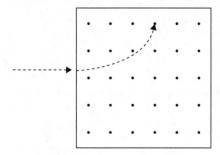

(A) The electric field would be directed into the page.
(B) The electric field would be directed toward the top of the page.
(C) The electric field would be directed toward the bottom of the page.
(D) The electric field would be directed out of the page.

414. In the illustration below, an electron enters a magnetic field from the right. Which of the following statements best describes the path of the electron as it travels through the field?

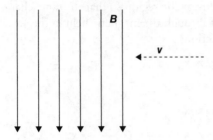

(A) It travels straight through the field undisturbed.
(B) It travels in a circle starting out of the page.
(C) It travels in the direction to which the magnetic field points.
(D) It travels in a circle starting into the page.

415. The illustration below shows a beam of protons entering a magnetic field at angle x. Which of the following expressions can be used to determine the magnitude of the magnetic force on each proton as the beam enters the magnetic field?

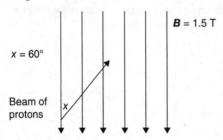

(A) $e(v \cos 60°)B$
(B) $e(v \sin 60°)B$
(C) evB
(D) The magnetic force would be zero.

416. In the illustration below, a cathode ray tube is set up between the magnetic poles of a horseshoe magnet. The tube shoots electrons from left to right between the poles. Which of the following statements describes the path of the beam of electrons?

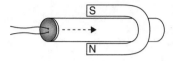

(A) The electrons will curve upward toward the north pole as they reach the region between the poles.

(B) The electrons will curve downward toward the south pole as they reach the region between the poles.

(C) The electrons will maintain a straight path at constant speed through the region between the poles.

(D) The electrons will not move closer to either pole but will curve outward toward the open end of the magnet and away from the magnet.

417. In the illustration below, a very long copper wire is positioned so that it lies between the poles of a strong horseshoe magnet. What is the effect of the magnet on the electrons in the metal wire?

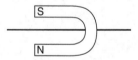

(A) The electrons begin to move to the right.

(B) The electrons begin to move to the left.

(C) The electrons begin to curve to one side of the wire.

(D) The magnet does not affect the charges in the wire.

418. A charged particle moves into a region with a uniform magnetic field and is observed to move in a circular path in the field. A second charged particle is sent into the field in the same direction but at twice the speed. What difference in the particles' paths will be observed?

(A) There will be no difference in the paths of the two particles.

(B) The second particle will move in a circle with a smaller radius.

(C) The second particle will move in a circle with a larger radius.

(D) The second particle will not move in a circular path in the magnetic field.

419. In the illustration below, a positive charge is placed at rest in the middle of a uniform magnetic field that is directed into the page, in the –z direction. What will be the direction of the subsequent motion of the charge?

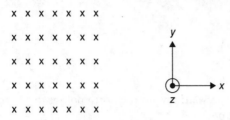

(A) The charge will move upward on the page, in the +y direction.
(B) The charge will move to the right, in the +x direction.
(C) The charge will move into the page, in the –z direction.
(D) The charge will not move.

CHAPTER 11

Geometric Optics

420. A beam of red light and a beam of blue light that shine on the surface of a piece of glass at the same incident angle are refracted at different angles as the beams enter the glass. The correct observation and best explanation is:

(A) the red-light frequency changes by a larger amount, so red light has a smaller refracted angle than blue light.

(B) the blue-light frequency changes by a larger amount, so blue light has a smaller refracted angle than red light.

(C) the red-light wavelength is reduced by a smaller amount, so red has a smaller refracted angle than blue

(D) the red-light wavelength is reduced by a smaller amount, so red light has a larger refracted angle than blue light.

421. The image formed by a plane mirror for a real object is:

(A) the same size as the object and inverted relative to the object.

(B) the same size as the object and upright relative to the object.

(C) smaller than the object and inverted relative to the object.

(D) smaller than the object and upright relative to the object.

422. The image formed by a convex (diverging) mirror by a real object is:

(A) the same size as the object and inverted relative to the object.

(B) the same size as the object and upright relative to the object.

(C) smaller than the object and inverted relative to the object.

(D) smaller than the object and upright relative to the object.

423. The image formed by a convex (converging) lens by a real object located inside the focal length of the lens is:

(A) the same size as the object and inverted relative to the object.
(B) the same size as the object and upright relative to the object.
(C) larger than the object and inverted relative to the object.
(D) larger than the object and upright relative to the object.

424. The image formed by a concave (converging) mirror by a real object located inside the focal length of the mirror is:

(A) smaller than the object and inverted relative to the object.
(B) smaller than the object and upright relative to the object.
(C) larger than the object and inverted relative to the object.
(D) larger than the object and upright relative to the object.

425. In a condition called myopia, or nearsightedness, the lens of the eye creates the image inside the eye at too short a distance from the lens. In other words, the image forms at a point between the lens and the retina. In order to correct this so that the person can see distant objects, the person may:

(A) wear concave lenses that will bring light rays to a closer focus.
(B) wear convex lenses that will extend the focus farther from the lens.
(C) wear concave lenses that will extend the focus farther from the lens.
(D) wear convex lenses that will bring light rays to a closer focus.

426. Chromatic aberration by a lens is the dispersion of white light to produce a fringe of colors around an image. Which statement is an explanation for this phenomenon?

(A) The frequencies change as white light goes through the lens, and blue frequencies change more than red frequencies.
(B) The frequencies change as white light goes through the lens, and red frequencies change more than blue frequencies.
(C) Different color components of white light have different focal lengths since each color has a unique index of refraction.
(D) The lens has a constant index of refraction for every color, but some colors bend more as they exit the lens back into air.

427. The three primary colors of light—that is, the colors that can be combined to produce white light—are:

(A) red, blue, and yellow.
(B) red, yellow, and green.
(C) blue, yellow, and green.
(D) red, blue, and green.

428. White light entering a glass prism may be separated into its component colors—a phenomenon called dispersion—because:

(A) each color undergoes a different frequency change as the light goes from the prism back into air.

(B) each color has a different index of refraction in the glass.

(C) longer wavelengths are refracted more than shorter wavelengths, separating the colors.

(D) the red end of the spectrum refracts at a larger angle than the violet.

429. An object is placed at the focal point of a thin convex lens. Which of the following statements best describes the image that forms?

(A) The image is real, forming at the focal length on the side of the lens opposite the object.

(B) The image is virtual, forming at twice the focal length on the same side of the lens as the object.

(C) The image is real, forming at twice the focal length on the side of the lens opposite the object.

(D) No image will form.

430. A thin diverging lens has a virtual focal length of 12 cm. An object is placed 6 cm from the center of the lens. Which of the following are properties of the image?

(A) Real, inverted, 4 cm from the lens

(B) Virtual, upright, 6 cm from the lens

(C) Virtual, upright, 4 cm from the lens

(D) Real, inverted, 6 cm from the lens

431. In the illustration below, an object at the position of the arrow is 1.5f from the center of a thin convex lens, where f is the focal length. Where will the image form?

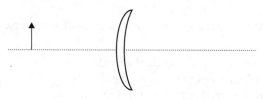

(A) At a distance f to the right of the lens

(B) At a distance f to the left of the lens

(C) At a distance 2f to the right of the lens

(D) At a distance 3f to the right of the lens

432. If an optical medium has an average index of refraction of 1.5 for white light, it can be concluded that a ray of white light traveling into the medium:

(A) has two-thirds the frequency it would have in a vacuum.
(B) has two-thirds the speed it would have in a vacuum.
(C) must change its direction.
(D) has 1.5 times the wavelength it would have in a vacuum.

433. The thin concave lens in the illustration has a virtual focal length *f*. An object, represented by the arrow, is positioned at a distance 1.5*f* from the center of the lens. Where will the image form?

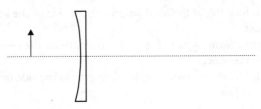

(A) At a distance 3*f* to the right of the lens
(B) At a distance 3*f* to the left of the lens
(C) At a distance 3*f*/5 to the left of the lens
(D) At a distance 3*f*/5 to the right of the lens

434. An object that looks blue when viewed under a white light source will appear to be which color when illuminated by white light and viewed through a yellow filter?

(A) Orange
(B) Black
(C) Red
(D) Green

435. When white light travels from air into a glass prism and is dispersed into colors:

(A) blue light refracts over a smaller angle than red.
(B) all frequencies of light travel at the same speed.
(C) green light changes wavelength more than blue.
(D) blue light has a lower speed than red.

436. For total internal reflection to occur at the interface between two different materials, all of the following conditions must be met EXCEPT:

(A) the incident path of the light must be from a medium of higher index of refraction to a medium of lower index of refraction.

(B) the incident angle must always be less than the critical angle.

(C) the incident angle must be the critical angle when the refracted angle is 90°.

(D) the critical angle must be equal to arcsin n_2/n_1, where n_1 is the incident medium.

437. The image in a plane mirror of a person standing a distance d in front of the mirror appears to the person to be:

(A) upright, real, and a distance d away.

(B) upright, virtual, and a distance $2d$ away.

(C) vertically inverted, virtual, and a distance $2d$ from the mirror.

(D) vertically inverted, real, and a distance $2d$ from the person.

438. In the illustration, four rays from the top of an object strike a mirror and reflect. Each ray and its reflection is shown using a different style of line. Which ray construction does NOT lead to a correct location of the image for the converging mirror shown?

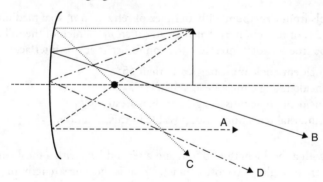

(A) A
(B) B
(C) C
(D) D

439. As a ray of light moves from a medium of lower index of refraction into a medium of higher index of refraction,

(A) speed decreases, while frequency and wavelength remain the same.
(B) speed and wavelength decrease, while frequency remains the same.
(C) speed and wavelength increase, while frequency remains the same.
(D) speed and frequency decrease, while wavelength remains the same.

440. Which of the following scenarios is NOT possible?

(A) A concave mirror produces a real image.
(B) A plane mirror produces a virtual image.
(C) A convex mirror produces a virtual image.
(D) A concave lens produces a real image.

441. An object placed a distance d_o in front of a convex mirror with a focal length $-f$ produces an image that is one-half the size of the original object. What is the magnitude of the focal length?

(A) $d_o/2$
(B) $2d_o$
(C) $2d_o/3$
(D) $d_o/3$

442. Light travels from a medium with an index of refraction n_1 to a medium with an index of refraction n_2 that is greater than n_1. Which of the following must be true for total internal reflection to occur at this interface?

(A) The incident angle must be greater than $45°$.
(B) The incident angle must be less than $45°$.
(C) The incident angle must be greater than arcsin n_2/n_1.
(D) Total internal reflection is not possible in this situation.

443. One lens with a focal length of 0.5 m and a second lens with a focal length of 0.25 m are brought into close contact. What is the lens strength, in diopters, of the combination of the two lenses?

(A) 2
(B) 4
(C) 6
(D) 8

444. Which of the following statements provides the cause of and a possible solution for spherical lens aberration?

(A) Spherical aberration is produced when a lens is not perfectly spherical, causing light to focus at multiple points. Both sides of the lens should be ground so that it is perfectly spherical.

(B) Spherical aberration is produced when a lens bends different wavelengths of light by different amounts, causing multiple focal points. Making the lens more spherical will cause red light to bend more, reducing the effect.

(C) Spherical aberration is produced when the lens is ground so that the focal length is greater than $R/2$, where R is the radius of curvature. Grinding the lens so that it is spherical but has less curvature will improve focus.

(D) Spherical aberration is produced when a spherical lens bends light from the edges to a closer focal point than light passing through closer to the center. Making the lens nonspherical will improve focus.

445. Which of the following statements describes the eye of a myopic (nearsighted) person and a possible solution?

(A) In nearsightedness, light passing through the eye's lens is focused in front of the retina; that is, the focal length of the lens is less than the distance from the lens to the retina. A convex lens will increase the focal length to correct it.

(B) In nearsightedness, light passing through the eye's lens is focused behind the retina; that is, the focal length of the lens is more than the distance from the lens to the retina. A convex lens will increase the focal length to correct it.

(C) In nearsightedness, light passing through the eye's lens is focused behind the retina; that is, the focal length of the lens is more than the distance from the lens to the retina. A concave lens will decrease the focal length to correct it.

(D) In nearsightedness, light passing through the eye's lens is focused in front of the retina; that is, the focal length of the lens is less than the distance from the lens to the retina. A concave lens will increase the focal length to correct it.

446. A biology student inspects a slide by using a microscope that has a 5× eyepiece lens and by setting the objective lens at 10×. An object on the slide that is 0.3 mm in diameter will appear to have what diameter?

(A) 0.15 cm
(B) 0.45 cm
(C) 1.5 cm
(D) 4.5 cm

447. A student is making a refracting telescope from two lenses. First, the student tests each lens and determines that the objective lens focuses light from distant objects at a point 15 cm from the lens. The eyepiece lens focuses light from distant objects at a point 5 cm from the lens. How far from each other does the student need to place the two lenses in order to form an image in the eye of the person looking through both lenses at a distant object?

(A) 75 cm
(B) 40 cm
(C) 20 cm
(D) 3 m

PART 5

Atoms, Nuclear Decay, Electronic Structures, and Atomic Chemical Behavior

CHAPTER 12

Atomic Nucleus

448. What does the symbol $_2\text{He}^4$ for the element helium mean?

(A) An atom of helium has 2 protons and 4 electrons.
(B) A helium nucleus has 2 protons and 4 neutrons.
(C) A helium nucleus has 2 protons and 2 neutrons.
(D) An atom of helium has 2 protons and a total of 4 charged nucleons.

449. Which of the following statements is NOT true regarding atomic nuclei?

(A) All atomic nucleons are protons and neutrons.
(B) All atomic nuclei have an approximately constant density regardless of their composition.
(C) All nuclei of a given element have the same number of protons.
(D) All nuclei of a given element have the same total number of nucleons.

450. Which of the following is a fundamental particle?

(A) Proton
(B) Neutron
(C) Electron
(D) Deuteron

451. Which of the following is NOT an isotope of hydrogen?

(A) Protium
(B) Deuterium
(C) Tritium
(D) Quaternium

452. Which of the following nuclear transformations is NOT possible?

(A) Decay of a neutron into a proton and an electron
(B) Capture of an electron by a proton to produce a neutron
(C) Emission of a positron by a proton to produce a neutron
(D) Decay of a proton into a neutron and an electron

453. What is the general pattern for the number of neutrons in stable isotopes?

(A) The most stable isotopes always have an equal number of protons and neutrons in the nucleus.
(B) The ratio of neutrons to protons in stable isotopes tends to increase as atomic number increases.
(C) The ratio of neutrons to protons in stable isotopes tends to decrease as atomic number increases.
(D) There seems to be no general pattern for the ratio of neutrons to protons for stable isotopes as the sizes of nuclei increase.

454. What is the weak nuclear force?

(A) The force that loosely binds outer-shell electrons to the nucleus of an atom
(B) The force that holds the nucleus together
(C) The force that causes protons in the nucleus to repel each other
(D) The nuclear force responsible for beta decay

455. Which of the following fundamental forces is considered to be the strongest at short ranges?

(A) Gravitational force
(B) The weak nuclear force
(C) The strong nuclear force
(D) Electromagnetic force

456. As a result of the emission of an alpha particle, an atomic nucleus:

(A) increases its atomic number by 2 and increases its mass number by 4.
(B) decreases its atomic number by 2 and decreases its mass number by 4.
(C) increases its atomic number by 2 and decreases its mass number by 4.
(D) decreases its atomic number by 2 and increases its mass number by 4.

457. As a result of the emission of a beta particle, an atomic nucleus:

(A) increases its atomic number by 2 and increases its mass number by 1.
(B) increases its atomic number by 1 but doesn't change its mass number.
(C) increases its atomic number by 1 and decreases its mass number by 1.
(D) decreases its atomic number by 1 and increases its mass number by 1.

458. During radioactive emission of gamma radiation in which no other particles are emitted, the gamma photons are emitted in pairs. Which conservation law would be defied if only one gamma photon were emitted?

(A) Conservation of mass
(B) Conservation of charge
(C) Conservation of linear momentum
(D) Conservation of energy

459. The radioactive element radium-224 has a half-life of 3.66 days. Which of the following statements is true regarding one nucleus of radium after 3.66 days?

(A) Half of the nucleus has decayed.
(B) The nucleus will decay only when a second nucleus is brought into contact with it.
(C) There is a 50% chance that the nucleus will have decayed.
(D) The nucleus won't decay prior to 3.66 days but should decay after that time.

460. What nuclear transformation occurs during beta decay?

(A) A proton decays into a neutron and an electron.
(B) An electron and a proton combine to form a neutron.
(C) A neutron decays into a proton and an electron.
(D) An electron and a neutron combine to form a proton.

461. The chart below shows the decay curve for a 100 g sample of polonium-210. Which of the following best estimates the half-life of ^{210}Po?

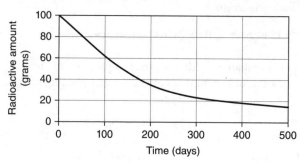

(A) 500 days
(B) 250 days
(C) 180 days
(D) 140 days

462. Particles with mass may be given off by a nucleus through the process of radioactive decay, thus reducing the mass of the nucleus. Which of the following is NOT one of these particles?

(A) Gammas
(B) Positrons
(C) Electrons
(D) Alpha particles

463. One step in the radioactive decay series of uranium-235 to lead-207 is the decay of bismuth-215. In this step, what is produced when $_{83}Bi^{215}$ gives off an alpha particle and a beta particle?

(A) $_{85}At^{218}$
(B) $_{82}Pb^{211}$
(C) $_{83}Bi^{211}$
(D) $_{84}Po^{211}$

464. A radioactive sample is placed in a cloud chamber so that the paths of radioactive decay products can be seen as "tracks" in the chamber. A magnetic field is set up across the cloud chamber to help identify the decay products. Which of the following radioactive decay products would never change direction in the magnetic field?

(A) Alpha particles
(B) Beta particles
(C) Gamma rays
(D) Positrons

465. In the nuclear fission reaction

$$_{92}^{235}U + _{0}^{1}n \rightarrow \ _{56}^{139}Ba + _{36}^{94}Kr + \underline{\quad} + energy$$

a uranium atom is bombarded with a neutron to produce an atom of barium and an atom of krypton. What is the other product of this reaction?

(A) An electron
(B) Two electrons
(C) A proton
(D) Three neutrons

466. In a nuclear fusion reaction, four protons (hydrogen nuclei) combine to form a helium nucleus, two neutrinos, and another product.

$$4{}_1^1\text{H} \rightarrow {}_2^4\text{He} + 2{}_0^0\eta + \underline{} + \text{energy}$$

What is the other product of this reaction?

(A) A helium nucleus
(B) Two protons
(C) Two positrons (positive electrons)
(D) Two beta particles (negative electrons)

467. According to some scientists, the fusion of deuterium with tritium to create helium-4 may be a source of energy in the future since the reaction gives off large amounts of energy.

$$ {}_1\text{H}^2 + {}_1\text{H}^3 \rightarrow {}_2\text{He}^4 + \underline{} + \text{energy}$$

What is the other product of this reaction?

(A) A proton
(B) A neutron
(C) An electron
(D) A positron

CHAPTER **13**

Electronic Structure

468. The graph below represents data from a photoelectric effect experiment. Estimate the minimum (cutoff) frequency of light that will cause the ejection of electrons from zinc.

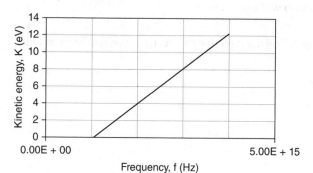

(A) 5.0×10^{14} Hz
(B) 2.5×10^{15} Hz
(C) 2.0×10^{15} Hz
(D) 1.0×10^{15} Hz

469. In the illustration below, a proton moves from the left toward the right into a uniform magnetic field that is directed into the page, in the –z direction. What will be the direction of the subsequent motion of the charge?

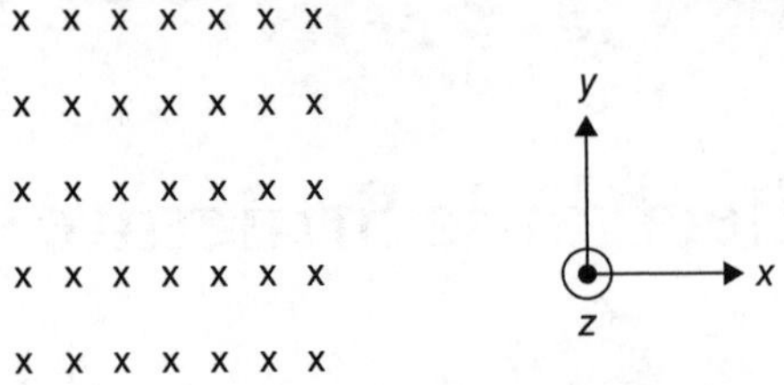

(A) The proton will move upward on the page, in the +y direction.
(B) The proton will move to the right, in the +x direction.
(C) The proton will move into the page, in the –z direction.
(D) The proton will not move.

470. Which of the following equations correctly expresses the momentum of a photon?

(A) $p = \dfrac{hf}{c}$

(B) $p = \dfrac{h}{c}$

(C) $p = hf$
(D) $p = h\lambda$

471. The Heisenberg Uncertainty Principle states that since particles can behave like waves, if the momentum of a particle is known with great precision, it is impossible to know the particle's _____ with the same great precision.

(A) speed
(B) wavelength
(C) position
(D) mass

472. One difference between typical particles and photons of light is that:

(A) only photons can have wavelengths, and particles do not have wavelengths.
(B) only particles have momentum, and photons do not have momentum.
(C) only photons have zero rest mass, and particles do not have zero rest mass.
(D) only photons have energy, and particles do not have energy.

473. Only one electron at a time may have a specific set of quantum numbers that identify the energy state in an atom. Thus, when an atom is in its ground state, not all electrons may occupy the lowest energy states. This is a partial statement of:

(A) the Pauli Exclusion Principle.
(B) the Heisenberg Uncertainty Principle.
(C) Einstein's special theory of relativity.
(D) Schrödinger's equation.

474. As the wavelength of a photon increases, its momentum:

(A) decreases since its speed will decrease.
(B) increases since its speed will increase.
(C) stays the same since photon momentum is not affected by wavelength.
(D) decreases since photons of longer wavelength have lower energy.

475. Circulating electric currents at the atomic level cause some materials to be magnetic. Materials that have no net magnetic field but that can become magnetic if they are placed in an external magnetic field—with the magnetic alignment in the same direction as the external field—are called:

(A) ferromagnetic.
(B) diamagnetic.
(C) paramagnetic.
(D) geomagnetic.

476. Materials that have no net magnetic field but that can become magnetic if they are placed in an external magnetic field—with the magnetic alignment of domains within the material in the opposite direction from the external field—are called:

(A) ferromagnetic.
(B) diamagnetic.
(C) paramagnetic.
(D) geomagnetic.

477. Which of the following statements best describes the magnetic field of Earth?

(A) Earth's magnetic field may be related to an iron-nickel core and the spin of the planet.
(B) Earth's magnetic field lies along the direction in which the north magnetic pole of a compass points.
(C) Earth's magnetic field has its current south magnetic pole in northern Canada.
(D) All of the above.

478. The strong magnetic field of a material such as neodymium is due primarily to:

(A) how electrons are paired in atoms of the material.
(B) the spin nature of electrons in the atom.
(C) the alignments of atoms within the material.
(D) all of the above.

479. Under certain conditions, a particle-antiparticle pair (such as an electron and a positron) can annihilate each other, converting all the mass of the particles into two gamma photons. If m is the mass of each particle, which of the following equations can be used to determine the frequency of each photon?

(A) $f = \dfrac{2mc^2}{\lambda}$

(B) $f = \dfrac{mc^2}{2h}$

(C) $f = \dfrac{mc^2}{h}$

(D) $f = \dfrac{2mc^2}{h}$

480. In which of the following cases would a uniform magnetic field B exert the largest magnitude of force on a charged particle?

(A) The charge is $3q$ and is placed stationary in the magnetic field.
(B) The charge is $2q$ and is moving at velocity v directly along the magnetic field lines.
(C) The charge is q and is moving at velocity v perpendicular to the magnetic field lines.
(D) The charge is q and is moving at an angle of $60°$ to the direction of the magnetic field.

481. In the illustration below, a helium nucleus is momentarily at rest in the middle of a uniform magnetic field that is directed into the page, in the $-z$ direction. What will be the direction of the subsequent motion of the nucleus?

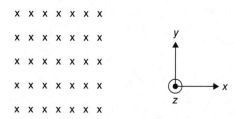

(A) The nucleus will move upward on the page, in the $+y$ direction.
(B) The nucleus will move to the right, in the $+x$ direction.
(C) The nucleus will move into the page, in the $-z$ direction.
(D) The nucleus will not move.

CHAPTER 14

Thermochemistry and Thermodynamics

482. According to the first law of thermodynamics (the law of conservation of energy for thermodynamic systems), an increase in the temperature of a system during an adiabatic process is due to:

(A) energy added to the system to increase the temperature of the molecules.

(B) work done by the molecules of the system in expanding themselves.

(C) work done by an external force on the system, increasing the kinetic energy of the molecules.

(D) any energy transfer from one part of the system to another.

483. How much energy must be added or removed to allow 2 moles of an ideal gas to expand isothermally from 1 m³ to 3 m³?

(A) An amount equal to the work done by the gas must be removed.

(B) An amount equal to the work done by the gas must be added.

(C) An amount equal to the product of pressure and volume must be added.

(D) No energy must be added or removed: $Q = 0$.

484. An ideal gas at pressure P, volume V, and temperature T undergoes an isothermal process that changes the pressure to $2P$. What is the new volume of the gas?

(A) $\frac{1}{2}V$

(B) V

(C) $2V$

(D) $4V$

485. A system of ideal gas molecules contains 2 moles of gas. Eighty joules of work is done in compressing the gas as the gas gives off 25 J of energy. Then the gas is allowed to expand, doing 40 J of work on its surroundings. What is the net change in the internal energy of the gas as a result of these processes?

    (A) +145 J
    (B) −15 J
    (C) +15 J
    (D) +45 J

486. Which of the following statements is true regarding the change in internal energy (ΔU) of a system of an ideal gas?

    (A) Internal energy will increase if work is done on the system during an isobaric process.
    (B) Internal energy will decrease if work is done by the system during an isovolumetric process.
    (C) Internal energy will increase if energy is added to the system and work is done on the system.
    (D) Internal energy will increase if energy is added during an isothermal process.

487. Chamber X, a very large reservoir of gas at a temperature of 400 K, comes into thermal contact with chamber Y, a very large reservoir of gas at 300 K. During a certain time interval, 500 J of heat transfer occurs from chamber X to chamber Y. Which of the following statements is true regarding entropy in this situation?

    (A) The magnitude of the entropy change of chamber X is greater than the magnitude of the entropy change of chamber Y.
    (B) The magnitude of the entropy change of chamber Y is greater than the magnitude of the entropy change of chamber X.
    (C) The magnitudes of the entropy changes of chambers X and Y are equal.
    (D) Once the chambers come to equilibrium, there has been no net change in entropy.

488. Two isolated chambers of an ideal gas are in thermal contact with each other, chamber X at a higher temperature T_1 and chamber Y at a lower temperature T_2. If heat is transferred directly from chamber X to chamber Y,

(A) the heat transfer out of chamber X is greater than the heat transfer into chamber Y.
(B) the magnitude of the change in entropy of each chamber is the same.
(C) the magnitude of the change in entropy of chamber X is greater than the magnitude of the change in entropy of chamber Y.
(D) the magnitude of the change in entropy of chamber X is less than the magnitude of the change in entropy of chamber Y.

489. The thermal conductivity of water is 0.609 W/m·C°, that of oil is 0.145 W/m·C°, and that of alcohol is 0.202 W/m·C°. Students are designing a container to maintain a beaker of boiling water at a constant temperature inside the container. The students decide to set the beaker into a liquid bath. With which of the following actions would the students be most successful in keeping the water boiling?

(A) Set the beaker into oil at 90°C.
(B) Set the beaker into alcohol at 80°C.
(C) Set the beaker into water at 90°C.
(D) Set the beaker into water at 80°C.

490. Which of the following methods of energy transfer is due to the motion of fluids of varying densities?

(A) Conduction
(B) Convection
(C) Radiation
(D) Insulation

491. A hot liquid can be cooled more quickly by stirring it with a silver stick. Which of the following actions would be even more effective in cooling the liquid?

(A) Replace the stick with one twice as long and half the diameter.
(B) Replace the stick with one half as long and twice the diameter.
(C) Replace the stick with one twice as long and twice the diameter.
(D) Replace the stick with one half as long and half the diameter.

492. The rate at which energy transfers by conduction from a hot chamber to a cold chamber through a steel rod may be increased by:

(A) substituting a rod with the same dimensions but made of a material with a higher specific heat.

(B) decreasing the temperature of the hot chamber and increasing the temperature of the cold chamber.

(C) substituting a shorter steel rod of the same diameter.

(D) substituting a thinner steel rod of the same length.

493. One method of heat transfer is radiation, which is transfer of energy by electromagnetic waves. This method is sometimes called:

(A) gamma radiation.

(B) infrared radiation.

(C) visible light.

(D) ultraviolet radiation.

494. Which of the following statements describes the mechanism at the molecular level that causes the handle of a metal spoon placed into a kettle of very hot soup to become too hot to touch?

(A) The molecules in the end of the spoon that is in the soup begin to move faster as they gain energy from the soup, so those molecules move to the handle of the spoon, exciting other molecules in the handle of the spoon and making the handle feel hotter to the touch.

(B) The molecules in the end of the spoon that is in the soup absorb radiation from the hot soup that is transmitted as thermal energy to the handle of the spoon.

(C) The molecules in the end of the spoon that is in the soup move farther apart as they gain energy from the soup, making that end of the spoon less dense. As molecules from the handle move to the other end of the spoon to balance out the density, the handle becomes less dense and thus feels hotter.

(D) The molecules in the end of the spoon that is in the soup have more kinetic energy as they gain energy from the soup. They are moving faster and collide with molecules near them more often, giving them kinetic energy and so on, until the molecules in the handle have higher kinetic energy, too.

495. A solid door is made of a material with a thermal conductivity of 0.1 W/m·C° and has the dimensions 2 m × 1 m × 2 cm thick. The inside temperature is 70°C, and the outside temperature is 20°C. Determine the rate of heat transfer through the door.

(A) 10 J/s
(B) 140 J/s
(C) 200 J/s
(D) 500 J/s

496. Which of the following quantities does NOT normally increase with an increase in temperature?

(A) Electrical resistance
(B) The speed of sound in air
(C) The density of a gas
(D) The pressure of a gas at constant volume

497. At room temperature, a brass ball has the same diameter as the inside opening of a brass ring, so the ball just barely fits through the ring. What happens if the ball and the ring are heated together to a much higher temperature?

(A) The ball gets larger while the inside diameter of the ring gets smaller.
(B) The ball gets larger while the inside diameter of the ring gets larger.
(C) The ball gets larger while the inside diameter of the ring remains constant.
(D) The ball's diameter remains constant while the inside diameter of the ring increases.

498. A metal ruler is made of a material that has a coefficient of linear expansion of $12 \times 10^{-6}/C°$. If the ruler is heated from 70°C to 100°C, by what percentage does the length of one centimeter on the ruler increase?

(A) About 1%
(B) Between 0.5% and 1%
(C) Between 0.01% and 0.5%
(D) Less than 0.01%

499. A square metal plate 10 cm on a side is made of a material that has a coefficient of linear expansion of $10 \times 10^{-6}/C°$. If the plate's temperature is increased from 70°C to 80°C, what is the new area of the plate?

   (A) 100.00 cm^2
   (B) 100.01 cm^2
   (C) 100.10 cm^2
   (D) 101.00 cm^2

500. During which step of the process shown in the graph below is work done on the gas?

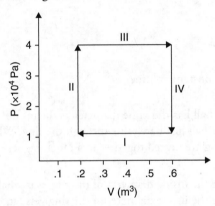

   (A) I
   (B) II
   (C) III
   (D) IV

ANSWERS

PART 1: TRANSLATIONAL MOTION, FORCES, WORK, ENERGY, AND EQUILIBRIUM

Chapter 1: Translational Motion

1. (C) The units on the left side of the equation are $(m/s)^2$, or m^2/s^2. On the right side of the equation, the units on acceleration are m/s^2, and the units on displacement are m; thus, the units on the right side are $(m/s^2)(m)$, or m^2/s^2. The correct answer is also quickly recognizable from the familiar equation $v_f^2 = v_o^2 + 2as$ for the case where v_o^2 is equal to zero.

2. (B) Graph II shows a power curve, or the relationship "y versus x^2." Graph I might represent the shape of an inverse curve, or the relationship "y versus $1/x$." Graph III might represent the shape of a root curve, or the relationship "y versus square root of x." Answer IV is a distractor—it is not a good representation of a mathematical curve (perhaps coming closest to a decreasing exponential function or a graph of a circle centered on $(0,0)$ with x and y both positive).

3. (A) Analysis of units can be an important tool for determining the meaning of slope and area in situations where you have some difficulty understanding the meanings of these quantities. Slope is "rise over run," or y axis quantity divided by x axis quantity. In this case, the slope is newtons per meter (N/m), which might be the spring constant, for example, if the graph is spring force versus spring extension. The area under the graph has units determined by multiplying the units on the axes. In this case, the units are newton-meters (N·m), which would be the work done in stretching a spring a given distance for the example described.

4. (B) First, convert centimeters to meters; this needs to be done in every case where you want to determine work or energy in joules when using newtons for force. One meter is equivalent to 100 cm, so the decimal point is moved two places to the left in each case to convert centimeters to meters. In answer A, force times distance is $(5)(2)$, or 10 J. In answer choice B, force times distance is $(5)(0.2)$, or 1.0 J—which is the correct answer. In answer choice C, force times distance is $(50)(0.002)$, or $(50)(2)/1{,}000$, which is 0.1 J. In answer choice D, force times distance is $(5)(0.02)$, or 0.1 J.

5. (C) The prefix *micro-* means one millionth, or 1×10^{-6}, while the prefix *mega-* means one million, or 1×10^6. One meter is equivalent to one million micrometers, and one megameter is equivalent to one million meters. Therefore, one megameter is equivalent to one million times one million, or one trillion micrometers (that's 1×10^{12}). Another way to determine this is the unit cancellation method:

$$\frac{(1 \times 10^6 \, \mu m)}{1 \, m} \times \frac{(1 \times 10^6 \, m)}{1 \, Mm} = \frac{1 \times 10^{12} \, \mu m}{1 \, Mm}$$

Using the unit cancellation method to convert units, each fraction multiplied is an "equivalent," where the numerator and the denominator are equal, so we're essentially multiplying by one in each case. Then cancel the units in the numerator and the denominator to determine the units in the answer.

6. (A) By multiplying the quantities as shown, making sure to square the units on Y, and canceling a meter in the numerator with the unit meter in the denominator, you get the units as shown in answer choice A. You might recognize the unit combination in answer choice A as equivalent to 1 newton. (It's useful to remember that 1 newton is equal to 1 kg·m/s^2.) You might also recognize this formula as a method of calculating centripetal force on an object of mass m (in kg) moving at speed v (in m/s) in a circle of radius R (in meters). The force is the result, measured in newtons.

7. (D) From the answer choices, it's apparent that we need to make a substitution for newtons. As noted before, it's helpful to remember that 1 newton is equal to 1 kg·m/s^2. Substituting this for the quantity X, substituting kg/m for the quantity Y, and canceling gives us the square root of meters squared per second squared. Taking the square root of that produces m/s:

$$\sqrt{\frac{\left(\dfrac{\text{kg} \cdot \text{m}}{\text{s}^2}\right)}{\left(\dfrac{\text{kg}}{\text{m}}\right)}} = \sqrt{\left(\frac{\text{kg} \cdot \text{m}}{\text{s}^2}\right)\left(\frac{\text{m}}{\text{kg}}\right)} = \sqrt{\frac{\text{m}^2}{\text{s}^2}} = \text{m/s}$$

Believe it or not, this is a real determination for the speed of a wave on a string, where X represents the tension in the string (in newtons) and Y represents the linear density of the string (in kg/m). The speed, indeed, turns out to be in meters per second.

8. (A) If the quantities n, R, and T are constant in the equation $PV = nRT$, then the product PV is equal to a constant. P and V are therefore inversely proportional to each other. Graph I represents an inverse proportion of the form xy = constant, so this is the correct answer choice. Graph II represents the form $y = kx^2$, where k is a constant. Graph III represents $y = k\sqrt{x}$, where k is a constant. Graph IV is a distractor (perhaps coming closest to a decreasing exponential function or a graph of a circle centered on (0,0) with x and y both positive).

9. (C) If length is the independent variable and period is the dependent variable, then the equation is of the form "period as a function of length." Period would be plotted on the y axis, and length would be plotted on the x axis, and the graph would be of the form $y = k\sqrt{x}$, which is Graph III. Graph I represents an inverse proportion of the form xy = constant, so this is an incorrect answer choice. Graph II represents the form $y = kx^2$, where k is a constant. Graph IV is a distractor (perhaps coming closest to a decreasing exponential function or a graph of a circle centered on (0,0) with x and y both positive).

10. (B) The graph is of the form $y = kx^2$, so squaring all the values of X given in the data and plotting "Y versus X^2" should produce a linear graph. A linear graph can also be produced by plotting "Y^2 versus X."

11. (B) Vectors are added from tip to tail, with the resultant or sum being measured from the beginning of the first vector to the end of the second vector, as shown below by the dashed line from the start of vector X to the end of vector Y.

12. (B) Express the plane's displacement in terms of components north of A and east of A. The first portion of the flight is 300 km north with no east component. The second portion of the flight can be considered in terms of components of a right triangle with acute angles of 45°. Since this type of triangle has sides with length ratios of 1-1-$\sqrt{2}$, the sides must be 1,000 km, 1,000 km, and 1,400 km (since $\sqrt{2}$ = 1.4). This means that the components are 1,000 km east and 1,000 km north. Adding these values to the first portion of the flight, the displacement is 1,300 km north and 1,000 km east. (Note: It's helpful to recognize the length ratios for the sides of "special" triangles such as the one here.)

13. (C) Since the two forces are at right angles, they can be considered to be components of the resultant force, so we recognize a 3-4-5 right triangle. The net force is 50 N. Then Newton's second law, $\Sigma F = ma$, is used to find the acceleration.

$$a = \frac{\Sigma F}{m} = \frac{50 \text{ N}}{35 \text{ kg}} = 1.4 \text{ m/s}^2$$

14. (C) The magnitude of the resultant of two vectors (such as these) that are perpendicular to each other can be found using the Pythagorean theorem. Since the question asks only for speed, which is not a vector, the direction of the resultant is not part of the answer.

$$R = \sqrt{A^2 + B^2} = \sqrt{200^2 + 70^2}$$

15. (C) The resultant vector of vector A minus vector B would be the addition of vector A to the negative of vector B. The negative of a vector has the same magnitude, but the vector is in the opposite direction. The addition of A to –B is shown as a dashed arrow below:

16. (D) The slope of the line is the acceleration, and since the slope is constant, the acceleration is constant. Any two points on the line can be used to determine the slope, which is negative:

$$\text{Slope} = \frac{\Delta y}{\Delta x} = \frac{0-6 \text{ m/s}}{6 \text{ m/s}-0} = -1 \text{ m/s}^2$$

17. (D) We can find the acceleration by using the equation $\Delta x = v_0 t + \frac{1}{2}at^2$ for the first interval, with initial velocity equal to zero: $2 \text{ m} = 0 + \frac{1}{2}a(4 \text{ s})^2$. The acceleration, then, is $\frac{1}{4} \text{ m/s}^2$. Now use this acceleration to find the final velocity after that first interval:

$$v_f = v_0 + at = 0 + (\frac{1}{4} \text{ m/s}^2)(4 \text{ s}) = 1 \text{ m/s}$$

Now we can apply the original equation again for the second interval, with initial velocity 1 m/s, to find the distance traveled:

$$\Delta x = v_0 t + \frac{1}{2}at^2 = (1)(4 s) + \frac{1}{2}(\frac{1}{4})(4 s)^2 = 6 \text{ m}$$

There is a shortcut method. An object starting from rest and accelerating at a constant rate will travel distances in equal intervals of time that are in the ratio of the odd numbers: 1, 3, 5, 7, etc. In this case, the first distance was 2 m, so the distance traveled during the second equal time interval is 3 times 2, or 6 m. (This shortcut method, sometimes called "Galileo's law of odd numbers," is very useful for objects from rest under the influence of the gravitational force.)

18. (C) For a graph with velocity on the y axis and time on the x axis, the slope would be $\Delta y/\Delta x$ or $\Delta v/\Delta t$. This ratio would have units of m/s/s, which are units of acceleration. Since only a single point is designated, the slope for this point is the instantaneous acceleration, or acceleration at that instant in time.

19. (D) In choice A, the acceleration is centripetal and is constant. In choice B, the acceleration could be constant and positive, while in choice C, the acceleration could be constant and negative. So choice D correctly indicates that any of the three could be correct.

20. (D) Answer choices A, B, and C could be true. If the line is horizontal, the velocity is constant. If the plot is diagonal, for example, the slope is the acceleration, which is constant. If the line is a horizontal line at $v = 0$, then both velocity and acceleration are zero.

21. (C) A parabolic path is defined by an object in free motion in two dimensions if there is a constant net force on the object in one dimension and no net force in the second dimension. If there is no net force in one of the dimensions, then there is no acceleration ($\Sigma F = ma$) and constant velocity. In the second dimension, there would be a constant force, which means constant acceleration in that dimension. An object projected into the air at an angle to the ground will take a parabolic path if we disregard any frictional effects due to air.

22. (C) The area between the graph line and the x axis is the change in position. For this graph, the area is positive and is equal to $(\frac{1}{2})(6 \text{ m/s})(6 \text{ s})$ since the shape is a triangle. The displacement, then, is 18 m. Further, the area for the time interval from 6 to 10 s is negative (-8 m), so the total displacement or change in position for the time from $t = 0$ to $t = 10$ is equal to 10 m. This graph tells us that the object moved in the positive direction for the first 6 s and then in the negative direction for the next 4 s.

23. (D) The slope of a tangent line at the time $t = 7$ s is the velocity, which in this case is negative. We can estimate the slope, or "rise over run," by approximating the curve as a line from the point (6, 10) to (7.4, 0). Thus, the closest estimate of the velocity is $-10/1.5$, which is about -7 m/s.

24. (B) According to this graph, the object starts moving forward from a zero position of $x = 10$ m at a velocity of about 5 m/s (the slope). The object decreases its velocity from $t = 0$ to $t = 3$, reaching a velocity of zero at $t = 3$ s. The object then turns around at $t = 3$ s and increases its velocity in the negative direction from $t = 3$ to $t = 10$ s, reaching a point 30 m behind the zero position and 40 m behind the point where it started.

25. (A) The acceleration of the air rocket, due to the gravitational force exerted on it, is downward during the rocket's entire trip—which by our definition is always negative. The velocity vector, describing the direction of motion of the rocket, is by our definition positive while the air rocket is on its way upward and negative as it falls back down.

26. (A) Assuming negligible air friction, the ball's vertical motion is upward during the first 2 s of its motion and downward for the next 2 s. Its vertical motion is independent of its horizontal motion, so it travels upward until the vertical component of its velocity is zero and then falls for 2 s. Therefore, at a time 2 s after it leaves the ground, the ball has only its horizontal component of velocity, which is 20 m/s cos 60°, or 10 m/s.

27. (B) Once the stone leaves the thrower's hand, it is under the influence only of the gravitational force, which produces a downward force and a downward acceleration. The acceleration is the same at every moment during the stone's trip upward and back down again, and that constant acceleration is 9.8 m/s².

28. (A) Solve for time, t, in the equation for the vertical motion of the wheel. Since the vertical motion is independent of the horizontal motion, the speed of the wheel horizontally as it falls does not affect the time it takes to drop to the ground.

$$\Delta y = v_{oy}t + \tfrac{1}{2}at^2$$
$$-500 \text{ m} = 0 + \tfrac{1}{2}(-10 \text{ m/s}^2)t^2$$
$$t = 10 \text{ s}$$

29. (D) When the rocket is fired vertically, its vertical velocity is maximum, so the rocket reaches its maximum height. When it is fired at an angle of less than 90 degrees, only the vertical component determines the vertical height, and the vertical component of the velocity becomes less as the angle becomes less. The rocket's time in the air is determined by its altitude, so the time is maximum when the vertical velocity is maximum. When it is fired at an angle of 60 degrees to the ground, the vertical velocity component is less than v and air time is less than t.

30.

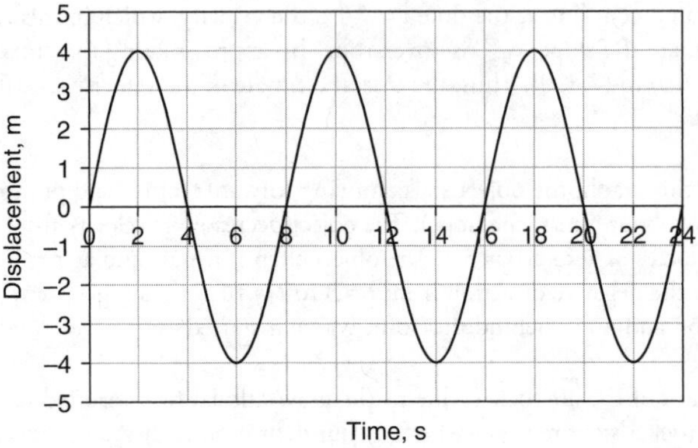

Displacement, m vs Time, s

(C) At $t = 0$ s and again at $t = 4$ s, the displacement is zero, so the net force and acceleration are zero. However, at $t = 6$ s, the displacement is a maximum downward, so the force and acceleration are a maximum upward.

31. (D) The time it takes the rock to fall to the ground depends only on the height of the building and is independent of the horizontal speed.

$$\Delta y = v_{oy}t + \tfrac{1}{2}at^2$$
$$-h = 0 + \tfrac{1}{2}(-g)t^2$$
$$t = \sqrt{\frac{2h}{g}}$$

32. (D) If there is no air friction, horizontal acceleration is zero, but the vertical acceleration is a constant value of g downward at every point during the path. Thus, the acceleration is never zero. The horizontal speed remains constant. Vertical speed is maximum at A, decreases to zero at C and then increases to a maximum at E just before it lands. Obviously, the height is at a maximum at point C.

33. (C) Since the wind vector and the plane vector are at right angles, the resultant vector can be determined using the Pythagorean theorem:

$$v = \sqrt{v_w^2 + v_p^2} = \sqrt{100^2 + 10^2}$$

It's easy to see—even without the final calculation—that the resultant speed is closer to 101 km/h than to 110 km/h. The direction will not be due northeast (since the wind causes the plane to veer east). The resultant direction will be a small angle since the tangent of the angle is the wind speed divided by the plane's airspeed. That small angle is east of north.

34. (C) The boat's resultant path is the addition of the boat's velocity vector (pointing across the river) and the river's velocity vector (pointing to the right). Path 3 is the most logical resultant of these vectors, so the boat will move downstream before reaching the other side of the river. You should also recognize that the boat and velocity vectors, 6 m/s and 8 m/s, are in a ratio of 3 to 4, so they make the legs of a right triangle. This is one of the "special" right triangles, a 3-4-5 right triangle, so the resultant velocity vector follows the same ratio. The boat will move downstream at a speed of 10 m/s.

35. (A) Since the block is in parabolic motion from the time it leaves the table until it hits the floor, its acceleration in the vertical direction is g, and there is no acceleration in the horizontal direction.

36. (C) The horizontal and vertical motions of the block are independent, linked only by time (since both components of motion occur during the same time). The horizontal component of velocity remains constant at 2 m/s during the block's trip to the ground. The vertical velocity increases as the block falls with an acceleration of g. We'll use $g = 10$ m/s^2 to estimate the final vertical velocity. Note that the initial vertical velocity is zero since the block leaves the roof moving only horizontally.

$$v_f^2 = v_o^2 + 2as$$
$$v_f^2 = 0 + (2)(10 \text{ m/s}^2)(5 \text{ m}) = 100$$
$$v_f = 10 \text{ m/s}$$

37. (C) The mass attached to a pendulum does not affect the period. Doubling the length will increase the period by a factor of $\sqrt{2}$, according to the equation:

$$T = 2\pi\sqrt{\frac{L}{g}}$$

38. (A) As the mass on the spring oscillates, its velocity is zero at the amplitude of the oscillation, or where the mass "turns" to change direction, much like a ball that has been thrown into the air turns to come back down. The velocity is zero, then, at the times 2 s, 6 s, 10 s, 14 s, 18 s, and 22 s on this graph. Another way to think of this is that the velocity is zero when the kinetic energy is zero; at the amplitude of its oscillation, the potential energy of the oscillator is maximum, so kinetic energy is zero.

Chapter 2: Forces, Torque, and Equilibrium

39. (D) First, find the acceleration of the car by finding the change in velocity and dividing by time. This can be done without a calculator by determining that the change in speed is 40 m/s. Then divide the change in speed by time to determine that the acceleration is 10 m/s^2. Then apply Newton's second law of motion, using the mass of the car and the acceleration, to find the magnitude of the force. (Of course, both the acceleration and the force are negative because the velocity of the car is reduced, but the problem is asking just for the magnitude of the average force.)

$$\bar{a} = \frac{\bar{v}_f - \bar{v}_0}{t} = \frac{30 \text{ m/s} - 70 \text{ m/s}}{4 \text{ s}} = -10 \text{ m/s}^2$$

$$\bar{F} = m\bar{a} = (500 \text{ kg})(-10 \text{ m/s}^2) = -5,000 \text{ N}$$

40. (B) The acceleration of an object or system is directly proportional to the net force exerted on the object or system and inversely proportional to the mass:

$$\Sigma F = ma$$

$$a = \frac{\Sigma F}{m}$$

On this plot of acceleration versus force, the slope would be $1/m$. Using the data point (4,10), since the best-fit line is easy to read at that point, the slope is $\Delta y / \Delta x$ or 10/6. Since this is $1/m$, the mass is 6/10 kg, or 0.6 kg.

41. (C) According to Newton's third law of motion, for every action there is an equal and opposite reaction, with action and reaction forces on separate bodies. In this case, the force of the car pulling forward on the trailer is matched by the force of the trailer pulling backward on the car.

42. (D) Apply Newton's second law, $\Sigma F = ma$. The product ma is equal to 10 N, so the net force has to be 10 N. The friction force (backward) must be 2 N, so the sum of 12 N forward and 2 N backward must be 10 N.

43. (C) If we consider the frame of reference where one axis is along the surface of the ramp, the sum of all forces on the box that are parallel to the ramp must equal zero if the box is to remain stationary. The component of W that points downward along the ramp is $W \sin \theta$. This component has to be equal to the two forces directed upward along the ramp, which are the tension T and the friction force F_F.

44. (D) As the ramp angle is increased, the normal force from the ramp decreases. Since friction depends on the coefficient of friction (which doesn't change) and normal force, the friction force decreases as the normal force decreases. As the ramp is tilted, more of the weight of the block is supported by the string, so tension increases.

45. (A) Use Newton's second law of motion, $\Sigma F = ma$, to solve for tension. To find the mass of the elevator, divide the weight in newtons by g. The mass is 1,000 kg.

$$\Sigma F = T - W = ma$$

$$T = W + ma = 10,000 \text{ N} + (1,000 \text{ kg})(3.0 \text{ m/s}^2) = 13,000 \text{ N}$$

46. (D) Use Newton's second law of motion, $\Sigma F = ma$, to solve for acceleration.

$$a = \frac{\Sigma F}{m} = \frac{10\ \text{N}}{15\ \text{kg}} = 0.67\ \text{m/s}^2$$

47. (D) Use Newton's second law of motion $\Sigma F = ma$ and substitute values given to solve for acceleration: $a = F/m = (10\ \text{N})/(2\ \text{kg}) = 5\ \text{m/s}^2$. Then use the acceleration and time to find the change in velocity: $at = \Delta v$. The change in velocity is 5 m/s² times 5 seconds, or 25 m/s. The change in velocity in answer choice D, from 20 m/s to 45 m/s, is correct.

48. (D) When visualizing this, remember that the vectors 30 N north and 40 N east are components of the resultant vector that accelerates the object. Think of a 3-4-5 right triangle, where the hypotenuse would be the resultant of 50 N due northeast. Then use Newton's second law of motion to find the acceleration (which is also due northeast):

$$a = \frac{\Sigma F}{m} = \frac{50\ \text{N}}{35\ \text{kg}} = 1.4\ \text{m/s}^2$$

49. (B) Consider the three connected blocks as a system with a total mass of 6 kg. Using the equation $F = ma$, the acceleration must be 2 m/s². Since this indicates that the answer must be B or C, we know that the tension in the string attached to the 1-kg block has to accelerate only that block, so it must be less than 12 N; there is no need to actually calculate it. (Using $F = ma$ to find the tension, multiply the 1-kg mass times the acceleration to find a tension of 2 N.)

50. (B) When the elevator is accelerating upward, there are two forces on the person—the gravitational force downward and the normal upward force of the scale on the person. For the person to accelerate upward, there has to be more force upward on the person than downward ($\Sigma F = ma$). The scale reading is equal to the weight of the person when he or she is in equilibrium—either stationary or moving up or down at constant speed. The scale reading is more than the person's weight when the person is accelerating upward, and the scale reading is less than the person's weight when the person is accelerating downward. The scale would read zero only if the scale and the person were in free fall.

51. (C) Examine the forces on the 200-N frame. The forces are vectors and must be considered in each direction separately. In the y direction, the only force downward is 200 N. In the upward direction, each of the two components of tension supports half of that, so the vertical component of each tension is equal to 100 N. Using the 1-1-$\sqrt{2}$ relationship in a right triangle that has 45° angles, we determine that the components are each 100 N and that the tension (hypotenuse) must be 100$\sqrt{2}$, which is 100 times 1.4, or about 140 N. This is also the answer that is most reasonable.

52. (C) Apply Newton's second law and substitute for acceleration:

$$\Sigma F = ma$$

$$a = \frac{\Delta v}{\Delta t}$$

$$\Sigma F = \frac{m\Delta v}{\Delta t}$$

$$10 \text{ N} = \frac{(2 \text{ kg}) \, \Delta v}{5 \text{ s}}$$

$$\Delta v = 25 \text{ m/s}$$

53. (C) The weight of the rock is the gravitational force of the planet on the rock:

$$F_G = \frac{GMm}{R^2}$$

On Earth, the force is 12 N. If the rock is taken to the hypothetical planet, everything in the equation is the same except the mass of the planet, M. On the other planet, M becomes $4M$, so the gravitational force is four times as much, or 48 N.

54. (B) To determine the expression for gravitation acceleration, g, set your weight on the surface, which is mg, equal to the gravitational force between you and the Earth on the surface. Then cancel and solve for g:

$$mg = \frac{GMm}{R^2}$$

$$g = \frac{GM}{R^2}$$

Substitute $\tfrac{1}{2}M$ for M and $2R$ for R (remembering to square!) to find that the new expression is one-eighth as much as the original expression for g.

55. (B) The gravitational force and gravitational acceleration—like other quantities such as intensity of light and electrical force—follow an inverse square law—an important rule to remember. This rule states that the quantity decreases as the inverse of the square of the factor by which distance increases. In this case, the distance doubles, so the inverse of the square of 2 is ¼. Thus, the gravitational acceleration is ¼ as great, or 0.6 m/s². If the distance had been 3 times as much, the acceleration would have been ⅑.

56. (D) On the surface, the satellite is a distance r from the center of Earth. Its weight on the surface is $W = mg$, or 1,000 N. At the orbit insertion point, the satellite is $4r$ above the surface, which is 5 times as far from the center of Earth, so it weighs 1/25 as much. Remember that the gravitational force, like many other quantities in physics, follows an inverse square law since r^2 is in the denominator of the equation (see equation below). So the satellite weighs 1/25 of 1,000 N, or 40 N.

$$F_\text{G} = \frac{GMm}{R^2}$$

57. (D) Find the x coordinate and the y coordinate of the center of mass separately, using the formula and the total mass of the three objects, 10 g.

$$x_\text{com} = \frac{m_1 x_1 + m_2 x_2 + m_3 x_3}{m_\text{total}} = \frac{(2)(0) + (6)(5) + (2)(2)}{10} = 3.4$$

$$y_\text{com} = \frac{m_1 y_1 + m_2 y_2 + m_3 y_3}{m_\text{total}} = \frac{(2)(7) + (6)(6) + (2)(2)}{10} = 5.4$$

58. (C) The kinetic energy at the bottom of the ramp is equal to the gravitational potential energy at the top of the incline minus the energy lost to thermal energy due to friction.

59. (B) The potential energy stored in a spring is $\frac{1}{2}kx^2$, where x is the displacement of the spring from its equilibrium position. Without a calculator, the best approach is to write out the decimals as fractions and cancel: $\frac{1}{2}(200)(5/100)(5/100) = (100)(5/100)(5/100) = 25/100$ or 0.25 J.

60. (A) Use $\Sigma F = ma$ on the system of blocks, in the horizontal direction. The net external force on the system of three blocks is 9 N, which is the vector sum of 12 N to the right and 3 N to the left. The total mass of the system is 6 kg, which is the total mass of all three blocks. Use $\Sigma F = ma$ and solve for acceleration:

$$\vec{a} = \frac{\Sigma \vec{F}}{m} = \frac{9 \text{ N}}{6 \text{ kg}} = 1.5 \text{ m/s}^2$$

Now apply Newton's second law again—this time only on the 1-kg block.

$$\Sigma \vec{F} = m\vec{a} = (1 \text{ kg})(1.5 \text{ m/s}^2) = 1.5 \text{ N}$$

If the net force on the 1-kg block is 1.5 N and the friction force (to the left) on the block is 1 N, then the tension (to the right) in the string is 0.5 N.

61. (A) First, apply Newton's second law of motion to the system of both boxes. The accelerating force is the weight of the hanging box, $mg = 100$ N. The force acting against the motion is the friction force on the 20-kg box: $F_f = \mu N = \mu mg = (0.2)(20 \text{ kg})(10 \text{ m/s}^2) = 40$ N. So the net force on the system of two boxes is 60 N. Calculate the acceleration of the system:

$$\vec{a} = \frac{\Sigma \vec{F}}{m} = \frac{60 \text{ N}}{30 \text{ kg}} = 2 \text{ m/s}^2$$

Now apply Newton's second law to the 10-kg mass only, using the acceleration we have just calculated:

$$\Sigma F = mg - T = ma$$
$$(10\text{ kg})(10\text{ m/s}^2) - T = (10\text{ kg})(2\text{ m/s}^2)$$
$$100 - T = 20$$
$$T = 80\text{ N}$$

62. **(C)** The coefficient of friction is a value less than 1, so answer choice A is incorrect. The coefficient of kinetic friction is generally considered to be less than the coefficient of static friction between an object and a surface, so answer choice D is incorrect. As long as the object moves across the surface, the coefficient of kinetic friction has a set value, regardless of speed, so answer choice B is incorrect. Additionally, rolling friction is less than sliding friction between two similar surfaces, so answer choice C is the correct statement.

63. **(B)** Use Newton's second law of motion, remembering that the mass of the box is 10 kg if the weight of the box (on Earth) is 100 N since $W = mg$:

$$\Sigma F = ma$$
$$F_{pulling} - F_{friction} = ma$$
$$30\text{ N} + F_{friction} = (10\text{ kg})(2\text{ m/s}^2)$$
$$F_{friction} = 10\text{ N}$$

If the box had been pulled at constant speed, the net force would be zero, and the friction force would be equal to the pulling force.

64. **(A)** As the angle of the ramp is increased, the normal force of the ramp on the box decreases. Think about it: when the ramp becomes vertical, the gravitational force on the box is also vertical, so the box does not exert any normal force on the ramp—and by Newton's third law, the ramp does not exert any normal force on the box. The friction force depends upon the coefficient of friction and the normal force. If the normal force becomes less as the ramp is tilted, then the friction between the two surfaces also decreases.

65. **(C)** Let's talk this one through using a "system approach." By Newton's second law, the net force on the system of boxes must be enough to accelerate the boxes. The system of boxes has a mass of 6 kg, so the net force must be equal to mass times acceleration (*ma*), or 3 N. The friction force on the boxes is equal to the coefficient of friction times the normal force of the surface on the boxes. Since the surface is level, the normal force is equal to the weight of the boxes ($F_N = mg = 60$ N). The friction force is equal to μF_N, or 6 N. We determined previously that the net force must be 3 N, so the pulling force must be 9 N.

$$F_{pulling} - F_{friction} = ma$$
$$9\text{ N} - 6\text{ N} = (6\text{ kg})(0.5\text{ m/s}^2)$$

66. (A) As the parachutist falls due to the force of gravity exerted on her, velocity increases. However, as the velocity of the parachutist increases, the friction force of air (air drag) on the parachutist increases. Once the friction force increases to the point where the friction force upward on the parachutist is equal to the gravitational force downward, the parachutist is in equilibrium—since there is no longer a net force—and there is no longer an acceleration. The parachutist then falls at a constant velocity downward (called the terminal velocity). Answer choice A is a true statement. In answer choice B, if the gravitational force is greater than the friction force of air, then the parachutist is not only falling downward but still accelerating downward, so she is not falling at terminal velocity. Answer choice C cannot be true at terminal velocity because if the friction force (which is upward) is greater than the gravitational force, the parachutist would be accelerating upward. Answer choice D cannot be true because as long as the parachutist is moving (i.e., falling) through air, there will be a frictional force of air on her.

67. (C) To start the box moving, the pulling force must be just large enough to overcome the friction force; friction force is equal to 40 N. The normal force, assuming a level surface, is equal to the weight of the box, which is mg. At this point, use the equation $F_F = \mu F_N$ to solve for the coefficient of friction, μ.

$$\mu = \frac{F_F}{F_N} = \frac{40\,\text{N}}{mg} = \frac{40\,\text{N}}{100\,\text{N}} = 0.40$$

68. (C) Using the formula $F_F = \mu F_N$, use the diagram to determine the values for the friction force and the normal force. Since the box is sliding at constant speed, this is an equilibrium situation; thus, the sum of the forces in each direction is zero. The frame of reference to use here is setting the x axis parallel to the incline and the y axis perpendicular to the incline. The forces parallel to the incline must add to zero, so the friction force, F_F, is equal to the force component 20 sin 40°. The forces perpendicular to the surface must also be equal to each other, so the normal force, F_N, is equal to 20 cos 40°. Substituting:

$$\mu = \frac{F_E}{F_N} = \frac{20\sin 40°}{20\cos 40°}$$

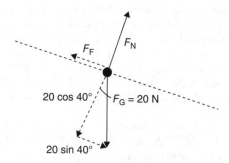

69. (C) Since the applied force is three times as far from the fulcrum, the force needs to be only one-third the weight of the heavy box is order to balance it or move it at constant speed (both equilibrium conditions). However, the input work and output work must be the same, according to conservation of energy principles.

$$W_{input} = W_{ouput}$$
$$F_{input}d_{input} = F_{ouput}d_{output}$$

If the input force, F, is one-third the output force (or weight of the box), then the input distance must be three times the output distance. Each end of the board changes position in the same amount of time, so the input force must move three times as far in the same amount of time—and is moving three times as fast.

70. (B) The bottom pulley is a single movable pulley, which has a mechanical advantage of 2. We can see this if we remember that the tension throughout the rope has to be the same and that there are two ropes supporting the weight. Therefore, each rope attached to the bottom pulley is supporting one-half the weight, and the tension in each part of the rope is $\frac{1}{2}W$. That is, the tension in the rope pulling downward and the force F is $\frac{1}{2}W$. (The upper pulley has a mechanical advantage [MA] of 1. It simply changes the direction of the force and does not multiply the force.)

The total mechanical advantage is the product of the MA of each pulley, which is 1 times 2 or 2. This pulley system multiplies the input force by 2 and is able to lift twice as much as the input force. We conclude again that $W = 2F$.

Now, we have to remember that energy has to be conserved and that work input has to equal work output (assuming no frictional losses in the pulleys). Work equals force times distance. Since the input force is one-half the output force (or weight lifted), the input force has to move twice as far as the output weight is lifted:

$$W_{input} = W_{ouput}$$
$$F_{input}d_{input} = F_{ouput}d_{output}$$

71. (B) The weight of the object is mg. The mechanical advantage of the movable pulley, which is attached to the object, is 2. We can determine this by examining the forces on the pulley itself—there are two tension forces upward and one gravitational force downward. Lifting the object at constant speed is an equilibrium situation; that is, the net force is zero since there is no acceleration. Therefore, each of the ropes attached to the movable pulley is pulling upward with one-half the weight of the object. The single fixed pulley attached to the ceiling has a mechanical advantage of 1 since it only changes the direction of the force. The total mechanical advantage of a pulley system is the product of the mechanical advantages of the individual pulleys, which is 1×2 or 2. This means that the pulley system here multiplies the input effort by 2, enabling the operator of the machine to use one-half the force that is being moved.

Another way to think of this is to remember that the tension throughout the rope has to be the same, if we ignore the weight of the rope itself. If the person pulls downward with $\frac{1}{2}mg$, the tensions in the parts of the rope attached to the movable pulley are each also $\frac{1}{2}mg$, but there are two of them pulling upward. Therefore, the $\frac{1}{2}mg$ effort on the right can lift mg on the left.

72. (C) The single fixed pulley attached to the tree limb has a mechanical advantage of 1; it only changes the direction of the force. The weight of the children is 400 N ($W = mg$), so the father must pull downward with a force of 400 N to lift them at constant speed. Recognize that constant speed is an equilibrium situation in which the net force is zero (i.e., there is no acceleration), so the force pulling upward on the children is equal in magnitude to the gravitational force downward.

73. (A) The gravitational acceleration g on the surface of any planet varies in direct proportion to the mass of the planet and in inverse proportion to the radius of the planet squared (since the radius of the planet is the distance between the planet and any object on its surface). The mass of the object on the surface does not affect the value of g. The equation describing this relationship can be derived by setting the weight of any object on the surface, mg, equal to the gravitational force between the planet (of mass M) and the object (of mass m), where R is the radius of the planet:

$$mg = \frac{GMm}{R^2}$$
$$g = \frac{GM}{R^2}$$

74. (C) The new location of the object is twice as far from the center of Earth as it had been on the surface. Since the gravitational force and gravitational field follow inverse square laws, the object would weight one-fourth as much as it does on the surface. That is, the distance, which is twice as much, is squared to get 4, and the new quantity is the inverse of that, or one-fourth as much. Many quantities in physics, such as light intensity, sound intensity, electric force, and electric field, follow inverse square laws with distance.

75. (A) Though the object would, indeed, weigh one-sixth as much on the surface of the moon as it does on Earth, the mass of the object would not change.

76. (B) Because of its motion in a circle on the rotating Earth, an object on the surface has a centripetal force equal to the quantity mv^2/R, which is provided by the gravitational force toward the center of Earth—the gravitational force of the Earth on the object. However, since the Earth rotates, an object on the surface is constantly accelerating centripetally and therefore is not in an inertial frame of reference. In this accelerating frame of reference, the object is trying to move outward, seeming to experience a centrifugal force that decreases the net force toward the center of Earth. (Note that this outward force exists only in a noninertial frame of reference.) Thus, the effective value of g decreases slightly.

In answer choice A, the sun and moon would each, at times, exert gravitational forces on the object that are away from the center of Earth, decreasing the net force on the object; however, since Earth, the sun, and the moon change positions relative to each other as they orbit, that effect would not consistently be less.

77. (C) The easiest way to examine this is to start with a value for the gravitational field, g, for the smaller planet:

$$g_s = \frac{GM}{R^2}$$

The larger planet has 3 times the radius of the smaller planet, so its volume is 27 times the volume of the smaller planet. (The volume of a sphere is $4/3\pi R^3$.) Since the densities of the two planets are the same, the ratio of mass/volume must be the same for both planets. That means that the larger planet also has to have 27 times the mass of the smaller planet. Now substitute these values to determine a value for g for the larger planet:

$$g_L = \frac{G(27M)}{(3R)^2} = \frac{3GM}{R^2}$$

The larger planet has 3 times the value of g, so the object will weigh 3 times as much, or 90 N.

78. (D) Use M for the mass of Earth and m for the mass of the object and substitute $300,000M$ for the mass of the sun in the equation for gravitational force. Substituting $100R$ for the radius of the sun, we see that the answer is 30.

$$F_{earth} = \frac{GMm}{R^2}$$

$$F_{sun} = \frac{G(300,000M)m}{(100R)^2} = \frac{30\,GMm}{R^2}$$

79. (A) Density is equal to mass divided by volume. Since object A and object B have the same radius, they have the same volume. Therefore, object A, with twice the density, must have twice the mass of object B. In the formula to calculate the gravitational force between objects A and C or between objects B and C, the force between objects B and C will be twice as large.

80. (A) First, we can see that the net gravitational force on object A, due to the other two objects, will be the addition of the force of B on A to the force of C on A, and the net force will be to the right. Next, we see that the magnitude of the net gravitational force on object C will be less since both objects A and B are attracting object C to the left—but the distances are greater, and thus the net force will be less. The third step is to recognize that the net gravitational force on object B will also be less than the net force on A since object A is attracting B to the left and object C is attracting B to the right.

81. (A) First, we know that the 4-kg object located at $x = 6$ has four times the mass of the object at $x = 0$. By examination of the following equation, we can see that the distance between objects in the formula is squared, so doubling the distance in the denominator and squaring it would cancel the quadrupled mass in the numerator. Basically, this means that the magnitude of the force on the 3-kg object due to the 4-kg object would be equal to the magnitude of the force on the 3-kg object due to the 1-kg object if the 4-kg object were twice as far away from the 3-kg object. Positioning object B at $x = 2$ would accomplish this. Checking this with the formula below, you can see that the two quantities are equal.

$$F_G = \frac{GMm}{R^2}$$

$$F_{4\text{ kg on B}} = \frac{G(4\text{ kg})(3\text{ kg})}{(4\text{ units})^2}$$

$$F_{1\text{ kg on B}} = \frac{G(1\text{ kg})(3\text{ kg})}{(2\text{ units})^2}$$

82. **(D)** When the satellite is in orbit, the distance between Earth and the satellite (which is used in the gravitational formula to calculate force) is 4 Earth radii. The altitude above the surface must be added to the radius of Earth to get the total distance between them. This orbital radius is 4 times the distance when the satellite is on the surface of Earth. Since the gravitational force follows an inverse square relationship, the force on the satellite in orbit is $(1/4)^2$, or $1/16$, the force that Earth exerts on the satellite when it is on the surface.

83. **(A)** According to Newton's third law of motion, the force that one object exerts on a second object is equal in magnitude to the force that the second object exerts on the first object.

84. **(B)** Once the satellite is moving in a stable circular orbit, only Earth's gravitational force is required to provide the centripetal force. Answer choice A is incorrect because without any force exerted on the satellite, it will take a linear path as a result of its own inertia. Answer choice C is incorrect because the satellite will move tangentially in its orbit as a result of its own inertia (which is not a force). Answer choice D is incorrect because the gravitational force of Earth on the satellite provides the centripetal force to keep the satellite moving in a circle; the centripetal force is not a separate force.

85. **(D)** The gravitational force of Earth on the satellite provides the centripetal force to keep the satellite in orbit. Use this to derive an equation for the velocity of the satellite in orbit as a function of the distance, R, between the center of the satellite and the center of Earth.

$$\frac{GM_{\text{Earth}}m_{\text{satellite}}}{R_{\text{orbit}}^2} = \frac{m_{\text{satellite}}v^2}{R_{\text{orbit}}}$$

$$v = \sqrt{\frac{GM}{R}}$$

The original value for the orbital radius R is a total of 4 Earth radii—3 Earth radii above the surface plus 1 Earth radius to the center. If the new speed is one-half as much, then the value for R inside the radical needs to be 4 times as great so that taking the square root makes v equal to one-half as much. The new orbital radius, then, must be 4 times the original, or 16 Earth radii from the center of Earth. This is definitely more than 4 Earth radii above the surface.

86. **(C)** For the speed of the object to remain constant, the centripetal force must be constant since centripetal force is equal to mv^2/R and we can assume that the mass and the radius will be constant in the circular path. At the top of the circle, the centripetal force is

provided by the tension in the string and the weight of the object—both toward the center of the circle. At the bottom of the circle, the tension is toward the center and the weight of the object is away from the center, so the tension must be larger. At the bottom, the tension is providing the centripetal force *and* keeping the object from falling downward as a result of its own weight. It is possible for the tension to be zero, as in answer D, since the weight of the object provides the centripetal force at the top of the motion, but it does not have to be zero, as implied in answer D.

87. (C) The centripetal force is provided by a force toward the center of the turn. Both the gravitational forces and the normal forces are perpendicular to the surface, so they are both perpendicular to the radius of the turn and do not provide the centripetal force. Inertia is not a force. As the automobile goes around the turn, its attempted motion is along a tangent (outward), so the friction force opposes that motion—inward toward the center, providing the centripetal force to keep the vehicle in the turn.

88. (D) When the string is cut, the ball will take a tangential path at the speed of 1 m/s as it also falls to the floor, gaining vertical speed due to the gravitational force exerted on it. The ball will then hit the floor at a speed greater than 1 m/s.

89. (D) The minimum speed at the top of the vertical circle for ball A is the speed at which the weight (mg) of the ball alone provides the centripetal force. For the speed to be minimum, the tension in the string must be zero, and the speed is

$$mg = \frac{mv^2}{R}$$
$$v = \sqrt{gR}$$

Now, student B has a string that is $2R$ in length, so the speed is $\sqrt{2}$ times that of ball A, even without any tension in the string. An added tension in the string will only increase the speed, so none of the conditions will allow student B to match the speed of ball A.

90. (B) Assuming that the nickel is moving at constant speed in the circle, that speed is equal to the distance around the circle ($2\pi R$) divided by the time for each circle (1 s).

$$v = \frac{2\pi R}{t} = \frac{2\pi(0.10 \text{ m})}{1 \text{ s}} = 0.2\pi \text{ m/s}$$

91. (A) Set the gravitational force between Earth and the satellite equal to the expression for centripetal force, remembering that the distance used in both formulas must be the total distance from center to center, which is $R + h$:

$$\frac{GMm}{(R+h)^2} = \frac{mv^2}{(R+h)}$$
$$\frac{GM}{(R+h)} = v^2$$

92. (D) Creating a banked curve that is higher on the outside allows a component of the normal force of the road on a vehicle to be directed toward the center of the curve, increasing the force centripetally. Answer choice A is not most effective because smaller vehicles will still not be able to negotiate the curve; appropriate speed does not depend upon the mass of the vehicle (since mass cancels in the calculations). Answer choice B is not correct because banking the road so that it is higher on the inside will actually increase the problem. If the road is lower on the outside of the curve, a component of the normal force is directed outward. Answer choice C is not correct since decreasing the radius increases the centripetal force necessary to keep the car on the road ($F = mv^2/R$).

93. (B) At the equator, the radius of the circle on which the location is rotating is the radius of Earth. At 60° latitude, the distance to the center of Earth is approximately the same, but the circle on which the location is moving is one-half the distance to the axis of rotation, as shown below. The time for one complete rotation is the same everywhere, but reducing the radius of the circle to one-half also decreases the speed to one-half.

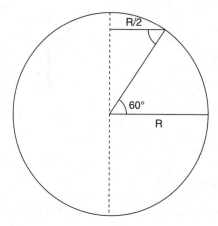

94. (D) In order to examine the factors that affect the washer as it moves in a circle, remember that it is the friction force of the turntable surface on the washer that provides the centripetal force.

$$F_{fr} = F_c$$
$$\mu mg = \frac{mv^2}{R}$$
$$v = \sqrt{\mu gR}$$

We can see from the equation that mass is not a factor, so stacking washers or reducing the mass of the washer, as in answer choices A and B, would not have an effect. In answer choice C, putting lubricating oil between the washer and the surface would decrease the coefficient of friction between the turntable and washer surfaces, so the washer would slide off more easily. Therefore, D is the only answer choice.

95. (B) As the pendulum oscillates, the tension force on the object is directed toward the center of the arc, and the gravitational force is directed downward toward the floor. Since the pendulum has its maximum speed at the bottom of its swing (when gravitational potential energy has been converted to kinetic energy), the tension is maximum. The tension at the bottom of the pendulum's swing (diagram on the left) is equal to the weight of the object on the string plus the centripetal force necessary to keep the object moving in a circle at that velocity. The tension cannot be constant, as in answer choice A, since the speed is changing and the direction of the gravitational force on the object is also changing. As shown in the diagram on the right, the tension is equal to the component of the gravitational force opposite (which is less than mg) plus the centripetal force, which is also less since the speed is less.

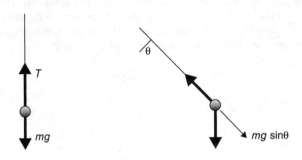

At the bottom: $T - mg = \dfrac{mv^2}{R}$

At an angle: $T - mg \sin \theta = \dfrac{mv^2}{R}$

When the pendulum is at an angle, v is less and $mg \sin \theta$ is less than mg.

96. (C) Answer choice A is true because the centripetal force on the satellite is, by definition, toward the center of the orbit in order to keep the satellite moving in a circle. Answer choice B is correct by Newton's third law of motion—for every action there is an equal and opposite action on another object. Answer choice D is true because there is a constant centripetal acceleration—that is, a change in direction of the velocity vector—as the satellite moves in a circle. Answer choice C is not correct for the same reason that answer B is correct.

97. (A) The forces on the small object inside the cone are shown: mg downward, a normal force perpendicular to the inside surface, and friction upward along the inside surface opposing the attempted slide of the object downward. The only force that would be directed toward the center of the circle in which the object is moving would be a component of the normal force, as described in answer choice A.

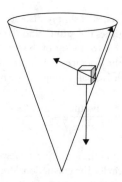

98. (C) If the object moves at constant speed in the circle and the angle remains constant, then there is an equilibrium (i.e., no acceleration) in the vertical direction. If that is the case, then the net force on the object in the vertical direction must be zero. There are only two forces on the object in the vertical direction—the gravitational force downward on the object (mg, or 0.25 kg times g) and the component of the tension in the string that is upward, $T \cos 60°$. Setting these two equal to each other and solving for T gives us:

$$T = 0.25 \, g/\cos 60°$$

99. (C) By Newton's universal law of gravitation, any two objects in the universe exert forces of equal magnitude on each other. Thus, the moon exerts the same force on the Earth as the Earth exerts on the moon, with the forces along a line between their centers and in opposite directions.

100. (B) For the value of gravitational acceleration, g, to be less, the shuttle must be farther from Earth. The gravitational force is equal to the "weight" of the shuttle, mg:

$$\frac{GM_{\text{Earth}} m_{\text{satellite}}}{R_{\text{orbit}}^2} = mg$$

$$g = \frac{GM_{\text{Earth}}}{R_{\text{orbit}}^2}$$

Next, we determine the relationship between the speed of the shuttle in its orbit and the distance of the shuttle from Earth. This can be derived by remembering that the gravitational force provides the centripetal force for the shuttle's circular orbit:

$$\frac{GM_{\text{Earth}} m_{\text{satellite}}}{R_{\text{orbit}}^2} = \frac{m_{\text{satellite}} v^2}{R_{\text{orbit}}}$$

$$v = \sqrt{\frac{GM}{R}}$$

We conclude that for the orbital radius to be greater (providing a lower value of g), the speed in orbit must be less.

101. (B) In a circular orbit, the speed is simply distance divided by time. The distance is the circumference of a circle, 2π times the radius, and the time for each orbit is the period, T. It is crucial here to remember that the radius of the orbit is the center-to-center distance, which is the radius of Earth plus the distance of the space debris from Earth (assuming that the radius of the space debris itself is small enough to be negligible).

$$v = \frac{\text{distance}}{\text{time}} = \frac{2\pi(R+r)}{T}$$

102. (C) A force toward the center of the arc of the curve would provide the centripetal force necessary for the car to move in a circle. The gravitational force (or weight of the car) is toward the center of Earth, so choice A is not the answer. With the ice, there is no friction force, so choice B is not the answer. Inertia is not a force; as a matter of fact, inertia will describe the tendency of the car to move in a straight line off of the curve if there is no centripetal force. If you draw a free-body diagram of the car on the banked surface, the normal force is perpendicular to the surface with one vertical component that is equal to the weight of the car and one horizontal component that is directed inward toward the center of the circle (the centripetal force).

103. (B) Essentially, this is an application of Newton's second law of motion, with the net force equal to the sum of the tension force toward the center of the circle (or up) and the weight of the stone away from the circle (or down). The acceleration is the centripetal acceleration.

$$\Sigma F = ma$$

$$T - mg = \frac{mv^2}{R}$$

$$120 - mg = \frac{mv^2}{1.2}$$

104. (D) The mass of the object is not needed in the calculation of centripetal acceleration:

$$v^2/R = a_{cen} = \frac{(20 \text{ m/s})^2}{100 \text{ m}} = 4 \text{ m/s}^2$$

105. (B) The mass of the object is not needed in the calculation of centripetal acceleration, v^2/R. When radius and speed are both doubled, the speed is squared in the numerator, so the new acceleration is $4/2$ times as great, or twice as great.

106. (A) The net force at the bottom of the stone's path is the difference between the tension T (upward) and the weight of the rock mg (downward). This net force is used in Newton's second law, remembering that the acceleration in this case is the centripetal acceleration.

$$\Sigma F = T - mg = ma$$

$$T - mg = \frac{mv^2}{R}$$

$$T = (2 \text{ kg})(10 \text{ m/s}^2) + \frac{(2 \text{ kg})(4 \text{ m/s})^2}{0.2} = 20 + 160 = 180 \text{ N}$$

107. (C) Use the centripetal force equation: $F = mv^2/R$. Cutting the radius in half on the right side, since radius is in the denominator, effectively multiplies the right side by 2. Doubling the force multiplies the left side by 2. Thus, there is no effect on the speed, v.

108. (B) An object moving in a circle at constant speed is constantly changing direction, so its velocity (which is a vector) is not constant. If the object is moving at constant speed, it has no tangential acceleration—only an inward radial (or centripetal) acceleration.

109. (B) If the two satellites are in orbits at different distances from Earth, they must be moving at different speeds. Since the force providing the centripetal force must be the gravitational force, set the two expressions equal to each other to determine the relationship between velocity and orbital radius:

$$\frac{GM_{Earth}m_{satellite}}{R_{orbit}^2} = \frac{m_{satellite}v^2}{R_{orbit}}$$

$$v = \sqrt{\frac{GM}{R}}$$

We can see that the speed in orbit, v, is inversely proportional to the orbital radius, so the satellite orbiting nearer to Earth must be moving faster. Using the equation for centripetal acceleration, $a = v^2/R$, the centripetal acceleration must get larger as the orbital radius gets smaller. The masses of the satellites cancel and are not factors in the calculations.

110. (D) Momentum, p, is equal to mv. Kinetic energy, K, is equal to $\frac{1}{2}mv^2$. Assuming that the mass stays constant, doubling the momentum means that the velocity was doubled. Now we look at the kinetic energy. Since the velocity term in K is squared, doubling the velocity would make the amount of kinetic energy four times is much as it was before. This is easier to see if we derive an expression for kinetic energy in terms of momentum:

$$p = mv, \text{ so } v = \frac{p}{m}$$

$$K = \frac{1}{2}mv^2 = \frac{1}{2}m\left(\frac{p}{m}\right)^2 = \frac{p^2}{2m}$$

111. (D) Change in momentum, Δp, is equal to $m\Delta v$, as long as mass remains unchanged. Using this in answer choice D, we have $m\Delta v/m$, which is Δv. Answer choice A would be equal to $m\Delta v/t$, which is rate of change in momentum or force. Answer choice B is force multiplied by time, which should be recognized as change in momentum—or impulse. Answer choice C is equal to force over time, and not change in velocity.

112. (C) On the air track, we can assume that all the motion is in one dimension. Thus, we are able to use one momentum equation to show conservation of momentum during the collision of the carts. This can be done mentally first by adding the momenta, $p = mv$, for the two carts and setting momentum to the right as positive and momentum to the left as negative. Before the collision, the net momentum is $(2)(1) + (1)(-3)$, or a net of -1.

So the momentum after the collision must also be –1. The 2-kg cart has a momentum of –4 kg·m/s, so the 1-kg cart has to have a momentum of +3 for the momenta to add to –1. Thus, the 1-kg cart has to be moving at 3 m/s to the right.

$$\Sigma p_0 = \Sigma p_f$$

$$m_1 v_{1_0} + m_2 v_{2_0} = m_1 v_{1f} + m_2 v_{2f}$$

$$(2\text{ kg})(1\text{ m/s}) + (1\text{ kg})(-3\text{ m/s}) = (2\text{ kg})(-2\text{ m/s}) + (1\text{ kg})(v)$$

$$v = 3\text{ m/s}$$

113. (D) In a totally inelastic collision, the colliding objects stick together to form one object. Even though kinetic energy is not conserved in an inelastic collision, we can assume that momentum is conserved. Making the velocity to the right positive and the velocity to the left negative, the net momentum before the collision is $2mv + -4mv$, which is $-2mv$. Therefore, the net momentum after the collision must be $-2mv$. The combined objects after the collision have a mass of $2m$, so the velocity of the objects afterward must be $-v$, which is to the left.

$$\Sigma p_0 = \Sigma p_f$$

$$m_1 v_{1_0} + m_2 v_{2_0} = (m_1 + m_2)v_f$$

$$m(2v) + m(-4v) = 2mv_f$$

$$v_f = -v$$

114. (D) It's important here that the skaters are on ice, as this implies no friction on the skaters. So in the absence of an external force on the two skaters, linear momentum will be conserved. The momentum before they push off each other is zero, so the total momentum after they start moving must be zero. They must move in opposite directions so that the sum of their momenta—one negative and one positive—are still zero.

$$p_{\text{original}} = p_{\text{final}}$$

$$0 = m_1 v_1 + m_2 v_2$$

$$0 = (40\text{ kg})v_1 + (50\text{ kg})v_2$$

$$\frac{v_1}{v_2} = -\frac{5}{4}$$

115. (C) By Newton's second law of motion, force is equal to the rate of change in momentum: $F = \Delta p/\Delta t = m\Delta v/\Delta t$. If the mass of the car is the same both times and the contact time is the same both times, then the force is proportional to the change in velocity. For an elastic collision, the final velocity is the negative of the initial velocity (since it's in the opposite direction), so $\Delta v = -2v$. If the initial velocity, v, is doubled, then the force exerted on the wall is doubled.

116. (C) This is a totally inelastic collision, where momentum is conserved but kinetic energy is not conserved. We don't need to know the mass of each cart, as the masses will cancel in the solution. Using conservation of linear momentum:

$$p_{original} = p_{final}$$
$$m_1 v_1 + 0 = (m_1 + m_2) v_2$$
$$m(2 \text{ m/s}) + 0 = (2 \text{ m}) v_2$$
$$v_2 = 1 \text{ m/s}$$

117. (C) From chart A, the final velocity of cart A is about −2.2 m/s, and its initial velocity is about +1.2 m/s. The collision contact starts at $t = 0.3$ s and ends at 0.6 s, so the time of contact is 0.3 s. The force is calculated as the rate of change in momentum, so, as shown below, the force is about 11.0 N. From chart B, the final velocity of cart A is about −1.2 m/s, and its initial velocity is about +2.2 m/s. Remember that since the motion sensors face each other, a positive velocity for sensor A is in the same direction as a negative direction for sensor B, that is, away from the sensor is recorded as positive. We estimate the contact time from both charts to be about 3.0 s (the same from both charts). The two carts exert the same amount of force on each other, so we really only have to use one chart to determine the force.

$$\bar{F} = \frac{\Delta \bar{p}}{\Delta t} = \frac{m(v_f - v_o)}{t}$$

$$\text{Chart A: } \bar{F} = \frac{(1 \text{ kg})(-2.2 \text{ m/s} - 1.2 \text{ m/s})}{0.3 \text{ s}}$$

$$\text{Chart B: } \bar{F} = \frac{(1 \text{ kg})(-1.2 \text{ m/s} - 2.2 \text{ m/s})}{0.3 \text{ s}}$$

118. (C) Change in momentum is called impulse, but the rate at which momentum changes is force. This is really a statement of Newton's second law of motion:

$$\bar{F} = \frac{\Delta \bar{p}}{\Delta t}$$

119. (B) The area under the graph line here is the change in momentum, $m\Delta v$, which is called impulse. The impulse is equal to force times time, $F\Delta t$. In the equation below, you can see that $F\Delta t = \Delta p$. The area above is a triangle, with area $= \frac{1}{2}bh$. To find the area, you would multiply the time of contact by one-half the maximum force, which is the average force. It's important to note that the racket exerts the same force on the ball that the ball exerts on the racket and that the ball and the racket also exert equal and opposite impulses on each other.

$$\bar{F} = \frac{\Delta \bar{p}}{\Delta t}$$
$$\bar{F}\Delta t = \Delta \bar{p}$$

120. (A) Use the equation below, which is a statement of Newton's second law of motion. The change in momentum is the same in both situations, the car's mass stays the same, and the initial and final velocities are the same. Therefore, cutting the time in half means doubling the force applied to stop the car.

$$\bar{F} = \frac{\Delta \bar{p}}{\Delta t}$$

$$\bar{F}\Delta t = \Delta \bar{p}$$

121. (A) Newton's second law of motion can be stated in terms of change in momentum:

$$\Delta \bar{F} = \frac{\Delta \bar{p}}{\Delta t}$$

The car's momentum change will be the same regardless of time, that is, from momentum mv to momentum equal to zero when it stops. The key to less force on the occupants during the stop is increasing the time—which decreases force. An air bag increases the stopping time of the person who moves into the bag after it is deployed. Answer choice B is not true because the person does not move as far when an air bag is in place—even though the second part, decreasing acceleration, would be helpful. Answer choice C is not correct because the softness of the air bag doesn't explain the physics in terms of increased time and reduced force. Answer choice D tries to imply that large forces in opposite directions on a person would provide a net force of zero, and we know that this is not logical.

122. (C) The area under the graph is the change in momentum of the object since $Ft = m\Delta v$. Dividing by the mass of the object will provide the change in velocity. (We'll assume that the forward motion of the object toward the wall is the positive direction, so the change in momentum and the change in velocity are in the negative direction.)

$$F = \frac{m\Delta v}{\Delta t}$$

$$\Delta v = \frac{F\Delta t}{m} = \frac{\text{area}}{m} = \frac{\frac{1}{2}(5\text{ N})(1.0 \times 10^{-3}\text{ s})}{0.25\text{ kg}} = 0.01\text{ m/s}$$

123. (D) Assuming that the time of contact between the ball and the target is about the same and also assuming a collision that is nearly elastic so that the ball rebounds at about the same speed as it hit, doubling the speed of the throw will double the force on the target:

$$F = \frac{m\Delta v}{\Delta t} = \frac{m(v_f - v_o)}{\Delta t} = \frac{m(-v_o - v_o)}{\Delta t} = -\frac{2mv_o}{\Delta t}$$

$$F' = \frac{m\Delta v}{\Delta t} = \frac{m(2v_f - 2v_o)}{\Delta t} = \frac{m(-2v_o - 2v_o)}{\Delta t} = -\frac{4mv_o}{\Delta t} = -4F$$

We have calculated the force of the target on the ball (which is negative), so the force of the ball on the target is positive.

124. (A) If there are no external forces, then linear momentum is conserved. However, if the collision is totally inelastic, the objects will stick together upon impact, and part of the kinetic energy is converted to thermal energy of the objects. Kinetic energy is not conserved in inelastic collisions.

125. (A) Linear momentum depends on both mass and velocity: $p = mv$. If either of these quantities changes, momentum changes. Thus, velocity could remain constant while the mass of the system changes, producing a change in momentum.

126. (A) In elastic collisions, both momentum and kinetic energy are conserved. In inelastic collisions, however, only momentum is conserved; kinetic energy is not conserved. In a totally inelastic collision, kinetic energy is not conserved, and the colliding objects stick together during the collision.

127. (C) In an elastic collision between two particles of equal mass, there are several possibilities: (1) If one particle is stationary and a second particle hits it head-on, the second particle will transfer its momentum to the first particle, so the second particle stops in the position of the first particle. (2) If both particles are moving when they collide head-on, they will exchange speeds. (3) If one particle is initially stationary, as in the example given, and a second particle hits it off-center, the two particles will move off at right angles to each other. Their speeds do not necessarily have to be equal—only if they each move off at an angle of 45° to the original direction of motion will they be equal. The proof of this last case is not difficult because when the conservation of kinetic energy equation is written, the masses cancel to leave a Pythagorean relationship between the velocities: $v^2 = v_1^2 + v_2^2$.

128. (A) Kinetic energy is lost during a collision in the sense that the energy is converted into other forms of energy, such as thermal energy of the molecules of the colliding object, or into sound or light. For example, when two objects collide, we may hear the sound of the collision. That sound energy, which is really thermal energy of molecules, comes from the kinetic energy of the moving objects prior to the collision, so the objects have less kinetic energy after the collision. That is the definition of an inelastic collision. Momentum may be conserved, but kinetic energy is not conserved.

129. (B) When two objects collide head-on and elastically, the motion will all be along a line, or in one dimension, and both momentum and kinetic energy will be conserved during the collision. That the masses are equal means that they will cancel during the derivation and we need to consider only velocities. Answer choice (A) cannot be correct because kinetic energy is conserved during elastic collisions, and in this case there would be no kinetic energy after the collision. Answer choice (C) would be impossible in the situation where one object was moving faster than the other prior to the collision; it could not collide and then have the same velocity after the collision since that would imply that it was moving in the same direction at the same speed after hitting another object. Answer choice (D) cannot be correct if the objects collide head-on since the motion would be entirely in one dimension.

130. (A) Since the electron now has kinetic energy, the photon has less energy than it did before the collision. The energy of a photon is equal to hf or hc/λ, where h is Planck's constant, f is the frequency of the photon, and λ is the wavelength of the photon. If the photon has less energy, it has a longer wavelength when it recoils.

131. (D) The force exerted by the rubber ball will be greater than the force exerted by the dart. Force equals the rate of change in momentum. For the dart, the change in momentum is from mv to zero. For the elastic ball, the change in momentum is from mv to $-mv$, so the change in momentum is $-2mv$—twice the change in momentum of the dart and twice the force. Then we need to consider where to place the ball when it hits. Hitting the block at the top exerts more torque on the brick (force times distance from the pivot, which is at the bottom of the block). Hitting the block with the elastic ball near the top of the block is most likely to knock it over.

132. (C) The coefficient of restitution (e) describes the ratio of velocity after two objects collide to the ratio of velocity before the objects collide. The floor doesn't move a measurable amount as a result of the collision, so we use the ratio of v_{after} to v_{before} for the ball to determine the coefficient. We don't have those velocities, but we can use the heights given to determine the velocities, using conservation of mechanical energy. When the ball is dropped, its gravitational potential energy is converted to the kinetic energy that the ball has when it hits the floor. Also, the kinetic energy that the ball has after it hits the floor is converted to gravitational potential energy when the ball rises again to its maximum height. We can use either conversion to derive an expression for velocity:

The final and initial velocities are in opposite directions, so they have opposite signs. The negative sign in the above formula for e assures us that the value for e is positive.

133. (A) Use Newton's second law to solve for v:

$$F = \frac{m\Delta v}{\Delta t} = \frac{m(v - v_o)}{t}$$
$$Ft = mv - mv_o$$
$$v = \frac{Ft + mv_o}{m} = \frac{Ft}{m} + v_o$$

134. (D) The center of mass of the rocket will continue to follow the path described by the first launch, which is 30 m forward from the launch site. When the rocket splits, there is no net external force in the horizontal direction, so momentum will be conserved in the direction of motion. Therefore, if the larger piece has momentum mv and lands 3 m short of the predicted (center of mass) landing site, then the smaller piece, with momentum $\frac{1}{2}mv$, would land twice as far on the other side of the predicted (center of mass) landing site, so the smaller piece lands 6 m farther, or at 36 m.

135. (C) Linear momentum must be conserved in each dimension. Before the collision, the only momentum is in the positive x direction, with no momentum in the y direction. After the collision, ball 2 has a momentum component in the negative y direction, so ball 1 must have a momentum component in the positive y direction so that the sum is still zero. Only answer choice C has a momentum component in the positive y direction.

136. (C) Use conservation of mechanical energy, with the gravitational potential energy (U) before the ball is dropped equal to the kinetic energy (K) just before the ball hits the floor, to find the velocity before the ball hits the floor the first time:

$$\Delta U = \Delta K$$
$$mgH = \frac{1}{2}mv_o^2$$
$$v_0 = \sqrt{2gH}$$

Then use the coefficient of restitution to compare the velocities before and after the ball hits the floor, with the velocity afterward equal to $-v$:

$$e = 0.5 = -\frac{v_f}{v_o} = \frac{v}{\sqrt{2gH}}$$
$$v = \frac{1}{2}\sqrt{2gH}$$

Now find the velocity when H is doubled:

$$v_{new} = \frac{1}{2}\sqrt{2g(2H)} = \sqrt{2gH}$$

This value is twice the original, or $2v$.

137. **(C)** You may already know that in elastic collisions of two objects of equal mass, the objects exchange velocities, so answer choice C is obvious. However, a proof of this follows to show that (1) linear momentum is conserved and (2) kinetic energy is conserved:

(1) $p_o = p_f$

$$mv_{oA} + mv_{oB} = mv_{fA} + mv_{fB}$$

Cancel the equal masses:

$$(6 \text{ m/s}) + (-4 \text{ m/s}) = v_{fA} + v_{fB}$$
$$v_{fA} = 2 - v_{fB}$$

(2) $K_o = K_f$

$$\frac{1}{2}mv_{oA}^2 + \frac{1}{2}mv_{oB}^2 = \frac{1}{2}mv_{fA}^2 + \frac{1}{2}mv_{fB}^2$$

Cancel the equal masses and $\frac{1}{2}$:

$$v_{oA}^2 + v_{oB}^2 = v_{fA}^2 + v_{fB}^2$$
$$(6 \text{ m/s})^2 + (-4 \text{ m/s})^2 = v_{fA}^2 + v_{fB}^2$$

Substitute:

$$52 - (2 - v_{fB})^2 = v_{fB}^2$$
$$52 - 4 + 4v_{fB} - v_{fB}^2 = v_{fB}^2$$
$$2v_{fB}^2 - 4v_{fB} - 48 = 0$$
$$v_{fB}^2 - 2v_{fB} - 24 = 0$$

Factor:

$$(v_{fB} - 6)(v_{fB} + 4) = 0$$
$$v_{fB} = 6 \text{ or } -4$$

When we substitute for the velocity of the other cart, we determine that cart A has a velocity of –4 m/s when cart B has a velocity of 6 m/s and that cart A has a velocity of 6 m/s when cart B has a velocity of –4 m/s. Only one of these combinations is possible. The second combination is not possible because the carts would have to "pass" each other—and that is not possible on the track.

Thus, we prove our original quick and very important solution: when two objects of equal mass collide elastically and head-on (as on a track), they exchange velocities.

138. (A) To conserve both momentum and kinetic energy, the first nickel stops and transfers all its momentum to the second nickel, which moves along a line with the first nickel's velocity. In answer choice B, momentum and kinetic energy would be conserved mathematically, but this is an unreal situation that does not account for the force the first nickel exerts on the stationary nickel. In answer choice C, you might think that both momentum and kinetic energy could be conserved if the numbers were right, but this is again an unreal solution that wouldn't happen in an elastic head-on collision of two objects of equal mass. Answer choice D is the solution if the nickels hit off-center and not head-on.

139. (A) The two nickels exert equal forces on each other when they collide but in opposite directions. That explanation is clear for answer choice A: the force of the second nickel on the first stops the first nickel, and the equal amount of force of the first nickel on the second causes that nickel to start moving with the same momentum that the first nickel had before the collision. The forces are in line with each other in a head-on collision, so the subsequent motions are along a line.

140. (D) By conservation of momentum principles, the carts move away from each other in opposite directions with the same momentum. Since cart A has twice the mass, it will have half the velocity of cart B and in the opposite direction, so cart B has a higher velocity. However, regardless of their horizontal velocities, the carts start at the same height from the floor, so they will hit the floor at the same time. The time in the air depends only on the height, not on the horizontal speed or mass of the object.

141. (D) We have to consider the components of the velocities in order to conserve linear momentum in the east-west (x) direction and in the north-south (y) direction. The two objects will combine to form one object in a totally inelastic collision, so there is only one 6-kg object moving after the collision. The x component of the new object's momentum is equal to only the original momentum in the x direction: (4 kg)(10 m/s) or 40 kg·m/s west. The y component of the new object's momentum is equal to only the original momentum in the y direction: (2 kg) (5 m/s) or 10 kg·m/s north. The resultant of these is calculated with the Pythagorean theorem:

$$R = \sqrt{R_x^2 + R_y^2} = \sqrt{10^2 + 40^2} = \sqrt{1,700} = 41 \text{ m/s to the northwest}$$

The actual direction of motion is at an angle that is more west than north since the west (or x) component is much larger: $\tan \theta = (10/40)$ and $\theta = 14°$ north of west.

142. (B) First, use conservation of momentum to determine the final velocity of the 2.0-kg cart. Then calculate the kinetic energy of each cart, both before and after the collision. Finally, add the kinetic energies of the two carts before and after the collision to determine the change in total kinetic energy during the collision. That change in kinetic energy is assumed to be the loss to thermal energy of the surroundings during the collision.

(1) $p_o = p_f$

$m_A v_{oA} + m_B v_{oB} = m_A v_{fA} + m_B v_{fB}$

$(1.5 \text{ kg})(2 \text{ m/s}) + (2.0 \text{ kg})(-2 \text{ m/s}) = (1.5 \text{ kg})(-1 \text{ m/s}) + (2.0 \text{ kg})v_{fB}$

$v_{fB} = 0.25 \text{ m/s}$

(2) $K_o = K_f$

$\frac{1}{2} m_A v_{oA}^2 + \frac{1}{2} m_B v_{oB}^2 = \frac{1}{2}(1.5 \text{ kg})(2 \text{ m/s})^2 + \frac{1}{2}(2.0 \text{ kg})(-2 \text{ m/s})^2 = 7.0 \text{ J}$

$\frac{1}{2} m_A v_{fA}^2 + \frac{1}{2} m_B v_{fB}^2 = \frac{1}{2}(1.5 \text{ kg})(-1 \text{ m/s})^2 + \frac{1}{2}(2.0 \text{ kg})(0.25 \text{ m/s})^2 = 1.0 \text{ J}$

$\Delta K = K_f - K_o = 1.0 - 7.0 = -6.0 \text{ J}$

Note that the negative sign on the answer indicates that kinetic energy was lost from the system, but the question just asked "how much," so the sign is not necessary on the answer.

143. (C) First, use conservation of momentum to determine the final velocity of the combined carts, which now move as one object. Then calculate the kinetic energy of each cart before the collision and of the combined carts after the collision. Finally, find the kinetic energies of the two carts before and of the combined carts after the collision to determine the change in total kinetic energy during the collision. That change in kinetic energy is assumed to be the loss to thermal energy of the surroundings during the collision.

(1) $p_o = p_f$

$m_A v_{oA} + m_B v_{oB} = m_A v_{fA} + m_B v_{fB}$

$(1.5 \text{ kg})(2 \text{ m/s}) + (2.0 \text{ kg})(-2 \text{ m/s}) = (1.5 \text{ kg} + 2.0 \text{ kg})v_f$

$v_f = -0.33 \text{ m/s}$

(2) $K_o = K_f$

$\frac{1}{2} m_A v_{oA}^2 + \frac{1}{2} m_B v_{oB}^2 = \frac{1}{2}(1.5 \text{ kg})(2 \text{ m/s})^2 + \frac{1}{2}(2.0 \text{ kg})(-2 \text{ m/s})^2 = 7.0 \text{ J}$

$\frac{1}{2}(m_A + m_B)v_f^2 = \frac{1}{2}(3.5 \text{ kg})(-0.33 \text{ m/s})^2 = 0.2 \text{ J}$

$\Delta K = K_f - K_o = 0.2 - 7.0 = -6.8 \text{ J}$

The negative sign means that kinetic energy was lost from the system—in this case, most if it, so the carts are moving very slowly after the collision.

144. (B) A few insights here make what seems like a lengthy problem much simpler. Since the blocks are identical (i.e., have the same mass) and their trajectories are such that the horizontal velocities of the blocks are at right angles, we can assume an elastic collision between the two blocks. In this special case, both linear momentum and kinetic energy are conserved in the horizontal plane. We don't need to be concerned about rolling motion or friction on the track since we are calculating only the linear velocity of the block just before it hits. (Note, however, that momentum and kinetic energy are not conserved vertically as the blocks fall since the gravitational force is an intervening external force in that dimension.) The Pythagorean theorem in this case can be used to relate the original velocity of the block coming down the ramp (v_0) to the velocities of the two blocks immediately after the collision. (1) Use the height of the desk to determine the time it takes the blocks to fall to the floor. (2) Use the horizontal distances along with this time to determine the velocities. (3) Use the Pythagorean theorem to relate the velocities.

$$(1)\ t = \sqrt{\frac{2h}{g}} = \sqrt{\frac{2(1\text{ m})}{9.8\text{ m/s}}} = 0.45\text{ s}$$

$$(2)\ v_1 = \frac{d_1}{t} = \frac{0.5}{0.45\text{ s}} = 1.1\text{ m/s}$$

$$v_2 = \frac{d_2}{t} = \frac{0.25}{0.45\text{ s}} = 0.55\text{ m/s}$$

$$(3)\ v_o^2 = (1.1\text{ m/s})^2 + (0.55\text{ m/s})^2$$

$$v_o = 1.2\text{ m/s}$$

The solution seems very math intensive, but it can be made easier if you remember that it takes an object about ½ s to fall one meter from rest near Earth's surface and use that to calculate the velocities of the blocks after the collision. Additionally, the Pythagorean calculation can be estimated since the sum of the squares of the velocities is just a little over 1, and so the square root is closer to 1 than to the other answer choices.

145. (D) Since the track is level at the point of collision, linear momentum is conserved in the horizontal plane, as there are no external forces (such as friction or gravitational force) applied to the system. However, once the blocks collide and begin to fall, the gravitational force is an external force that changes both momentum and kinetic energy. Answer choice A cannot be true since kinetic energy is not conserved as the blocks fall; as they fall, gravitational potential energy is converted to additional kinetic energy. Answer choice B cannot be true since the gravitational force increases both momentum and kinetic energy as the blocks fall. Answer choice C cannot be true since the gravitational force exerted on the blocks as they fall increases their momentum, and thus linear momentum is not conserved in the vertical direction, or third dimension.

146. (D) Since each velocity vector is the same, the momentum vector for each piece will be its mass time its velocity. Therefore, each momentum vector is longer by a factor of the mass. For example, the momentum vector for the 3-g piece is three times the size of the momentum vector for the 1-g piece. Since the explosion takes place on a level table, the gravitational force is not in the plane of the table, and so momentum is conserved in the plane of the table. Momentum must be considered in each direction on the plane. In this case, we'll consider the components in the left-right direction separately from the components in the up-down direction. Answer choice A cannot be correct because the momentum of the 3-g piece in the up direction is not balanced in the down direction, so momentum is not conserved. Answer choice B cannot be correct because the up component of the momentum of the 1-g piece will be far less than the down component of the momentum of the 3-g piece. Answer choice C cannot be correct because the momentum of the 1-g piece to the left will be far less than the sum of the components of the other two pieces to the right. Answer choice D is a possibility since the momentum in the up-down direction could add to zero, and the momentum in the left-right direction could add to zero.

147. (C) The net force on an object is zero if there is no acceleration in any dimension. In answer choice A, if the box is sliding down a frictionless ramp, it must be accelerating since there is no friction force on the box to oppose the component of the gravitational force that is accelerating the box down the ramp. In answer choice B, there must be an unbalanced centripetal force to keep the satellite in a circular path. In answer choice C, the box is sliding at constant speed, so the net force horizontally must be zero. In answer choice D, the hammer must be accelerating since there is no atmosphere on the moon to provide a drag force to keep the hammer from accelerating under the influence of gravity.

148. (A) Set up the problem so that the horizontal components of the tensions in all three posts add—as vectors—to zero. This will create a horizontal equilibrium to keep the post in an upright position. The horizontal component for each tension is equal to $T \cos 60°$. Since the first two vectors have horizontal components that are perpendicular to each other (east and north), we can use the Pythagorean theorem to determine the resultant. The third vector required to balance will have a horizontal component that is equal in magnitude to the resultant but in the opposite direction; it is called the "equilibrant." Answer choice A correctly uses the horizontal components to determine the magnitude of the tension in the equilibrant.

149. (C) First, make a diagram of the situation that shows the friction force directed up the ramp and parallel to the ramp, a weight force directed directly downward on the page, and a normal force on the box directed perpendicular to the ramp; the friction force of the ramp on the box is equal in magnitude to the component of the gravitational force that is parallel to the ramp, which is $10 \sin 30°$. Since the box is sitting stationary, the net force exerted on the box in the direction of motion must be zero.

150. (B) Since the ladder is in static equilibrium, the net force in each direction is equal to zero. Therefore, the normal force from the floor and the weight of the ladder are equal. The friction force from the floor is equal to the normal force from the wall. Also, the friction force is equal to the coefficient of friction times the normal force from the floor. The coefficient is less than 1, so the friction force must be less than the normal force.

151. (B) As an object oscillates on a spring, it is in equilibrium at the position where the forces on it are in balance, that is, where velocity is maximum, acceleration is zero, and displacement is zero.

152. (B) As the Ping-Pong ball accelerates due to the gravitational force exerted on it, the air drag force upward on the ball also increases. (Drag forces increase with the speed of an object moving through a fluid.) At terminal velocity, the air drag force is equal to the weight of the ball, and the ball is in equilibrium. Then the acceleration of the ball is zero, and the ball subsequently falls at constant speed, called the terminal velocity.

153. (D) The pendulum is in equilibrium in the horizontal direction since there are no forces in the x direction at the bottom of the motion if we exclude air friction. This does not, however, allow answer choice B to be correct, as there is no accelerating force at the bottom; the pendulum continues to move at that point due to the inertia of the pendulum bob. Additionally, the pendulum is in equilibrium in the vertical direction at the bottom of its swing since the tension upward must be equal to the weight of the pendulum bob plus enough force to provide the centripetal force to keep the pendulum moving in a circular path.

154. (C) This is an equilibrium situation. For the sled to move at constant speed down the hill, the net force on the sled must be zero. Answer choice A is not correct because inertia is not a force. Answer choice B is not correct because there is a force propelling the sled down the hill: the component of the gravitational force that is parallel to the hill. Answer choice D is not correct because a friction force must be present in the opposite direction from the gravitational force component directed down the hill if the sled is to be in equilibrium and move at constant speed.

155. (D) The force shown will cause the wheel to rotate clockwise, so the friction torque must be counterclockwise to create balanced torques and an equilibrium situation for the wheel to rotate at constant speed. The clockwise torque will be calculated using $\tau = R_1 F = (0.20 \text{ m})(100 \text{ N}) = 20 \text{ N·m}$. Thus, the counterclockwise torque must also be equal to 20 N·m. The axle radius is one-fourth as much, so the friction force must be 4 times as much as the applied force, or 400 N. However, the question asks for torque, not force, so the friction torque is 400 N times 0.05 m, or 20 N·m counterclockwise.

156. (C) Actually, the system will still balance if the center of mass of the system of sticks is anywhere to the left of the edge of the table so that gravitational force on that center of mass cannot exert a torque that will cause the sticks to fall. The center of mass of the system can be determined by taking the edge of the table as a "pivot" or "zero point." Since all of the sticks have the same mass, multiply that mass by the distance of the center of mass of each stick from the edge of the table, using anything to the left of the table edge as negative. Then, add all four results together. Add all four results. If the result is zero, the center of mass is above the pivot, so there is no net torque to cause the stick to rotate and fall. If the result is negative, the center of mass is over the table, so the system will balance. Additionally, each stick must have its center of mass above that of the object below it. Answer choice B will work, but it does not meet the condition that the top stick is entirely beyond the table edge.

157. (B) As the wheels roll, they are moving backward at the instant they touch the pavement, so the friction force from the pavement on the tires is forward. The friction force is the force that moves the car forward in the same way that the friction force from the floor is forward on your feet as you step—and it's that friction force that causes you to move forward.

158. (D) The torque you exert is your force, F, times the radius of the steering wheel. For the car, the torque is $30F$, and for the truck, it is $40F$. The increase is $10F$, and the percent increase is the amount of increase divided by the original:

$$\% \text{ increase} = \frac{\text{increase}}{\text{original}} = \frac{10F}{30F} = 33\%$$

This increase in torque using the same applied force makes it easier to drive the much larger truck.

159. (D) Using the edge of the roof as the pivot, the clockwise torque exerted by the acrobat on the board cannot be more than the counterclockwise torque exerted by the weight of the board, applied at its center of mass at the center of the board. The clockwise torque exerted by the acrobat (force times distance to the pivot) is $(60 \text{ kg})(9.8 \text{ m/s}^2)(x)$. The counterclockwise torque exerted by the board is $(20 \text{ kg})(9.8 \text{ m/s}^2)(2 \text{ ft})$. Note: Remember that one-third of the length of the board, or 4 ft, extends over the edge, so the center of the board is 6 ft from the end and 2 ft from the edge of the building. Therefore, $60x = 40$ and $x = 2/3$ ft, or 8 inches.

160. (B) Torque is force applied (which in this case will be the weight of the rider) times the distance from the downward applied force to the axle, measured horizontally: $\tau = (50 \text{ kg})(9.8 \text{ m/s}^2)(0.18 \text{ m}) = \text{about } (50)(10)(0.2) = 100 \text{ N·m}$. Of course, the torque applied by the rider changes as the pedal goes around in a circle. The maximum torque is applied when the pedal is farthest forward and moving downward; the average torque for any complete circle is probably closer to half of that value.

161. (B) To lift the weight slowly, the clockwise torque exerted by the object must be equal to the counterclockwise torque exerted by the lower arm: $\tau = R_\perp F = (0.3 \text{ m})(9.8 \text{ m/s}^2)(5 \text{ kg}) = 15 \text{ N·m}$.

162. (A) Torque is equal to force (in this case, the weight of the object) times the distance from the line of force to the pivot. The clockwise torque is due to the weight of the rod and the weight of the smaller object:

$$\tau = R_\wedge F = (0.5 \text{ kg})(10 \text{ m/s}^2)(0.7 \text{ m}) + (0.2 \text{ kg})(10 \text{ m/s}^2)(0.2 \text{ m}) = 3.9 \text{ N·m}$$

The counterclockwise torque is due to the weight of the larger object at the left end:

$$\tau = R_\wedge F = (1.0 \text{ kg})(10 \text{ m/s}^2)(0.3 \text{ m}) = 3.0 \text{ N·m}$$

The net torque is 0.9 N·m clockwise. (Using either $g = 9.8$ or 10 m/s^2 will lead to answer choice A.)

163. (D) For a condition of equilibrium, the object or system may be either stationary or moving at constant velocity, as long as acceleration is zero. The net torque and net force in every dimension must be zero.

164. (A) Forces C and D exert clockwise torques, and forces A and B exert counterclockwise torques. Torque is the product of force and radius in each case since the forces are all tangential (making them perpendicular to the radius). For record keeping, we'll make clockwise torques positive and counterclockwise torques negative:

$$\text{Torque C} = (30 \text{ N})(0.10 \text{ m}) = 3.0 \text{ N·m}$$
$$\text{Torque D} = (10 \text{ N})(0.10 \text{ m}) = 1.0 \text{ N·m}$$
$$\text{Torque A} = (20 \text{ N})(0.10 \text{ m}) = -2.0 \text{ N·m}$$
$$\text{Torque B} = (50 \text{ N})(0.02 \text{ m}) = -1.0 \text{ N·m}$$
$$\text{Net torque} = 1.0 \text{ N·m (clockwise)}$$

165. (A) Torque is equal to the applied force times the perpendicular distance to the axis of rotation. Since each torque is along a tangent and the tangent is always perpendicular to the radius, then in each case we'll multiply the force times the radius at the point $\tau = r_\perp F$. Assume that torques that cause clockwise rotations are positive and that torques that cause counterclockwise rotations are negative and add them to find the net torque. (The sign on the direction is arbitrary.)

$$\Sigma\tau = (10\text{ N})(0.3\text{ m}) + (30\text{ N})(0.3\text{ m}) - (50\text{ N})(0.1\text{ m}) - (20\text{ N})(0.3\text{ m}) = 1.0\text{ N}\cdot\text{m}$$
$$\Sigma\tau = I\alpha$$
$$1.0\text{ N}\cdot\text{m} = (4.0\text{ kg}\cdot\text{m}^2)(\alpha)$$
$$\alpha = 0.25\text{ rad/s}^2$$

166. (D) For the system to balance—that is, maintain rotational equilibrium—the net torque about the fulcrum (or pivot point) must be zero. In other words, the net clockwise torque on the rod must be equal in magnitude to the net counterclockwise torque. Without the added 1-kg mass, the clockwise torque ($\tau = F_\perp R$) is $mgR = (2\text{ kg})(9.8\text{ m/s}^2)(2/3L)$. The counterclockwise torque is $mgR = (6\text{ kg})(9.8\text{ m/s}^2)(1/3L)$. The net torque clockwise is $4gL/3$, and the counterclockwise torque is $6gL/3$. So to balance, we need to add $2gL/3$ to the right side, knowing that $m = 1$ kg.

$$\frac{2mgL}{3} = mgR$$
$$\frac{2L}{3} = R$$

Therefore, the extra 1-kg mass needs to be placed $2L/3$ from the pivot, meaning that it will be attached to the right end of the stick.

167. (D) First, construct a diagram of the situation, showing the forces that are being exerted on the bridge. (1) We know that the net force in the y direction (vertically) must be zero, so the two piers together must support the entire weight of the bridge plus the car, or $W = mg = (22{,}000\text{ kg})(10\text{ m/s}^2) = 220{,}000$ N. (2) Then position a fulcrum at one end (in this case, the left end) and set the clockwise and counterclockwise torques equal since the net torque on the bridge about any axis must be zero.

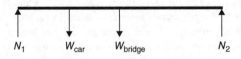

(1) $\Sigma F_y = 0$

$$N_1 + N_2 - W_{car} - W_{bridge} = 0$$
$$N_1 + N_2 = (22{,}000\text{ kg})(9.8\text{ m/s}^2) = 220{,}000\text{ N}$$

(2) $\tau_{cw} = \tau_{ccw}$

$(W_{car})(5\,m)+(W_{bridge})(10\,m) = N_2(20\,m)$

$(20{,}000\ N)(5\,m)+(200{,}000\ N)(10\,m) = N_2(20\,m)$

$N_2 = 105{,}000\ N$

Then: $N_1 = 115{,}000\ N$

168. **(D)** Use balanced torques to solve for the unknown mass of the meter stick:

$\Sigma \tau = 0$

$\tau_{cw} = \tau_{ccw}$

$(.35\ kg)(9.8\ m/s^2)(0.35\ m)+(m_{stick})(9.8\ m/s^2)(0.15\ m) = (0.80\ kg)(9.8\ m/s^2)(0.2\ m)$

$m = 0.25\ kg$

169. **(B)** First recognize that the net force in each direction must be equal to zero and that the net torque on the meter stick must be equal to zero. This problem becomes easier if you see the 1-2-$\sqrt{3}$ right triangle relationship since the length of the meter stick and the distance of the meter stick from the wall at the base are in a 1:2 ratio.

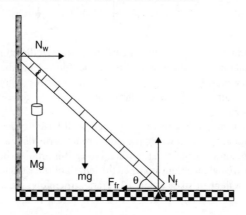

$\Sigma F_x = 0$, so $N_{wall} = F_{fr, floor}$

$\Sigma F_y = 0$, so $N_{floor} = W_{meter\ stick} + W_{hanging\ mass}$

Set a pivot where the meter stick meets the floor and set the clockwise and counterclockwise torques equal:

$\tau_{cw} = \tau_{ccw}$

$(N_{wall})(\sqrt{3}/2\ m) = (W_{meter\ stick})(0.25\ m)+(W_{object})(0.375\ m)$

$(N_{wall})(\sqrt{3}/2\ m) = (0.5\ kg)(9.8\ m/s^2)(0.25\ m)+(1\ kg)(9.8\ m/s^2)(0.375\ m)$

$N_{wall} = F_{fr, floor} = 5.7\ N$

Note: In each torque term, we've made sure that the force is multiplied by the perpendicular distance from the line of force to the fulcrum to determine the torque.

170. (B) The clockwise torque exerted by the person's downward force is equal (at a minimum) to the counterclockwise torque exerted by the lid of the can. Setting the torques equal.

171. (B) If the pivot is set at the connection of the beam to the wall, then the sum of the clockwise torques and the sum of the counterclockwise torques must be equal. By setting the pivot at this point, the force from the wall exerts no torque since the line of force runs through the pivot. (See the diagram below.) Answer choice B correctly shows each force applied to the beam multiplied by its lever arm (the perpendicular distance from the line of force to the pivot). Answer choices A and D ignore the force applied by the hinge between the beam and the wall in accounting for horizontal and vertical forces. Answer choice C has used the incorrect component to determine the lever arm for the tension.

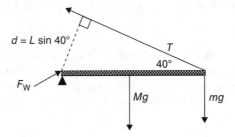

172. (D) For the ladder to remain stable, the net force in each direction must be equal to zero. The only vertical forces are the weight of the ladder (down) and the normal force from the floor (up), so they must be equal: $Mg = N_f$. The only horizontal forces are the normal force from the wall (right) and the friction force of the floor on the ladder (left), so these must be equal: $N_w = F_f$.

Since we are given only the mass of the ladder, we'll have to use torque to solve the problem. Set the pivot at the point where the ladder touches the floor and set the clockwise and counterclockwise torques equal to each other. Note: This problem becomes easier if you see the 1-2-$\sqrt{3}$ right triangle relationship since the length of the ladder and the distance of the ladder from the wall at the base are in a 1:2 ratio. Therefore, the height of the ladder on the wall is $\sqrt{3}$.

$$\tau_{cw} = \tau_{ccw}$$
$$(N_{wall})(\sqrt{3}\,\text{m}) = (m_{ladder})(g)(0.5\,\text{m})$$
$$N_{wall} = F_f = \frac{(6\,\text{kg})(9.8\,\text{m/s}^2)(0.5\,\text{m})}{\sqrt{3}} = 17\,\text{N}$$

173. (B) If the meter stick and the unknown object balance when the pivot is at the 60-cm mark, then the clockwise and counterclockwise torques exerted by the weight of the meter stick on one side and the unknown mass on the other side of the pivot must be equal. Each torque is equal to the weight of the object times its distance from the pivot. The torque due to the meter stick's weight is mgR, or $(0.1\text{ kg})(9.8\text{ m/s}^2)(0.10\text{ m}) = 0.10$ N·m. The torque due to the weight of the unknown mass is mgR, or $m(9.8\text{ m/s}^2)(0.2\text{ m})$. Since the distance of the unknown mass from the pivot is twice as much, its mass must be half as much as the stick's, or 50 g.

174. (C) Start with the bottom branch. The rectangle on the right exerts a torque of (0.1 kg) $(9.8 \text{ m/s}^2)(0.1 \text{ m}) = 1.0 \text{ N·m}$, so the torque on the left also has to be 1.0 N·m. The weight of the stick exerts a torque of $(0.01 \text{ kg})(9.8 \text{ m/s}^2)(0.1 \text{ m}) = 0.01 \text{ N·m}$, and the triangle exerts a torque of $(0.33 \text{ kg})(9.8 \text{ m/s}^2)(0.3 \text{ m}) = 0.99 \text{ N·m}$, so the total on the left is 1.0 N·m, for a total net torque of zero. These numbers work. Now use the entire weight of the bottom branch, which is $(0.143 \text{ kg})(9.8 \text{ m/s}^2)$, or 1.40 N, to determine torque in the top branch.

The torque on the right side of the connection is due to the weight of the bottom branch, so the torque is $(1.40 \text{ N})(0.3 \text{ m})$, or about 0.42 N·m. (Notice here that the length of the stick is 0.4 m and that the bottom branch is attached 10 cm from the center, so the lever arm, R, is 0.3 m.) The torque on the right due to the weight of the stick is $(0.01 \text{ kg})(9.8 \text{ m/s}^2)(0.1 \text{ m}) = 0.01 \text{ N·m}$, so the total torque on the right is 0.43 N·m. Thus, the torque on the left also has to be 0.43 N·m. Calculate: $m(9.8 \text{ m/s}^2) (0.1 \text{ m}) = 0.43 \text{ N·m}$ and $m = 0.44 \text{ kg or } 440 \text{ g}$.

175. (D) For the rod to balance, the torque exerted by the masses on each side of the pivot has to balance. The equation to calculate torque is $\tau = RF$, with R being the distance from the attachment of the object to the pivot and F being equal to the weight of the attached object. The distance R must be measured perpendicular to the force F, but in this situation, the rod will be horizontal when it is balanced, so the forces will all be vertical and perpendicular to the measured distances. When we balance the torques on each side, the force (or weight of each object) is equal to mg, but each term will have g in it, so we can cancel g in every term and simply examine mass times distance on each side of the pivot to see which answer choice will balance. In answer choice A, the sum of the torques on the right side is $(1)(1) + (2)(0.5)$ and the torque on the left side is $(3)(0.5)$, which doesn't balance. In answer choice B, the sum on the right side is $(1)(1) + (2)(0.5)$ and the torque on the left side is $(3)(2)$, which doesn't balance. In answer choice C, the sum on the right is $(1)(2) + (2)(1)$ and the torque on the left is $(3)(0.5)$, which doesn't balance. Checking answer choice D, the torque on the right is $(1)(2) + (2)(2)$, which does equal $(3)(2)$.

176. (C) Kinetic energy is equal to $\frac{1}{2}mv^2$. Since the object is accelerating as it falls, its velocity at any point after it falls can be determined using $v_f^2 = v_o^2 + 2ad$, where the acceleration, a, is equal to g and the initial velocity is zero, since the object has been dropped from rest. We can see that doubling the distance the object has fallen also doubles the square of the velocity. Since kinetic energy depends upon the square of velocity, we conclude that doubling the distance also doubles the kinetic energy.

Another way to determine this is to think in terms of energy conservation. As it is dropped, the object has gravitational potential energy. Halfway to the ground, the object has half as much potential energy as it had when it was dropped and half as much kinetic energy as it will have when it hits the ground.

177. (D) As the spring oscillates vertically, the object attached to it has maximum displacement when the object is at the top of its motion or at the bottom of its motion. When it has maximum displacement at the bottom, the net force on the object is maximum since $F = -kx$. If the net force is maximum, the acceleration is maximum. At the lowest point, the spring-mass system has maximum potential energy $(U = \frac{1}{2}kx^2)$ and minimum kinetic energy, so the velocity at this point in zero.

Chapter 3: Work and Energy

178. (C) The space vehicle moves more slowly in its orbit when it is farther from Earth. As the vehicle moves farther away, the gravitational force of Earth on the satellite is less, and this provides the centripetal force to keep the object in orbit. Therefore, if the centripetal force is less, the speed of the vehicle is less:

$$F_G = F_C$$
$$\frac{GM_{Earth}}{R^2} = \frac{mv^2}{R}$$
$$v = \sqrt{\frac{GM_{Earth}}{R}}$$

When the speed is less, the kinetic energy is less.

179. (B) The kinetic energy of the rock when it hits the ground will be the total of the original kinetic energy and the kinetic energy converted from gravitational potential energy during the fall. The closest answer is choice B, 100 J, as shown in the calculations.

$$K_{TOTAL} = K_o + \Delta U = \tfrac{1}{2}mv^2 + mgh = \tfrac{1}{2}(0.5 \text{ kg})(5.0 \text{ m/s})^2 + (0.5 \text{ kg})(9.8 \text{ m/s})(20 \text{ m})$$
$$= 104 \text{ J}$$

180. (D) Kinetic energy is $\tfrac{1}{2}mv^2$, so the change in kinetic energy (ΔK) is final K minus initial K, and the amount of time this takes is not a factor here:

$$\Delta K = K_f - K_o = \tfrac{1}{2}mv_f^2 - \tfrac{1}{2}mv_o^2 = \tfrac{1}{2}(2,000 \text{ kg})[(20 \text{ m/s})^2 - (10 \text{ m/s})^2] = 300,000 \text{ J}$$

181. (B) This question brings out the concept that energy can be measured in electron volts as well as in joules. One electron volt is equal to 1.6×10^{-19} J since one electron volt is the amount of energy gained by one electron moving through an electric potential difference of one volt. The answer here is just the product of the number of electrons and the electric potential difference:

$$\Delta K = q\Delta V = (1 \text{ e}^-)(12 \text{ V}) = 12 \text{ eV}$$

182. (D) Joules, ergs, and electron volts are all units of work or energy. The watt is a unit of power, or energy divided by time.

183. (B) The object has an initial kinetic energy due to its horizontal motion at the moment it starts falling. Therefore, answer choices C and D are not possible because they start at zero when time is zero. The relationship between kinetic energy and time is a curve since $K = \tfrac{1}{2}mv^2$, and the kinetic energy increases as the object falls the only possibility is answer choice B.

184. (D) Because of conservation of energy, the total energy of the block as it slides off the roof is the sum of its potential and kinetic energies. At the ground, all the mechanical energy is kinetic energy, so the kinetic energy at the bottom is equal to the total mechanical energy at the top, just before the fall.

$$E = mgh + \tfrac{1}{2}mv^2 = (2.0 \text{ kg})(10 \text{ m/s}^2)(4.0 \text{ m}) + (\tfrac{1}{2})(2.0 \text{ kg})(3.0 \text{ m/s})^2 = 89 \text{ J}$$

185. (C) The gravitational potential energy, mgh, is equal to 80 J. Just before the ball hits the floor, this gravitational potential energy has been converted to 80 J of kinetic energy. Then 10% of this, or 8 J, is converted to thermal energy during the collision with the floor, leaving 72 J of kinetic energy as the ball rebounds.

186. (A) The object has an initial kinetic energy due to its horizontal motion at the moment it starts falling. Then it adds kinetic energy as it falls. However, the largest height is at the right on the x axis, so as the object falls, we move left on the x axis to determine the kinetic energy. At height zero—just before the object lands—the object has the highest kinetic energy. The relationship between height and kinetic energy is linear since kinetic energy increases as potential energy decreases: $mgh = 1/2mv^2 = K$. In the other three answer choices, kinetic energy increases with the height, which does not happen as the object falls.

187. (D) Assuming no losses of energy due to air friction, mechanical energy is conserved. The kinetic energy as the rock hits the ground is equal to the total energy as the rock leaves the top of the building. The total energy at the top is kinetic energy plus gravitational potential energy.

188. (C) If the larger object moves downward 0.1 m, the smaller object has to move upward the same amount. The change in gravitational potential energy of the smaller object is equal to mgh, which is $(0.02 \text{ kg})(9.8 \text{ m/s}^2)(0.1 \text{ m}) = 0.02 \text{ J}$.

189. (B) Moving the object to a position two Earth radii above the surface means that the new distance between the centers of the objects has been tripled. The equation $U = mgh$ is an approximation for gravitational potential energy only when an object is located on the surface—and gives no real sense of the fact that a single object can't have potential energy. Gravitational potential energy is a property of a system of objects and depends upon the masses and relative positions of the objects. By examining the equation to determine the gravitational potential energy for two objects of masses M and m, we can see that tripling the distance between them will make the new value of U equal to 1/3 the original value:

$$U_G = \frac{-GMm}{R}$$

190. (C) As Earth orbits the sun, the total mechanical energy of the Earth-Sun system must remain constant. At a point in Earth's elliptical orbit when it moves closer to the Sun, Earth moves faster and has greater kinetic energy. Thus, the gravitational potential energy of the Earth-Sun system is decreased.

191. (D) Gravitational potential energy, U, for the original system is:

$$U_1 = \frac{-GMm}{R}$$

Now calculate the potential energy of the second system by doubling each mass and substituting one-half the distance between them:

$$U_2 = \frac{-G(2M)(2m)}{\frac{1}{2}R} = 8U_1$$

192. (C) Spring potential energy is equal to $\frac{1}{2}kx^2$. If the spring extension, x, is doubled, the potential energy is 4 times as much since the spring extension is squared.

193. (D) When the ruler is bent horizontally, it behaves like a spring and has elastic potential energy. Then when the ruler is released with the rock against it, the potential energy stored in the ruler is transferred to the rock, giving kinetic energy to the rock. When the ruler reaches its equilibrium position, it releases the rock, and the rock moves away with kinetic energy. Use the mass and velocity of the rock to determine its kinetic energy. Set the elastic potential energy of the ruler equal to the kinetic energy of the rock to determine the elastic constant, k:

$$\Delta U_{RULER} = \Delta K_{ROCK}$$
$$\frac{1}{2}kx^2 = \frac{1}{2}mv^2$$
$$k = \frac{mv^2}{x^2} = \frac{(0.1\text{ kg})(2.0\text{ m/s})^2}{(0.05\text{ m})^2} = 160\text{ N/m}$$

194. (B) Spring potential energy is dependent upon amplitude: $U = \frac{1}{2}kx^2$. At the peaks on the graph—either positive or negative—amplitude is the greatest because the spring displacement, x, is the greatest. At all other times, the displacement of the spring is zero, so the spring potential energy is zero.

195. (D) The spring equation is in the form $x(t) = A \cos \omega t$, where $\omega = 10$ rad/s and $m = 2$ kg:

$$\omega = \sqrt{\frac{k}{m}}$$
$$10\text{ rad/s} = \sqrt{\frac{k}{2\text{ kg}}}$$
$$k = 200\text{ N/m}$$

196. (D) Using conservation of energy, the potential energy of the ball-spring system is converted to kinetic energy of the ball: $\frac{1}{2}kx^2 = \frac{1}{2}mv^2$. Substituting mass ($m = 0.10$ kg), speed ($v = 10$ m/s), and displacement ($x = 0.10$ m), the spring constant, k, is equal to 1,000 N/m.

197. (C) The spring extension, x, is half the maximum extension at the amplitude of the oscillation. Spring potential energy is equal to $\frac{1}{2}kx^2$, so at the point that the extension is half the maximum, the potential energy is one-quarter of the maximum. Due to conservation of energy, if the potential energy is one-quarter, the kinetic energy must be three-quarters of the maximum.

$$K = \frac{3}{4} K_{max}$$
$$\frac{1}{2} mv^2 = (\frac{3}{4}) \frac{1}{2} mv_{max}^2$$
$$v^2 = (\frac{3}{4}) v_{max}^2$$
$$v = \frac{\sqrt{3}}{2} v_{max} = 0.7 \, v_{max}$$

198. (B) Some of the gravitational potential energy is converted to rotational kinetic energy, so the ball has a smaller proportion of its kinetic energy as translational kinetic energy. The ball will then land not as far from the table than predicted.

199. (C) The work done by the gravitational force is equal to the weight of the object (mg) times the vertical distance that the object drops (10 m). Since the gravitational force is a conservative force, the path length—or total distance that the object travels—does not matter. The gravitational force on the object is directed downward at all times during the object's trip down the hill, and the direction of displacement of the object is downward, so the product (or dot product) is positive.

Another way to think of this is the work-energy theorem. The work done by gravity is equal to the increase in kinetic energy. If we calculate the kinetic energy using the decrease in gravitational potential energy, the work is equal to mgh:

$$\Delta U = W = mg\Delta h = (2 \text{ kg})(9.8 \text{ m/s}^2)(10 \text{ m}) = 196 \text{ J}$$

200. (C) Use the concept that work done on the spring is equal to the applied force, F, multiplied by the displacement of the spring, x: $W = Fx$. To use this equation, we must recognize that the force is not a constant force. It requires more force to stretch a spring each unit of distance as the spring is stretched farther from equilibrium. Use the average force from the data in the graph, which is one-half times the maximum force, or one-half of 100 N. So the work is 50 N times 2 m, or 100 J.

Another way to think about this is to use the area under the line—a triangle—to calculate the work done (which would also be the potential energy of the spring system when stretched this distance). The area of the triangle is $A = \frac{1}{2}bh$, or $\frac{1}{2}(2 \text{ m})(100 \text{ N})$.

201. (D) Work is defined as force times displacement, with the force and displacement being in the same direction ($W = F \cdot s$). The velocity vector of the car at any moment is on a tangent to the circle, so the displacement vector is also a tangent. By definition, the centripetal force is inward, toward the center, along a radius—and the radius is always perpendicular to a tangent. Since there is no component of force in the direction of displacement, the product is zero and the work is zero.

Another way to think about this is the work-energy theorem, where work done is equal to the change in kinetic energy. The track is level and the speed is constant, so neither the kinetic energy nor the potential energy of the car changes during its motion. If there is no change in energy, then the work is zero.

202. (B) First, the work done by friction will be negative since it is in the opposite direction from the motion of the box. Work is defined as the product of force and displacement, using components of both that are along the same dimension: $W = F \cdot s = Fs \cos \theta$. Since both the friction force and the displacement of the box are parallel to the floor, the work in this case is the product of the friction force and the distance, d. By definition, the friction force is equal to the coefficient of friction times the normal force—and the normal force is equal to the weight of the box (mg) on a level surface.

$$W = -(F_f)(d) = -(\mu N)(d) = -\mu mgd$$

203. (A) The work done by the force on the box is: $W = F \cdot s$ or $W = Fs \cos \theta$. This means that to calculate work, we must use components of force and displacement that are along the same line. In answer choice A, the force and displacement are both parallel to the floor, so the maximum work is done by F in this case. In the other three answer choices, only a component of the force F is parallel to the floor, and since the component is always less than F, the work done in each of those cases is less.

204. (A) The friction force between the car's tires and the roadway is the only force in the right direction (toward the center of the circle in which the car is turning) to provide the centripetal force. Since the car is on a level road and since the friction force is equal to the coefficient of friction (μ) times the normal force (and the normal force of the road on the car is equal to the weight of the car), set the centripetal force equal to μmg. (Notice below that the mass of the car cancels.)

$$F_{fr} = F_{cent}$$
$$F_{fr} = \mu N = \mu mg$$
$$\mu mg = \frac{mv^2}{r}$$
$$\mu = \frac{v^2}{gr} = \frac{(10 \text{ m/s})^2}{(10 \text{ m/s}^2)(100 \text{ m})} = 0.1$$

205. (C) The work done by the target in stopping the arrow is equal to the loss in kinetic energy of the arrow. The kinetic energy is $\frac{1}{2}mv^2$, so the work equals $\frac{1}{2}(0.25 \text{ kg})(10 \text{ m/s})^2$, or 12.5 J. The work is force times distance, so the force can be determined by dividing the work by the distance: $W/d = F = 12.5 \text{ J}/0.04 \text{ m} = 312 \text{ N}$. The force of the arrow on the target is equal in magnitude to the force of the target on the arrow.

206. (D) As the ball leaves the top of the platform, its total energy is the sum of its kinetic energy and its gravitational potential energy. The easiest way to work this problem is to use conservation of mechanical energy. As the ball hits the ground, its total mechanical energy is the same as when it left the platform, except that it is now all in the form of kinetic energy.

$$K_{top} + U_{top} = K_{bottom}$$
$$\tfrac{1}{2} mv_{top}^2 + mgh_{top} = \tfrac{1}{2} mv_{bottom}^2$$
$$\tfrac{1}{2}(4.0 \text{ m/s})^2 + (9.8 \text{ m/s})^2 (10 \text{ m}) = \tfrac{1}{2} v_{top}^2$$
$$v_{bottom} = 14.6 \text{ m/s}$$

We have canceled the mass in every term, so the mass of the object does not affect the result.

207. (C) The friction force of the floor on the box does work in stopping the box. By the work-energy theorem, the work is equal to the loss in kinetic energy. We can estimate the coefficient of friction from the simple numbers provided. Notice that the mass of the box cancels, so changing the contents of the box to change the mass of the box will not affect the outcome.

$$W_{fr} = \Delta K$$
$$F_{fr} d = \tfrac{1}{2} mv^2$$
$$(\mu N)d = \tfrac{1}{2} mv^2$$
$$(\mu mg)d = \tfrac{1}{2} mv^2$$
$$\mu(9.8 \text{ m/s}^2)(1.0 \text{ m}) = \tfrac{1}{2}(2.0 \text{ m/s})^2$$
$$\mu \sim 0.2$$

208. (C) The boxes will travel the same distance. If the boxes are identical otherwise, we see that the masses of the boxes cancel in the solution below. It is the work done by the friction force of the floor on each box that stops the box. Set the work done by friction (which is negative) equal to the change in kinetic energy of the box (which is also negative).

$$W_{fr} = \Delta K$$
$$F_{fr} d = \tfrac{1}{2} mv^2$$
$$(\mu N)d = \tfrac{1}{2} mv^2$$
$$(\mu mg)d = \tfrac{1}{2} mv^2$$
$$d = \frac{v^2}{2g\mu}$$

As long as the boxes are moving at the same speed when they start the "race" and the coefficient of friction between each box and the floor is the same, they will move the same distance before coming to a stop.

209. (C) The maximum net work is done during a time interval in which the net change in kinetic energy is greatest. In answer choice A, the oscillating object moves from a position where spring potential energy is maximum and kinetic energy is zero to another position where potential energy is maximum. Therefore, the change in kinetic energy $(K_f - K_o)$ is zero and work is zero. In answer choice B, the oscillating object again moves from a position of zero kinetic energy to another position of zero kinetic energy, so the net work is zero. In answer choice D, the initial and final positions are at maximum amplitude, where kinetic energy is zero, so no net work is done on the object during this interval. In the correct answer choice (C), the spring force moves the object from amplitude (where $K = 0$) to equilibrium (where K is maximum). Therefore, the maximum amount of net work is done by the spring on the object.

210. (A) The block loses contact with the spring at the equilibrium, or relaxed, position of the spring, so the block has moved a distance of 5 cm (0.05 m) when it loses contact. The kinetic energy of the block at this point is equal to the spring potential energy of the spring/block system prior to release of the block minus the work done against friction in moving the block across the surface. The work done against friction is equal to friction force times the distance the block moves to equilibrium, and the friction force is equal to the coefficient of friction times the normal force. The normal force on this level surface is equal to the block's weight, *mg*.

$$U_{spring/block} = K_{block} + W_f$$
$$\tfrac{1}{2}kx^2 = \tfrac{1}{2}mv^2 + \mu mg$$
$$\tfrac{1}{2}(200 \text{ N/m})(0.05 \text{ m})^2 = \tfrac{1}{2}(0.5 \text{ kg})(v^2) + (0.02)(0.5 \text{ kg})(9.8 \text{ m/s}^2)(0.05 \text{ m})$$
$$v = 0.99 \text{ m/s}$$

211. (C) The potential energy of the spring/putty system when the toy is pushed down is equal to the gravitational potential energy of the system when it reaches its maximum height.

$$\Delta U_s = \Delta U_G$$
$$\tfrac{1}{2}kx^2 = mgh$$
$$\tfrac{1}{2}k(0.01 \text{ m})^2 = (0.02 \text{ kg})(9.8 \text{ m/s}^2)(0.08 \text{ m})$$
$$k = 320 \text{ N/m}$$

212. (D) The best answer choice is D because the satellite already has some gravitational potential energy with reference to the center of the Earth when it is on the surface. (Actually, the Earth-satellite system has gravitational potential energy.) The satellite also already has kinetic energy since it is moving in a circular path with Earth's surface. So the work necessary is equal to the sum of the changes in kinetic and potential energies. Answer choices A and C are easily eliminated because each answer involves adding force to energy.

213. (B) In answer choice A, the speed doesn't change, so no work is done to increase kinetic or potential energy. However, there is work done against friction, which is the friction force (μmg) times the distance moved: $W = \mu mgd = (0.05)(20)(10)(10) = 100$ J. In answer choice B, the work is equal to the change in gravitational potential energy:

$W = mgh = (20(10)(2) = 400$ J. In answer choice C, there is no work done (although this is tough to do!) since the person has caused no change in the energy of the box. In answer choice D, there is no work done against friction and no change in gravitational potential energy, so the work is equal to the change in kinetic energy of the box: $W = \frac{1}{2}mv^2 = \frac{1}{2}(20)(5)^2 = 250$ N.

214. (D) The change in gravitational potential energy is equal to the gain in kinetic energy of the ball as the ball hits the floor. The floor does work on the ball in bringing it to a stop, so the ball does an equal amount of work on the floor (since the forces are equal and opposite).

$$mgh = \frac{1}{2}mv^2 = F_{ave}d$$
$$(5 \text{ kg})(9.8 \text{ m/s}^2)(1 \text{ m}) = F(0.01 \text{ m})$$
$$F = 5,000 \text{ N}$$

215. (D) Power is defined as the rate at which work is done or the rate at which energy is produced. In this case, the energy produced is the kinetic energy of the car after 20 s.

$$P = \frac{W}{t} = \frac{\Delta K}{\Delta t} = \frac{\frac{1}{2}mv^2}{t} = \frac{\frac{1}{2}(2000)(40)^2}{20} = 80,000 \text{ W}$$

The prefix *kilo* means 1,000, so the answer is 80 kilowatts, sometimes abbreviated kW.

Another way to approach this type of problem is to use the equation $P = Fv$, where F is average force and v is change in velocity, with force and velocity being in the same direction. First, calculate the acceleration using $a = \Delta v/\Delta t$ and then use $F = ma$ to calculate the force. Finally, apply the force and the average velocity to the power equation:

1. $a = \dfrac{\Delta v}{\Delta t} = \dfrac{v_f - v_0}{t} = \dfrac{40 - 0}{20} = 2 \text{ m/s}^2$
2. $F = ma = (2,000)(2) = 4,000 \text{ N}$
3. $P = Fv_{ave} = (4,000)(20) = 80,000 \text{ W}$

216. (D) Power is the rate of energy use, or $P = E/t$. Therefore, the energy used is equal to power (in watts) times time (in seconds). There are 3,600 seconds per hour times 40 W, or 144,000 J.

217. (A) There are two ways to work this one. (1) Calculate the change in kinetic energy of the object and then calculate power as change in energy divided by time:

$$\Delta K = \frac{1}{2}m(v_f^2 - v_o^2) = \frac{1}{2}(2)(3^3 - 2^2) = 5 \text{ J}$$
$$P = \frac{\Delta K}{t} = \frac{5 \text{ J}}{10 \text{ s}} = 0.5 \text{ W}$$

(2) A second method uses the equation $P = Fv$, where F is average force and v is average velocity: If the acceleration is constant, we can assume that the force is constant and the average velocity is simply one-half the sum of the initial and final velocities:

$$P = Fv = (0.2 \text{ N})\left(\frac{3 \text{ m/s} + 2 \text{ m/s}}{2}\right) = 0.5 \text{ W}$$

Another possibility is using $F = ma$ to calculate the acceleration. Once the acceleration is known, determine the distance it takes for the force to accelerate the object the amount given. Then calculate the work done and calculate power as work divided by time.

218. (B) Power is equal to energy divided by time, so the slope of this graph line is the average power.

$$\text{Slope} = \frac{\Delta y}{\Delta x} = \frac{100 \text{ J}}{10 \text{ s}} = 10 \text{ W}$$

219. (A) According to the first law of thermodynamics, two systems at different temperatures that come into contact will transfer energy until the system is at thermal equilibrium—that is, all parts of the system are at the same temperature. If the two cubes are at the same temperature, then the larger cube contains more internal energy since internal energy (U) depends upon number of moles as well as temperature.

220. (C) Thermal energy will be transferred from the higher-temperature block to the lower-temperature block until thermal equilibrium is reached, at which point both blocks will have the same temperature. Regardless of the material of which the blocks are composed, if they are at the same temperature, the average translational kinetic energy of molecules in both blocks will be the same.

221. (C) Conservation of energy is stated by the first law of thermodynamics: $\Delta U = Q + W$. One complete cycle, starting at state A and returning the gas to state A, brings the gas back to its original conditions of pressure and volume. The ideal gas law, $PV = nRT$, shows that if P and V are unchanged after the cycle, then T is also back to its original value. If temperature doesn't change, then internal energy doesn't change ($\Delta U = 3/2nR\Delta T$). Now, going back to the first law equation, if ΔU is zero, then $Q = -W$ for a complete cycle.

The work for a complete cycle is the area confined by the closed curve. This is a triangle, so:

$$W = \text{area} = \tfrac{1}{2}bh = \tfrac{1}{2}(3 \text{ m}^3)(3,000 \text{ Pa}) = 4,500 \text{ J}$$

In this cycle, where work is the area between the line and the volume axis, the work during step AB is an expansion, which is larger than the work during step BC. Step AB is work done *by* the gas, and step BC is work done *on* the gas. No work is done on or by the gas is step CA since there is no change in volume ($W = -P\Delta V$). Therefore, the net work done by the gas requires energy, which means that energy must be added if this cycle is to go. This work is equal in magnitude to the heat exchange, which is 4,500 J.

222. (C) The internal energy change for the complete cycle is zero since the system is back to its original state conditions of P, V, and T. Since $\Delta U = Q + W$, the work for the complete cycle is equal to Q for the cycle. By the convention used here, expansion of the gas or work done by the gas on its surroundings is negative. Thus, we can see here that there is more work done by the gas in expanding in step BC than the positive work done in compressing the gas in step CA, so the net work in this complete cycle is negative. Using the equation above, $W = -Q$, so if the work for the cycle is negative, then Q for the entire cycle is positive (energy added):

$$Q = +78 - 50 - 20 = 8 \text{ kJ}$$

$$W = -Q = -8 \text{ kJ}$$

The net work for the cycle is the work done during step BC (negative) plus the work done during step CA, which is the area under the line BC.

$$W_{net} = -8 \text{ kJ} = W_{BC} - W_{CA}$$

$$W_{CA} = (4 \text{ m}^3)(1 \text{ kPa}) = 4 \text{ kJ}$$

$$W_{BC} = -12 \text{ kJ (The amount of work is 12 kJ.)}$$

223. (B) On a pressure versus volume diagram (P-V diagram), the net work done on or by the gas can be estimated by the area enclosed by the cycle. In this case, the work during step AB is done by the gas since the gas expands in volume during this step. In step BC, no work is done on or by the gas since there is no change in volume ($W = -P\Delta V$). During step CA, the gas is compressed by an external force, so volume decreases, and work is done on the gas. In each step, the area between the curve and the volume axis is the amount of work. The most work is done on the gas in step CA. Summing these areas and giving work done by the gas the opposite sign from the work done on the gas, the *net* area is the area enclosed. This area is approximately the area of a triangle: $\frac{1}{2}(1.5 \text{ m}^3)(8,000 \text{ Pa}) = $ approx. 6,000 J.

224. (D) The term *isothermal* means constant temperature, so the temperature does not change during the process. Using the ideal gas equation $PV = nRT$, doubling the pressure while keeping the temperature constant leaves only one other possibility—reducing the volume to one-half, which is not an answer choice.

225. (C) Apply the energy conservation law to examine each step: $\Delta U = Q + W$, where U is internal energy, Q is energy transferred into or out of the gas, and W is work done on the gas. For a step to be adiabatic, Q must be zero in the equation. Step AB is isovolumetric, and $W = P\Delta V$, so work must be zero. The temperature has to increase in AB using $PV = nRT$ (since P increases and $\Delta V = 0$), so AB is not isothermal. If $W = 0$ in AB and $\Delta U \neq 0$ (since $\Delta T \propto \Delta U$), then Q cannot be zero in step AB, and step AB is not adiabatic. Step CA is constant pressure, so both volume and temperature must decrease together, meaning that the step is not isothermal. In Step BC, P times V is the same (5 times 1 and 1 times 5), so temperature must also be constant, and Step BC is isothermal. Both pressure and volume change during Step BC, so it is neither isobaric nor isovolumetric. This leaves answer choice C.

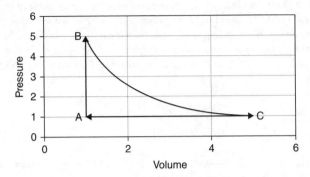

226. (D) Apply the energy conservation law to examine each step: $\Delta U = Q + W$, where U is internal energy, Q is energy transferred into or out of the gas, and W is work done on the gas. For a step to be adiabatic, Q must be zero in the equation. Step AB is isovolumetric, and $W = -P\Delta V$, so work must be zero. The temperature has to increase in AB (since P increases and $V = 0$), so U increases. Therefore, Q cannot be zero in step AB.

In step BC, the temperature is constant; since internal energy is proportional to temperature ($U = 3/2nRT$), ΔU must be zero for step BC. Since we can see that there is a volume change and work is done by the gas in expansion during this step, W is not zero and Q cannot be 0.

In step CA, there is a decrease in volume, so work is done on the system in compressing the gas. By the definition used above, this is positive work. However, the temperature has to decrease since V does not change and P decreases ($PV = nRT$); therefore, U decreases. In the equation above, Q must have a negative value in this step for conservation of energy (ΔU is – and W is +).

None of these processes can be adiabatic. An adiabatic process on a P-V diagram will be a curve much like the isothermal line for step BC, except that an adiabatic curve dips much lower, as the temperature of the gas drops quickly during expansion.

PART 2: IMPORTANCE OF FLUIDS FOR THE CIRCULATION OF BLOOD, GAS MOVEMENT, AND GAS EXCHANGE

Chapter 4: Fluids

227. (C) Since blood is not an ideal fluid, it has a viscosity greater than zero. Real fluids, such as blood, create flow patterns in a tube such that the speed of the fluid near the sides of the tube is nearly zero and the speed of the fluid is greatest near the center. Thus, a force is needed to keep the blood moving—which is provided by a pressure difference from one end of a vessel to the other.

228. (B) The total mass of blood flowing per second has to remain constant. When an arteriole branches, however, there is a much larger total area through which the blood can move, so the speed of blood flow in each capillary is less. This slower flow rate allows for more diffusion of gases through the capillary walls (in the lungs) or other materials (in other tissues in the body).

229. (B) Density is equal to mass divided by volume. The volume of oil displaced by the halite is the volume of the sample (since the piece is submerged). The density of the oil is not a factor in this calculation.

$$\rho = \frac{m}{V} = \frac{220\ \text{g}}{100\ \text{cm}^3} = 2.2\ \text{g/cm}^3$$

230. (B) If the block of wood floats 60% below the surface of the water, the block has a density 60% that of water (which is 1,000 kg/m³). The block's density is thus 600 kg/m³. If the alcohol is 90% as dense as water, the alcohol's density is 900 kg/m³. Then the block's density is 600/900 that of alcohol, so the block should float in the alcohol so that it is two-thirds under the surface. (This makes sense since the block will have to submerge slightly more in alcohol to displace enough alcohol to create a buoyant force equal to the block's weight.)

231. (B) The weight of fluid displaced by an object that is partially or fully submerged in the fluid is equal to the buoyant force of the fluid on that object. When an object floats, the buoyant force is equal to the object's weight in air. If the object floats only 75% submerged, then the object has to displace only three-fourths of its volume in order to displace a volume of fluid that weighs the same as the object weighs in air. Density equals mass divided by volume: $\rho = m/V$.

In other words, a volume of fluid that is 75% of the volume of the object weighs the same as the entire object. Thus, the fluid must be four-thirds the density of the object, and the object is three-fourths the density of the fluid. As a general rule, for an object that floats in a fluid, the depth to which the object floats gives an indication of the ratio of the density of the object to the density of the fluid.

232. (A) Liquid A has a specific gravity of 0.5, so it has a density that is half the density of water, or 500 kg/m³. If we know the density and the volume, we can find the mass of liquid A. (Remember that 1 ml is about 1 cm³, which is 1×10^{-6} m³.)

$$\rho = \frac{m}{V}$$

$$m = \rho V = (500\ \text{kg/m}^3)(60 \times 10^{-6}\ \text{m}^3) = 0.03\ \text{kg}$$

Next, find the mass of liquid B in the solution:

$$m = \rho V = (700\ \text{kg/m}^3)(40 \times 10^{-6}\ \text{m}^3) = 0.028\ \text{kg}$$

Then use the total mass and total volume to determine the density of the solution:

$$\rho = \frac{m}{V} = \frac{0.058\ \text{kg}}{100\ \text{ml}} = \frac{0.058\ \text{kg}}{(100 \times 10^{-6}\ \text{m}^3)} = 580\ \text{kg/m}^3$$

$$\text{Specific gravity} = \frac{\rho_{\text{solution}}}{\rho_{\text{water}}} = \frac{580\ \text{kg/m}^3}{1,000\ \text{kg/m}^3} = 0.58$$

233. (D) Answer choice D is a statement of Archimedes' principle, in the sense that the weight of the fluid displaced by the ball is equal to the buoyant force of the fluid on the ball. If the ball floats, the forces on the ball are in equilibrium, so the gravitational force on the ball (i.e., its weight in air) is equal to the buoyant force of the fluid on the ball. Since the ball must have only half of its volume submerged in order to displace a weight of fluid equal to the ball's weight, then the ball must be only half as dense as the fluid. (Density = mass/volume.) The weight of the ball equals the weight of the fluid displaced; the volume of fluid is half the volume of the ball, so the density of the fluid is twice the density of the ball.

234. (B) If the block has a density that is very close to the density of water and is at room temperature, it will sink in hot water. Hot water is less dense than water at room temperature, so the block will be more dense than the water and therefore will sink. As the block warms in the hot water, it will also become less dense and closer to the density of the water, so it will rise and float. Now the warm block will float in the second container of water if the water in that container is quite cold. Then, as the block cools off, it becomes more dense, and the water approaches room temperature, so the block rises and floats. The block is evidently slightly less dense than water when both are at room temperature.

235. (B) Since the bar is in equilibrium, the net force in the vertical direction is zero. The two tension forces, $2T$, are upward, and so is the buoyant force on the bar. The gravitational force, W, is the same whether the bar is in or out of water, so $2T + F = W$.

236. (D) Examine the forces on the rock when it is underwater: a spring force upward, buoyant force upward, and the gravitational force downward. The buoyant force is equal to the weight of the water displaced, which is the weight of 10 ml (10 g) of water: $W = mg = (0.01 \text{ kg})(9.8 \text{ m/s}^2) = 0.098 \text{ N}$. Now we can determine the weight of the rock, which is equal to the spring force plus the buoyant force: $W = 0.80 \text{ N} + 0.098 \text{ N} = 0.9 \text{ N}$. The mass of the rock is its weight divided by g: $m = W/g = 0.9 \text{ N}/9.8 \text{ m/s}^2 = $ about 0.09 kg. Converting this to grams, the answer is closest to 90 g.

Another way to think about this is that the apparent loss of weight of the rock when it is submerged is equal to the buoyant force on the rock. The buoyant force on a submerged object is equal to ρVg, where ρ is the density of the water and V is the volume of water displaced. Therefore, the buoyant force is:

$$F = \rho Vg = (1,000 \text{ kg/m}^3)(10 \times 10^{-6} \text{ m}^3)(9.8 \text{ m/s}^2) = 0.1 \text{ N}$$

The weight of the rock is the buoyant force plus spring force, or 0.9 N. The mass of the rock is 0.9 N divided by g, which is 0.09 kg or 90 g.

237. (C) If the ball floats 60% underwater, that means that it has to sink only that far to displace enough water to weigh the same as the ball's weight. The ball is 60% as dense as water, so it has a density of 600 kg/m³. The ball sinks 70% below the second liquid, so the ball is 70% as dense as the second liquid. Then 0.7 times the second liquid's density equals the density of the ball: $(0.7)(\rho) = 600 \text{ kg/m}^3$. The density of the second liquid is close to 860 kg/m³.

238. (B) If the ball floats, it is in equilibrium, with the buoyant force equal to the weight of the ball.

$$F_B = mg = \rho V g$$
$$mg = (0.020 \text{ kg})(9.8 \text{ m/s}^2) = 0.196 \text{ N}$$

239. (A) The total fluid pressure in each side of the tube will be the same at equilibrium. The total pressure of water plus oil plus atmospheric pressure on the left side must equal the total pressure of water plus atmospheric pressure on the right side. Since atmospheric pressure is essentially the same on both sides, we will consider only the pressure due to oil and water at the same depth on each side:

$$P_{\text{oil(left)}} + P_{\text{water(left)}} = P_{\text{water(right)}}$$
$$\rho_{\text{oil}} g h_{\text{oil}} + \rho_{\text{water}} g h_{\text{water(left)}} = \rho_{\text{water}} g h_{\text{water(right)}}$$
$$\rho_{\text{oil}}(0.10 \text{ m}) + (1000 \text{ kg/m}^3)(0.13 \text{ m}) = (1000 \text{ kg/m}^3)(0.19 \text{ m})$$
$$\rho_{\text{oil}} = 600 \text{ kg/m}^3$$

A "quick" method of working this type of problem is to see that 8 cm of oil has to have the same fluid pressure as 5 cm of water. Therefore, the oil is five-eighths as dense as water. We know that the density of water is 1,000 kg/m³, so the oil has a density of about 625 kg/m³.

240. (C) Absolute pressure is equal to the hydrostatic pressure of the water plus the atmospheric pressure. The surface area of the lake has no effect on the fluid pressure at the bottom of the lake.

$$P = P_{\text{atm}} + P_{\text{water}} = 1.01 \times 10^5 \text{ Pa} + \rho g h$$
$$P = 1.01 \times 10^5 \text{ Pa} + (1,000 \text{ kg/m}^3)(9.8 \text{ m/s}^2)(20 \text{ m}) = 3 \times 10^5 \text{ Pa}$$

The closest answer is 300,000 Pa, or 300 kPa.

Note: There is also a "quick estimate" method. Each 10-m depth of water is approximately 1 atmosphere, so the 20-m depth of water exerts a pressure of 2 atmospheres at the bottom of the lake. Then the absolute, or total, pressure is equal to 2 atm of water plus 1 atm of air above it. This total of 3 atm is closest to 300 kPa.

241. (A) Pressure exerted by a fluid is dependent only on the depth and density of the fluid: $P = \rho g h$. Total volume and surface area are not factors in pressure (although area is used to determine total force: $F = PA$). Lake A has greater pressure at the bottom since it has greater depth.

242. (C) Absolute pressure is the total pressure of all fluids above the given point of reference—in this case the pressure of water plus the pressure of the atmosphere:

$$P_{\text{abs}} = P_{\text{atm}} + P_{\text{water}} = 101 \text{ kPa} + \rho g h = 1.01 \times 10^5 + (1,000 \text{ kg/m}^3)(9.8 \text{ m/s}^2)(6 \text{ m})$$
$$= 161,000 \text{ Pa}$$

The area of the bottom of the tank is not a factor in the determination of pressure.

243. (D) A pitot tube uses difference in fluid flow pressure to determine speed (such as that of an airplane). Once the pressure of the fluid is measured at a given point, Bernoulli's equation is applied to calculate the speed of the fluid. This is useful in determining the airspeed of an airplane, for example.

244. (A) The continuity equation describes conservation of mass rate of flow: as the vessel narrows, the amount of blood flowing through it must remain constant, so the speed of flow increases. Then Bernoulli's equation describes conservation of energy; that is, as the speed of blood flow increases, the pressure decreases. This could explain a pressure drop that could affect how the valve operates.

245. (D) First, find the total, or absolute, fluid pressure on the bottom of the tank. Absolute pressure is the total pressure of all fluids above the given point of reference—in this case, the pressure of water plus the pressure of the atmosphere:

$$P_{abs} = P_{atm} + P_{water} = 101 \text{ kPa} + \rho gh = 1.01 \times 10^5 + (1,000 \text{ kg/m}^3)(9.8 \text{ m/s}^2)(6 \text{ m})$$
$$= 161,000 \text{ Pa}$$

Then use the relationship between force, pressure, and area to determine the force:

$$P = \frac{F}{A}$$
$$F = PA = (161,000 \text{ Pa})(50 \text{ m}^2) = 8,050,000 \text{ N}$$

Hint: This multiplication is easy without a calculator: multiply the pressure by 100 and then divide by 2.

246. (C) Assuming that air pressure is a small factor, calculate the pressure due to sea water at that great depth ($P = \rho gh$), then multiply pressure times area to determine force.

$$F = PA = \rho ghA = (1,025 \text{ kg/m}^3)(9.8 \text{ m/s}^2)(4,000 \text{ m})(1 \text{ m}^2) = 40,180,000 \text{ N}$$

247. (D) The total fluid pressure at the bottom of a lake is equal to the sum of the atmospheric pressure and the pressure of the water. Water pressure at a given depth depends only on density, depth, and the value of g:

$$P_{total} = P_{atm} + \rho gh$$

248. (C) The total pressure on the bubble at a depth of 21 m is approximately 3 atm. (Remember that each depth of 10 m of water exerts a pressure of 1 atm, so the total is about 2 atm of water plus 1 atm of air.) When the bubble reaches the surface, it only has 1 atm of pressure on it. When the pressure is reduced to one-third, the bubble will expand to 3 times its original volume (since $P_1 V_1 = P_2 V_2$ at constant temperature).

249. (C) Since there is no atmosphere on the surface of the moon, there will be no buoyant force on the balloon. With only a gravitational force, the balloon will sink, regardless of changes in volume or density.

250. (D) For water and most fluids, viscosity increases as the temperature is decreased. An increase in viscosity means that there are more intermolecular forces, decreasing the rate at which the molecules of the fluid can move past each other and decreasing flow rate.

251. (C) Since all other measurements are the same, the velocities are the ratios of difference in density (squared) over viscosity.

$$\text{For water: } v \propto \frac{(\Delta\rho)^2}{\eta} = \frac{(7500-1000)^2}{0.001}$$

$$\text{For oil: } v \propto \frac{(\Delta\rho)^2}{\eta} = \frac{(7500-900)^2}{0.1}$$

The numerators are close in value, so the ratio of water to oil can be estimated as the inverse of velocity—or about 100 to 1.

252. (D) Determine the speed of the water as it flows into the smaller pipe by using the continuity equation (conservation of mass). Changing the elevation of the pipe will change the pressure in the pipe, but the water speed remains the same since the amount of water flowing through the pipe per second must remain constant.

$$A_1 v_1 = A_2 v_2$$
$$\pi r_1^2 v_1 = \pi r_2^2 v_2$$
$$(0.1 \text{ m})^2 (4 \text{ m/s}) = (0.05 \text{ m})^2 v_2$$
$$v_2 = \frac{(0.1)^2 (4)}{(0.05)^2} = 16 \text{ m/s}$$

Hint: Since flow rate in a pipe is inversely proportional to area (and area is proportional to the square of radius), cutting the diameter of a pipe in half means that the area is one-quarter is much and the speed quadruples.

253. (C) When your thumb decreases the cross-sectional area of the opening of the hose, the speed of water flow must increase to conserve the mass rate of flow—a statement of the continuity equation, $A_1 v_1 = A_2 v_2$. However, the amount of water flowing out of the hose each second must remain constant to conserve the mass rate of flow.

254. (B) Use the formula shown below, where A is cross-sectional area ($\pi r^2/2$ in this case since the semicircular area is half the circular area and the trough is full of water) and v is the speed of water flow. The product of area and speed will give volume, V, per unit time, t. For this semicircular shape, the depth at the center is the radius, r. The answer choices are spread out enough in value that an estimate for the calculation yields the correct answer choice.

$$\frac{V}{t} = Av$$
$$V = Avt = (\tfrac{1}{2}\pi r^2)(vt) = \tfrac{1}{2}\pi(0.2 \text{ m})^2(3 \text{ m/s})(3{,}600 \text{ s}) = 680 \text{ m}^3$$

Note: Just to get the feel of how much water this is, each cubic meter is 1,000 liters, so the flow is 680,000 liters—about 180,000 gallons.

255. (D) Turbulence in fluid flow is defined by the Reynolds number which is directly proportional to the density of the fluid (ρ), the diameter of the obstacle encountered or the diameter of the pipe in which the fluid flows (D), and the velocity of the fluid (v) and is inversely proportional to the viscosity of the fluid. A higher Reynolds number indicates a greater likelihood that flow will become turbulent.

256. (A) Turbulence in fluid flow is defined by the Reynolds number, which is directly proportional to the density of the fluid (ρ), the diameter of the obstacle encountered or the diameter of the pipe in which the fluid flows (D), and the velocity of the fluid (v) and is inversely proportional to the viscosity of the fluid. As the Reynolds number increases, the fluid flow is more likely to become turbulent. The sudden increase in diameter as blood flows from a small vessel into a larger one can cause turbulence.

257. (B) Viscosity and surface tension are both properties of real fluids that are not found in ideal fluids. Assumptions made about ideal fluids include no frictional losses and no interactions between molecules. Viscosity arises in fluids due to friction between the moving fluid and a surface, and surface tension is due to attractive forces among the molecules of the fluid at its surface. Density is a property of both real and ideal fluids.

258. (B) Adding an inorganic salt would actually increase surface tension in water. Adding sugar to the water would have little or no effect on surface tension. Adding a surfactant would decrease surface tension, and heating the water would decrease surface tension.

259. (A) Using Bernoulli's equation, we can assume that the air pressure inside and outside of the container is approximately the same. There is no water flow (to speak of) inside the container and no water pressure outside, so we'll cancel those terms, leaving:

$$\cancel{P_{in}} + \rho g h_{in} + \tfrac{1}{2}\rho \cancel{v_{in}^2} = \cancel{P_{out}} + \rho g \cancel{h_{out}} + \tfrac{1}{2}\rho v_{out}^2$$
$$\rho g h_{in} = \tfrac{1}{2}\rho v_{out}^2$$
$$(9.8 \text{ m/s}^2)(0.45 \text{ m}) = \tfrac{1}{2}v^2$$
$$v = 3.0 \text{ m/s}$$

260. (D) First, use Bernoulli's equation to determine the pressure difference between the upper and lower surfaces of the airfoil. Then use the equation $P = F/A$ with the area of the airfoil to determine the force. Since the pressure below the airfoil is greater than the pressure above, the force is a "lift" force. In using the equation, we can assume that the atmospheric pressure ($\rho g h$) above and below the foil is not significantly different, so we can cancel it. The density of air is 1.29 kg/m^3.

(1) $P_B + \rho g h_B + \tfrac{1}{2}\rho v_B^2 = P_A + \rho g h_A + \tfrac{1}{2}\rho v_A^2$

$P_B + \tfrac{1}{2}\rho v_B^2 = P_A + \tfrac{1}{2}\rho v_A^2$

$P_B - P_A = \Delta P = \tfrac{1}{2}\rho v_A^2 - \tfrac{1}{2}\rho v_B^2$

$\Delta P = \tfrac{1}{2}(1.29 \text{ kg/m}^3)(50 \text{ m/s})^2 - \tfrac{1}{2}(1.29 \text{ kg/m}^3)(40 \text{ m/s})^2 = 580 \text{ Pa}$

(2) $P = \dfrac{F}{A}$

$F = PA = (580)(30) = 17,400 \text{ N}$

Note here that the pressure in the fluid flow is lower when the speed is higher and higher where the speed is lower. Airfoils are designed so that air flows faster over the top, meaning that there is lower pressure on the top and higher pressure underneath the airfoil, creating a pressure difference and a lift force.

261. (C) In applying Bernoulli's equation, assume that the kinetic energy of the fluid emerging from the hose ($\frac{1}{2}\rho v^2$) is equal to the potential energy of the fluid ($\rho g h$) when the water reaches maximum height. The individual water droplets behave like any small objects thrown into the air with a speed v. Solving:

$$\tfrac{1}{2}\rho v^2 = \rho g h$$
$$v = \sqrt{2gh} = \sqrt{(2)(9.8\ \text{m/s}^2)(2\ \text{m})} = 6\ \text{m/s}$$

262. (C) Bernoulli's equation is a statement of conservation of energy in fluid flow. This is easily proved by multiplying each term in the equation by volume and examining the units on each term:

$$P + \rho g h + \tfrac{1}{2}\rho v^2 = \text{constant}$$
$$PV + (\rho V)gh + \tfrac{1}{2}(\rho V)v^2 = \text{constant}$$
$$W + mgh + \tfrac{1}{2}mv^2 = \text{constant}$$

Since density times volume is equal to mass and pressure times volume is equal to work, we have made those substitutions, which reduces Bernoulli's equation to the work-energy theorem.

263. (D) First, determine the speed of air flow in the narrower tube, using the continuity equation, $A_1 v_1 = A_2 v_2$. Since the radius is cut in half and area depends on radius squared, the new area is one-fourth as much, so the air speed is 4 times as much, or 8.0 m/s. Also, since the air flow is horizontal, we can neglect the $\rho g h$ terms in Bernoulli's equation:

$$P_1 + \rho g h_1 + \tfrac{1}{2}\rho v_1^2 = P_2 + \rho g h_2 + \tfrac{1}{2}\rho v_2^2$$
$$P_1 + \tfrac{1}{2}\rho v_1^2 = P_2 + \tfrac{1}{2}\rho v_2^2$$
$$P_1 - P_2 = \Delta P = \tfrac{1}{2}\rho v_2^2 - \tfrac{1}{2}\rho v_1^2$$
$$\Delta P = \tfrac{1}{2}(1.29\ \text{kg/m}^3)[(8\ \text{m/s})^2 - (2\ \text{m/s})^2] = (\tfrac{1}{2})(\tfrac{4}{3})(60) = 40\ \text{Pa}$$

264. (B) Poiseuille's equation states that the volume rate of flow of a fluid (which is a measure of speed) is directly proportional to the pressure difference across the length of the tube in which the fluid is flowing (ΔP). Volume rate of flow is also directly proportional to the cross-sectional area of the tube and inversely proportional to the viscosity (η) of the fluid and the length (L) of the tube:

$$\frac{\Delta V}{\Delta t} = \frac{(\Delta P)\pi r^4}{8\eta L}$$

265. (D) If the heart pumps 5 liters per minute, multiply by the density to get 5.3 kg per minute. There are 24 times 60 minutes per day, so the total mass pumped by the heart is $(5.3)(60(24) = 7,632$ kg/day.

Chapter 5: Kinetic Theory of Gases

266. (A) As the molecules strike the wall, they exert a force on the wall due to the change in momentum of each particle: $F = \Delta p / \Delta t$. The force causes a pressure equal to the force divided by s the area of the wall. Answer choice B is a true statement, but it does not explain the pressure exerted by the molecules on the wall.

267. (C) The diatomic nitrogen molecules will have extra rotational or bond energy. Nitrogen and oxygen molecules don't have the polarity to explain the interactions. Ideal gases are considered to be point particles, and the diatomic nitrogen (and oxygen), which are components of air, don't come close to the point particle requirement.

268. (A) An isothermal decrease in volume means that the temperature does not change as the volume decreases. Since temperature is a measure of the average translational kinetic energy of the molecules, no change in kinetic energy or average speed of the molecules would occur during an isothermal process.

269. (D) The average velocity of the molecules will be multiplied by the square root of two. The temperature of a system is proportional to the average kinetic energy of molecules. Since kinetic energy is equal to $\frac{1}{2}mv^2$, velocity is directly proportional to the square root of temperature. If temperature is doubled, the new velocity is proportional to the square root of two times the temperature.

270. (B) The average kinetic energy of the molecules is proportional to the temperature of the gas. The average speed of the molecules stays the same since the temperature does not change. However, since the volume is smaller, molecules collide with the walls of the container more often, increasing the force and thus increasing the pressure.

271. (B) After absorbing energy during the heating process, the molecules use the energy to increase their kinetic energy. They have greater average speed, so collisions with the walls of the container are more frequent and exert more force on impact. However, since the volume of the container does not change, the molecules do no work. Internal energy is directly proportional to change in temperature: $\Delta U = 3/2nR\Delta T$. Therefore, answer choice B is correct. Answer choice D cannot be correct because the root mean square speed of molecules increases with the square root of temperature; kinetic energy is directly proportional to temperature.

272. (B) The average kinetic energy is also doubled since the average kinetic energy of molecules is directly proportional to absolute (or Kelvin) temperature.

273. (D) Ideal gas molecules do not necessarily expand isothermally when pressure is decreased. However, answer choices A, B, and C are true conditions for ideal gases.

274. (A) If no work is done on or by the gas, the quantity $P\Delta V$ is constant, so pressure does not change.

275. (D) As the temperature is increased, the distribution of the curve widens, with fewer particles at the peak of the curve. However, the area under the curve must remain constant. Answer choice B would mean no change in the average velocity of the molecules, which can't be true if the temperature increases. Answer choice A would represent the curve for a decrease in temperature. Answer choice C assumes no change in entropy, or randomizing of molecular speeds with increase in temperature.

PART 3: ELECTRICAL CIRCUITS AND THEIR ELEMENTS
Chapter 6: Electrostatics

276. (A) $1 > 2 > 3 > 4$. The electric potential on each sphere is directly proportional to the charge and inversely proportional to the diameter of the sphere. The largest sphere, for example, has the same charge on it as the other spheres, but the larger diameter of the sphere means that the charge is distributed over a larger surface area. The surface charge density is least for the largest sphere, so the largest sphere has the smallest electric potential.

277. (D) All the spheres have zero electric field inside. Since all the spheres are made of metal, any charge on each sphere moves to the outside surface once electrostatic equilibrium is reached. Thus, the electric field inside each sphere is zero.

278. (A) $1 > 2 > 3 > 4$. The electric field on the outer surface is directly proportional to the charge and inversely proportional to the surface area of the sphere. The largest sphere, for example, has the same charge on it as the other spheres, but the larger diameter means a larger surface area, so the largest sphere has the smallest electric field, and the smallest sphere has the largest. Another way to consider this is to use Gauss's law:

$$\oint \bar{E} \cdot d\bar{A} = \frac{Q_{enclosed}}{\varepsilon_o}$$

Since the enclosed charge is the same in every case, as the surface area becomes larger, the electric field becomes smaller.

279. (A) Each electron has a charge of 1.6×10^{-19} C. This charge per electron times the number of electrons equals the total charge on the balloon.

$$\frac{\text{Total charge}}{\text{Charge per electron}} = \text{Number of electrons}$$

$$\frac{1.6 \times 10^{-8}}{1.6 \times 10^{-19}} = 1 \times 10^{11}$$

280. (C) When the spheres come into contact, the charge is distributed evenly across both spheres. The net charge is now $-2Q$ after positive and negative charges cancel, with half of that charge on each sphere since the spheres are identical in size. When they are separated, each sphere then has a net charge of $-Q$.

281. (A) The key idea here is that the first rod did not touch the second rod. While the negatively charged rod was near the second rod, a polarization of charge occurred in the second rod, meaning that the charges in the rod separated. Electrons moved to the end of the rod that was farthest from the first rod, leaving the end nearest the first rod with a positive charge. Thus, the positive end of the second rod was attracted to the negatively charged rod. However, when the negatively charged rod was removed, the charge in the second rod was redistributed, and the net charge on the second rod remained neutral.

282. (B) The key idea here is that the first rod did not touch the second rod and was kept in place while the ground wire was cut. While the negatively charged rod was near the second rod, a polarization of charge occurred in the second rod, meaning that the charges in the rod separated. Electrons moved to the end of the rod that was farthest from the first rod and then to the ground, leaving the first rod with a positive charge. Since the negatively charged rod was kept near the second rod while the ground wire was cut, the separation of charge was maintained, so the second rod was left with a net positive charge.

283. (B) Since the sphere is made of a conducting material, charges can move easily. The excess charges will repel and move to the outer surface of the sphere, distributing evenly over the surface of the sphere. The insulating stand is nonconductive, so the charges are not able to move to the ground.

284. (C) Since the sphere is nonconducting, the negative charge transferred to the sphere remains in place at the point of contact with the rod.

285. (D) As shown below using Coulomb's law, multiplying each charge by 2 means that the electric force that each charged object exerts on the other is four times as great:

$$F_E = \frac{kq_1q_2}{R^2} = \frac{1}{4\pi\varepsilon_o}\frac{q_1q_2}{R^2}$$

$$F_E^{new} = \frac{kq_1q_2}{R^2} = \frac{1}{4\pi\varepsilon_o}\frac{(2q_1)(2q_2)}{R^2} = 4F_E$$

286. (A) As shown below using Coulomb's law, multiplying the distance between the charged objects by 4 means that the electric force that each charged object exerts on the other is one-sixteenth as great. This is application of the inverse square law; that is, if the objects are four times as far apart, the force is $(\frac{1}{4})^2$, or one-sixteenth.

$$F_E = \frac{kq_1q_2}{R^2} = \frac{1}{4\pi\varepsilon_o}\frac{q_1q_2}{R^2}$$

$$F_E^{new} = \frac{1}{4\pi\varepsilon_o}\frac{(q_1)(q_2)}{(4R)^2} = \frac{F_E}{16}$$

287. (D) Each of the four particles exerts the same attractive force on the electron. Because of the symmetry of the arrangement, the four force vectors effectively cancel one another, so there is no net force on the electron.

288. (A) The net electric force on q_2 is the sum of the force of q_1 on q_2, which is to the left, since the positive particle will attract the negative particle, and the force of q_3 on q_2, which is also to the left, since the negative particles will repel each other. Thus, we'll add the magnitudes of the two forces since they are both to the left. The calculation is made easier by the 1.0-m distances between charges. The calculation reduces to the following if the magnitude

$$\Sigma F_{E} = \frac{kq_1q_2}{R^2} + \frac{kq_3q_2}{R^2} = \frac{(9\times10^9\,\text{N}\cdot\text{m}^2/\text{C}^2)(2)Q^2}{(1\,\text{m})^2} + \frac{(9\times10^9\,\text{N}\cdot\text{m}^2/\text{C}^2)(4)Q^2}{(1\,\text{m})^2} = 6kQ^2$$

289. (B) The electric force in this case is the expression qE. Set the gravitational force, which is the weight (mg) of the droplet, equal to the electric force and solve for mass. Use $2e$, which stands for the charge of two electrons, for the charge, q:

$$F_G = F_E$$
$$mg = qE$$
$$m = \frac{qE}{g} = \frac{2eE}{g}$$

290. (B) First, recognize the symmetry of the situation. Since the charges on the x axis are located equidistant from the y axis, they are also equidistant from point P. The electric force vectors are outward from each charge on the x axis since they both exert forces of repulsion on the charge at point P—and on each other. The force vectors that are important at point P are shown in the solution diagram below. We can again see the symmetry of the x and y components of the electric force vectors: the x components are equal in magnitude and opposite in direction, so they cancel. Thus, the only effective electric force vectors at point P resulting from the charged particles on the x axis are the y components. These y components are equal in both magnitude and direction, so we can calculate one of the y components and double it to get the answer:

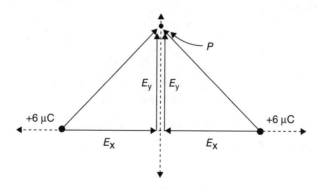

$$F = \frac{1}{4\pi\varepsilon_o}\frac{Q^2}{R^2} = \frac{kQ^2}{R^2} = \frac{(9\times10^9\,\text{N}\times\text{m}^2/\text{C}^2)(6\times10^{-6}\,\text{C})^2}{(3\sqrt{2}\,\text{m})^2}$$

$$F_y = F\sin45° = F\frac{\sqrt{2}}{2} = \frac{(9\times10^9\,\text{N}\times\text{m}^2/\text{C}^2)(6\times10^{-6}\,\text{C})^2}{(3\sqrt{2}\,\text{m})^2}\frac{\sqrt{2}}{2} = 0.0127$$

$$2F_y = (2)\frac{(9\times10^9\,\text{N}\times\text{m}^2/\text{C}^2)(6\times10^{-6}\,\text{C})^2}{(3\sqrt{2}\,\text{m})^2}\frac{\sqrt{2}}{2} = \frac{6\sqrt{2}}{2}\times10^{-3} = 0.025\,\text{N}$$

291. (D) The electric force of the proton on the electron is equal to and in the opposite direction from the force of the electron on the proton. It is calculated using Coulomb's law. The charge on the proton and on the electron is the same.

$$F = \frac{1}{4\pi\varepsilon_o}\frac{Q^2}{R^2} = \frac{kQ^2}{R^2} = \frac{(9\times10^9\,\text{N}\cdot\text{m}^2/\text{C}^2)(1.6\times10^{-19}\,\text{C})^2}{(5.29\times10^{-11}\,\text{m})^2} = 8.2\times10^{-8}\,\text{N}$$

292. (D) The electric force of the 12 protons in the nucleus on the electron is equal to and in the opposite direction from the force of the electron on the protons. It is calculated using Coulomb's law. The charge on each proton and on the electron is the same.

$$F = \frac{1}{4\pi\varepsilon_o}\frac{Q^2}{R^2} = \frac{kQ^2}{R^2} = \frac{(9\times10^9\,\text{N}\cdot\text{m}^2/\text{C}^2)(12)(1.6\times10^{-19}\,\text{C})^2}{(70\times10^{-12}\,\text{m})^2} = 5.6\times10^{-7}\,\text{N}$$

Note: The correct answer choice can be determined using powers of 10.

293. (C) First, recognize the symmetry of the situation. Since the charges are located equidistant from the y axis, they are also equidistant from point P. The electric field vectors are outward from each charge, and the only electric field vectors that are important at point P are shown in the solution diagram below. We can again see the symmetry of the x and y components of the electric field vectors; the x components are equal in magnitude and opposite in direction, so they cancel. Thus, the only effective electric field vectors at point P resulting from the charged particles are the y components. These y components are equal in both magnitude and direction, so we can calculate one of the y components and double it to get the answer:

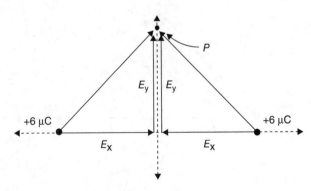

$$E = \frac{1}{4\pi\varepsilon_o}\frac{Q}{R^2} = \frac{kQ}{R^2} = \frac{(9\times10^9\,\text{N}\cdot\text{m}^2/\text{C}^2)(6\times10^{-6}\,\text{C})}{(3\sqrt{2}\;\text{m})^2}$$

$$E_y = E\sin 45° = E\frac{\sqrt{2}}{2} = \frac{(9\times10^9\,\text{N}\cdot\text{m}^2/\text{C}^2)(6\times10^{-6}\,\text{C})}{(3\sqrt{2}\;\text{m})^2}\frac{\sqrt{2}}{2}$$

$$2E_y = (2)\frac{(9\times10^9\,\text{N}\cdot\text{m}^2/\text{C}^2)(6\times10^{-6}\,\text{C})}{(3\sqrt{2}\;\text{m})^2}\frac{\sqrt{2}}{2} = \frac{6\sqrt{2}}{2}\times10^3 = 4.2\times10^3\;\text{N/C}$$

294. (C) Referring to the following equation, setting up and substitution with units gives:

$$E = \frac{1}{4\pi\varepsilon_o}\frac{Q}{R^2} = \frac{kQ}{R^2} = \frac{(9\times10^9\,\text{N}\cdot\text{m}^2/\text{C}^2)(2\times10^{-9}\,\text{C})}{(0.02\;\text{m})^2} = 4.5\times10^4\;\text{N/C}$$

295. (D) The electric field, which is defined as outward from a positively charged particle, is directed toward the center from each of the four particles. Since the charge of each particle is the same and since each particle is the same distance from the center, the vectors effectively cancel each other, creating a net electric field of zero at the center of the square. Thus, any charged particle placed at the center of the square would have no electric force exerted on it since $F = qE$.

296. (D) The net effect of this arrangement is zero since the field vectors at the center due to the positive charges are equal in magnitude and opposite in direction; therefore, those two vectors cancel. The same is true for the two negative charges. We say that this type of arrangement has "symmetry," and it's helpful to look for symmetry when examining any situation; in this case, we're looking for vectors that cancel each other.

297. (C) Once the metal surface of the sphere is charged, all charges are mobile and repel each other, so once equilibrium is established, the charges will distribute evenly on the outer surface of the sphere. All electric field vectors resulting from the charges will cancel inside the sphere, so there will be no electric field inside the sphere. (It's helpful to remember that the electric field inside any conductor will be zero.) Thus, the strongest field is just outside the sphere, getting weaker with greater distance from the sphere.

298. (B) The electric field will exert a force on the positive charges, moving them to the right side of the sphere: $F = qE$. That will leave the right side more positive and the left side more negative. Even if the field were strong enough to remove electrons, they would not move to the right, so answer choice D is not correct.

299. (C) When the sphere is put in the field, the field will exert a force on the charges within the sphere, separating and polarizing the charges so that the right side of the sphere will be more positive and the left side will be more negative. This concentration of charges increases the field on the left and right, altering the field so that it will be stronger in those regions (so we see a higher density of field lines on the left and right). However, there will be no electric field within the sphere.

300. **(D)** All statements are true except D. Since the charge is uniform on both plates, the electric field between the plates is constant. It is the electric potential that increases from the bottom to the top.

301. **(D)** The net electric field at point P is the vector sum of the field vector to the right from charged particle 1 and the field vector to the right due to the negative-charged particle 2. Thus, we can add the magnitudes of the field vectors since they are both to the right. The calculation is made easier by the 1-m distance between charges. The calculation reduces to:

$$\Delta E = \frac{kq_1}{r^2} + \frac{kq_2}{r^2} = \frac{k(q)}{1^2} + \frac{k(2q)}{1^2} = 3kq$$

302. **(D)** First, remember that the equation for the potential energy of two electric charges is equal to kQq/r. The amount of work required to assemble the group of charges would be equal to the sum of the potential energies of each pair of charges, taken two at a time. For the three positive charges, we would be adding three positive potential energies. For the three negative charges, we would be adding the same three quantities since the product of the two negative charges in each term would be positive. The amount of work in both cases would be the same. For the two positive charges and one negative charge, we would be adding one positive term and two negative terms—all of equal magnitude—so the net work would be less than in the first two cases. For the two negative charges and one positive charge, we are again adding one positive and two negative terms of equal magnitude.

303. **(C)** The electric field is inversely proportional to the square of distance, but electric potential is inversely proportional to distance by the following formulas:

$$E = \frac{kQ}{R^2} \quad \text{and} \quad V = \frac{kQ}{R}$$

304. **(B)** Electric potential is a scalar quantity that is directly proportional to charge: $V = kQ/r$. Positive and negative values of electric potential simply add numerically. Since the $-4q$ charge is twice as large, it should be twice as far from the "zero point" as the $2q$ charge. At $x = 4$, the potential from the negative charge is $-4kq/2$ or $-2q$. At $x = 4$, the potential from the $2q$ charge is $2kq/1$, or $+2kq$. These values will add to zero at $x = 4$.

305. **(D)** The magnitude of the change in electric potential is equal to Ed, from the equation $E = -\Delta V/\Delta d$, which does not depend on the magnitude of the charge. The path is measured along the direction of the field, using the component of the 0.02-m distance in the direction of the field.

$$V = (100)(0.02) \cos 60°$$

306. **(C)** A line drawn so that every point on the line has the same electric potential due to the three charges would be an equipotential line. The sum of the electric potentials due to the three charges would have to be the same at every point on the line:

$$\sum_{n=3} \frac{kQq}{r} = \text{constant}$$

Since all charges are the same, the distances from the charges to the equipotential line must be the same for every point on the equipotential line. This will be true for the line only if it is constructed from the center of the triangle, extending outward from the page perpendicular to the page.

307. (D) An equipotential due to both charged particles must be a set of points that are all of the same potential, found by adding the potentials due to each of the charges.

$$\Sigma V = \frac{kq}{r_1} + \frac{kq}{r_2} = kq\left(\frac{1}{r_1} + \frac{1}{r_2}\right)$$

By inspection, we can see cases for each of the three lines where the contribution due to one charge remains fairly constant while the contribution due to the other charge changes, causing varying values for the sum of the potentials.

308. (A) The mathematical calculation here is simple, involving only multiplication and operations with exponents, as long as the correct formula is used:

$$U = \frac{kq_1q_2}{r} \text{ or } \frac{1}{4\pi\varepsilon_o}\frac{q_1q_2}{r}$$

$$U = \frac{(9\times10^9)(3\times10^{-6})(3\times10^{-6})}{1\times10^{-2}} = 81\times10^{-1} = 8.1 \ J$$

The common mistakes on this one would be to square the distance, r, producing the incorrect answer choice C, or to use only one of the charges, leading to incorrect answer choice D. Incorrect answer choice B might arise from an incorrect operation with exponents.

Chapter 7: Circuits

309. (A) Current is the rate of flow of charge, so $I = \Delta Q/\Delta t = (3.6 \times 10^{-6})/(10 \times 10^{-3}) =$ 3.6×10^{-4} A. This is equal to 0.36×10^{-3} A, which is 0.36 mA.

310. (A) By definition, current is the rate of flow of charge, $I = \Delta Q/\Delta t$. If current is in amperes, charge is in coulombs, and time is in seconds, then 1 ampere is equal to 1 coulomb per second.

311. (C) The electric field is downward from the positive plate to the negative plate; the increase in electric potential is upward, toward the positive plate; and the force on a proton would be downward in the same direction as the electric field.

312. (C) The total resistance of the two resistors in series is 400 Ω. Then that 400 Ω is in parallel with 200 Ω. The quickest way to find this is to use "product divided by sum," which can be used for just two parallel resistors. So that is (400)(200)/600, which is 133 Ω. The parallel rule for addition of resistors can also be applied:

$$\frac{1}{R_T} = \frac{1}{R_1} + \frac{1}{R_2}$$

$$\frac{1}{R_T} = \frac{1}{400} + \frac{1}{200} = \frac{3}{400}$$

$$R_T = 133 \ \Omega$$

313. (D) When the current divides at the junction to the parallel branches, more current will go into the branch with the least resistance, so more current flows in the branch with the 200-Ω resistor. In the other branch, the same current will flow through the 100-Ω and 300-Ω resistors since they are in series.

314. (D) Resistance is directly proportional to length and inversely proportional to cross-sectional area. So the resistance is greatest when the ratio L/A is the greatest. With length $4L$ and area A, the ratio is greatest in answer choice D.

315. (D) The potential difference across bulb A is equal to the sum of the potential differences across bulbs B and C. From Kirchhoff's loop rule, the potential difference across each of the two branches must be the same. In answer choice A, the potential difference across bulb A is the greatest because bulb A has the largest current, but the second part of that answer statement is not true.

316. (A) Only the 200-Ω resistor will have a potential difference across it of 100 V. Since the battery has a potential difference of 100 V, by Kirchhoff's loop rule, the sum of potential differences around the large loop will equal zero, and thus the potential difference across the 200-Ω resistor must be 100 V. The sum of the potential differences across the 100-Ω and 300-Ω resistors is 100 V.

317. (B) If the total current from the battery is 0.75 A, the current will split at the junction, in an inverse proportion to total resistance in that branch. The 200-Ω resistor has half as much resistance as the two resistors in the other branch. The current will divide so that more current goes through the branch with smaller total resistance. The current will divide in three parts, with one-third going through the branch with a total resistance of 400 Ω and two-thirds going through the branch with a resistance of 200 Ω. Another way to do this is to use Kirchhoff's loop rule first to determine that the potential difference in the 200-Ω resistor must be 100 Ω. Then by Ohm's law ($I = V/R$), the current is 100/200, or 0.5 A. Therefore, both the 100-Ω and the 300-Ω resistors will each have a current of 0.25 A, and the 200 Ω resistor will have a current of 0.50 A.

318. (D) Since power is energy divided by time, then $E = Pt$, with power in watts and time in seconds. Multiplying the 40 W power times 3,600 s in one hour, $E = 144,000$ J.

319. **(B)** First, find the equivalent resistance, or total resistance of the two resistors. Since there are just two resistors in parallel, this can be done quickly using product over sum. So the total resistance is 18/9, or 2 Ω. Using Ohm's law, $V = IR$, the current must be 10 A. Because the resistance is in a ratio of 2:1, the current will split in the same ratio, with the larger current taking the path of least resistance. The current split is two-thirds of the current to the 3-Ω resistor and one-third of the current to the 6-Ω resistor. Thus, the current in the 3-Ω resistor is two-thirds of 10, or 6.7 A. *Alternative Method*: The sum of potential differences in any loop must be zero, so the potential difference in each of the resistors is 20 V. Using Ohm's law, $I = V/R = 20/3 = 6.67$ A.

320. **(B)** First, find the equivalent resistance of the three resistors. Start with the two resistors in parallel, using product over sum, which is $R^2/2R$, or $\frac{1}{2}R$. Then add the resistor in series to find the total resistance: $R_T = R + \frac{1}{2}R = \frac{3}{2}R$. Use Ohm's law to determine current from the battery: $I = V/R_T = V/(\frac{3}{2}R) = 2V/3R$. That total current splits equally into the two parallel branches so that the resistor on the far right gets one-half of this current, or $V/3R$.

321. **(D)** The total resistance of the two resistors in series is 50 Ω. Use Ohm's law to determine current: $I = V/R = 10/50 = 0.2$ A. Since the resistors are in series, all the current flows through each resistor. Again use Ohm's law, this time determining potential difference: $V = IR = (0.2\ \text{A})(20\ \Omega) = 4$ V. *Alternative method:* The 10-V potential difference across the resistors is split, with part of the difference in each resistor. Since both have the same current, we know that the smaller resistor will get the smaller share of the potential difference: two-fifths of the 10 V equals 4 V in the 20-Ω resistor, leaving 6 V in the 30-Ω resistor.

322. **(B)** If you apply Kirchhoff's loop rule, the sum of the potential differences for all elements in the circuit will be zero: $\varepsilon - IR - Ir = 0$. In this case, $\varepsilon = 12$ V, $r = 2\ \Omega$, $R = 16\ \Omega$, and I is the current.

$$12 - I(16) - I(2) = 0$$

$$I = 0.67\ \text{A}$$

323. **(D)** The emf of a battery minus the electric potential difference due to the internal resistance in the battery is the potential difference at the poles of the battery, or the voltage delivered to the external circuit:

$$V_{ext} = \varepsilon - Ir$$

$$10\ \text{V} = 12\ \text{V} - (1\ \text{A})(r)$$

$$r = 2\ \Omega$$

324. **(B)** First, find the equivalent resistance for the two parallel branches on the right. In those branches, the two bulbs in series on the far right have a resistance of 200 Ω, and that is in parallel with 100 Ω. Using product over sum, the equivalent in parallel is 20,000/300, or 67 Ω. Then the two bulbs on the left are in series with the parallel branches, so these are just added. The total resistance is $100 + 100 + 67 = 267\ \Omega$.

325. (C) The equivalent resistance, sometimes called total resistance, is the size of one resistor that could replace the combination of resistors and still deliver the same current and power to the external circuit. Start first with the two resistors at the right that are in parallel. To find the equivalent of two resistors (and only two resistors) in parallel, use product over sum, which is $100^2/200$, or 50 Ω. Then the third resistor is in series with the parallel combination, so we add the resistor in series to get a total of 150 Ω.

326. (D) Start first with the two parallel resistors at the bottom. You can use the parallel rule for addition of resistors in parallel, but the quickest method is to use product over sum, which is equal to $40^2/80$, or 20 Ω. Then add this to the resistances of the other two resistors, which are in series with this combination. The total resistance is 20 + 20 + 20 or 60 Ω.

327. (B) There is no mention here that the resistors used are equal to each other, so we cannot assume that the current splits equally in the branches. However, the potential difference across each branch must be the same (Kirchhoff's loop rule, or conservation of energy). In fact, as more resistors are added in parallel, the total resistance decreases.

328. (B) The resistance of a resistor is directly proportional to the product of resistivity and length and inversely proportional to cross-sectional area:

$$R = \frac{\rho L}{A}$$

Solve this for ρ to get answer choice B. When applying this formula, R is in ohms (Ω), ρ is in ohm-meters, L is in meters, and A is in square meters.

329. (D) The energy stored in a capacitor, C, is equal to $\frac{1}{2}CV^2$. If the potential difference, V, is one-half as much in the second case, the energy will be one-fourth of 100 μJ, or 25 μJ.

330. (B) The energy stored in a capacitor is $\frac{1}{2}CV^2$, where C is capacitance in farads (F) and V is electric potential difference in volts (V). The prefix *micro* (μ) means 10^{-6}.

$$U_C = \frac{1}{2}CV^2 = \frac{1}{2}(2000 \times 10^{-6}\,F)(10\;V)^2 = 0.1\;J$$

Answer choices C and D are distracters for those who might forget to incorporate the prefix μ into their calculations.

331. (A) With all other factors remaining constant (plate area and dielectric), doubling the distance between the plates requires work since the plates have opposite charges and attract each other.

332. (D) Since $U_C = \frac{1}{2}CV^2$, doubling the potential difference on the capacitor would quadruple the energy stored in the capacitor.

333. (D) Since charge is conserved in much the same way that current must be the same in all parts of a series circuit with resistors, the charge on each capacitor is the same. Then, since $Q = C/V$, the potential difference on each capacitor is proportional to the capacitance.

Therefore, the smaller capacitor has one-half the potential difference of the larger capacitor. By Kirchhoff's loop rule, the smaller capacitor will have a 10-V potential difference, and the larger capacitor will have a 20-V potential difference.

334. (A) The total capacitance for two capacitors in series is calculated in the opposite way from the way in which resistors in series are added. Use the product over sum rule (or reciprocal addition rule for just two components):

$$C_T = \frac{(2,000\times10^{-6})(4,000\times10^{-6})}{(2,000\times10^{-6})+(4,000\times10^{-6})} = \frac{8\times10^{-6}}{6,000\times10^{-6}} = 1,300\ \mu F$$

335. (A) The total capacitance for two capacitors in parallel is calculated in the opposite way from the way in which resistors in parallel are added. Simply add the capacitors in parallel, so the equivalent capacitance is 6,000 μF.

336. (D) The capacitance is changed when the dielectric (κ) is changed:

$$C = \frac{\kappa A}{d}$$

When the dielectric constant is one-half as much, the capacitance is reduced to one-half. Using the equation $Q = CV$, the charge on the capacitor will then be one-half since the voltage is the same in both cases.

337. (D) After a very long time, the capacitor has completely charged, so no more current flows through the resistor. With no current in the resistor, there is no potential difference (V) in the resistor (R), due to Ohm's law, $V = IR$. Therefore, by Kirchhoff's loop rule (or conservation of energy), the sum of the voltage changes around the loop has to be zero, and the voltage V_C on the capacitor has to be the same as the emf. Now, we know that $V_C = 20$ V and $C = 1,000\ \mu$F. Using the equation $Q = CV$, we can find Q: $Q = (1,000\ \mu$F) $(20$ V$) = 20,000\ \mu$C. The resistance has no effect on the final charge in this circuit; adding a resistor just slows the charging rate.

338. (C) After a long time, we can assume that the capacitor is completely charged, so no more charge moves in that branch of the circuit. However, the current still flows in the large loop that includes the two resistors. We need to find the potential difference across the bottom resistor in the diagram so that we can calculate the potential difference across the capacitor. The total resistance of the two resistors (which are now in series with each other) is 100 Ω. Using Ohm's law, $V = IR$, the current in the resistors is $I = V/R = 10/100 = 0.1$ A. Now calculate the potential difference in the bottom resistor, again using Ohm's law: $V = IR = (0.1$ A$)(50\ \Omega) = 5$ V.

Using the loop rule on the small loop on the left, the sum of the voltages must equal zero. (Even though there's no current flowing in the branch that contains the capacitor, there is still a voltage drop across the capacitor.)

$$\varepsilon - V_C - V_R = 0$$
$$10 - V_C - 5 = 0$$
$$V_C = 5\text{ V}$$

339. (A) When an electric potential difference is applied across the two ends of a metal wire, the resulting electric field causes electrons to move from one end of the wire to the other. Answer choice B is not true because the electrical conductivity is a property of the metal, not necessarily a function of the length of the wire. Answer choice C is not true because increasing the cross-sectional area of a wire will decrease resistance.

340. (A) In answer choice A, the power is equal to the change in potential energy divided by time, which is mgh/t, or $100/2 = 50$ W. In answer choice B, the power is equal to average force times average velocity, $P = Fv = 30$ W. In answer choice C, the power is equal to change in kinetic energy divided by time, or $P = \Delta K/t = 40/20 = 2$ W. In answer choice D, the electric power is equal to I^2R, or $(10)^2/10 = 10$ W.

341. (B) Power (P) is defined as the product of potential difference (V) and current (I). Since this question doesn't supply the current or ask for the current, use Ohm's law to substitute for current and then solve for power (in watts):

$$P = VI$$

$$V = IR \text{ and } I = \frac{V}{R}$$

$$\therefore P = \frac{V^2}{R} = \frac{(12)^2}{4} = 36 \text{ W}$$

342. (D) First, find the equivalent resistance of the four resistors. For the parallel pair, use product over sum to find the equivalent of the two 40-Ω resistors: $R = 40^2/80 = 20$ Ω. Add the two 20-Ω resistors, which are in series with the parallel pair of resistors, to find the total resistance: $R_T = 20 + 20 + 20 = 60$ Ω. Since we know the potential difference and the resistance, we can combine the power formula ($P = VI$) and Ohm's law ($V = IR$) to obtain the form that works best here: $P = V^2/R = (30)^2/60 = 15$ W.

343. (C) A voltmeter has very high internal resistance and should be connected in parallel with the component on which it is taking a measurement.

344. (D) An ammeter has very low internal resistance and should be connected in series with the component on which it is taking a measurement.

PART 4: HOW LIGHT AND SOUND INTERACT WITH MATTER

Chapter 8: Sound

345. (A) A transverse wave is one in which the oscillations of particles of a medium are perpendicular to the direction of propagation of the medium. A longitudinal wave is one in which the oscillations of a medium are along the same direction as the direction of propagation of the wave. Sound is an example of longitudinal waves. Compressional waves would describe the compressions of longitudinal waves.

346. (A) The waves travel from A to B, transferring energy to the person's ear, which makes the eardrum oscillate so that the person can hear the sound. However, the air molecules oscillate within a confined space, so the molecules transfer energy from one to another—

much like a lineup of dominoes—but the molecules don't travel beyond the amplitudes of their oscillations in place. Answer choice C describes a transverse oscillation, which is not the method by which sound travels. Answer choice D is not correct; the frequency remains the same, which defines the pitch of the sound. The amplitude may decrease with distance, however, causing the sound to be less loud as it travels farther.

347. (C) Blowing through an instrument increases the temperature of the air inside the instrument, which increases the speed of sound in the air inside the instrument. Assuming very little change in the dimensions of the instrument itself during this warming-up process, the wavelengths produced by specific notes would not change. Therefore, using the equation $v = f\lambda$, an increase in the speed of sound would correspondingly produce an increase in the frequency. We perceive an increase in frequency as higher "pitch."

348. (C) The two waves have the same amplitude, which is about 2 units. Wave A has a period of about 3 seconds—the time for one complete oscillation. Frequency is the inverse of period, so wave A has a frequency of $\frac{1}{3}$ Hz. Wave B has a period of about 2 seconds and a frequency of $\frac{1}{2}$ Hz, so the frequency of wave B is higher than that of wave A. The waves meet at crest and trough at about 3.8 s, where they would destructively interfere. At 4.2 s, the wave amplitudes are both zero, so they don't interfere. At 8.0 s, the waves are both in the same position, or in phase, so they constructively interfere.

349. (A) A maximum occurs at point B because the distance from each opening to point B is the same. Thus, the waves are still in phase with each other—and constructively interfere—at point B. For a maximum, or constructive interference of the waves, to occur at point A, the extra distance that the waves from one slit have to travel to point A compared to the distance the waves from the other slit have to travel would have to be one wavelength. We call this the "path length difference." For constructive interference, the path length difference needs to be a whole number of wavelengths so that the waves are in phase when they meet at that point.

Use the equation $m\lambda = d \sin \theta$, where m is the number of the maximum from the central maximum, λ is the wavelength, d is the slit spacing, and θ is the angle BPA. In this case, $m = 1$, λ is the unknown, d is 1 mm, and θ has a tangent of length AB divided by length PB.

$$m\lambda = d \sin\theta$$

$$\tan\theta = \frac{\overline{BA}}{\overline{BP}} = \frac{2 \text{ mm}}{100 \text{ mm}} = 0.02$$

$$\theta = 1.15$$

$$(1)(\lambda) = (0.001 \text{ m})\sin(1.15) = 2\times10^{-5} \text{ m or } 0.02 \text{ mm}$$

350. (C) Waves are in the same phase when they are in the same position, i.e., at the same amplitude and traveling in the same direction. The two oscillations start in the same position at $t = 0$, which is with an amplitude of 0 and moving toward the positive direction. In answer choice A, wave A is at 0 and moving toward the positive direction, and wave B is at 0 but moving toward the negative direction. In answer choice B, wave A is at an amplitude of 2, and wave B is at an amplitude of −2. In answer choice C, waves A and B are both at an amplitude of about −2 and moving in the same direction, so they are in phase. In answer choice D, wave A is near a maximum positive amplitude, and wave B is near zero.

351. (A) Moving the speaker twice as far away reduces the intensity to one-fourth since intensity of sound varies as the inverse square of distance. However, doubling the intensity at the source brings the intensity from one-fourth to one-half of the original.

352. (C) We can substitute the given value for intensity into the formula and calculate it easily since we know that log 100 = 2.

$$\beta = 10 \log \frac{I}{I_o} = 10 \log \frac{1 \times 10^{-10}}{1 \times 10^{-12}} = 10 \log 100 = 10(2) = 20 \text{ dB}$$

353. (C) It's not a bad idea to remember that the intensity is multiplied by 10 when the decibel level goes up by 10. The proof is shown below, where we can see that the intensity, I, for 50 decibels is 1×10^{-7} W/m² and the intensity for 60 decibels is 1×10^{-6} W/m².

$$\beta = 10 \log \frac{I}{I_o} = 60 = 10(6) = 10 \log 10^6 = 10 \log \frac{1 \times 10^{-6}}{1 \times 10^{-12}}$$

$$\beta = 10 \log \frac{I}{I_o} = 50 = 10(5) = 10 \log 10^5 = 10 \log \frac{1 \times 10^{-7}}{1 \times 10^{-12}}$$

354. (B) When the waves are added, or superimposed, their amplitudes at that point in time will add. At $t = 0$, the sum of the two amplitudes is 0 + 2, or 2 m. At $t = 7$, the sum of the two amplitudes is approximately 1.5 + 1.5, or 3 m. At $t = 9$, the sum of the two amplitudes is 0 + –2, or –2 m. And at $t = 12$, the sum of the two amplitudes is approximately 1.5 + (–1), or 0.5 m.

355. (D) The amplitude will add to zero when the centers of peaks of the waves are in the same position. Each wave is 1 m wide, so they will completely cancel when the centers are in the same position. At the point shown, the centers are at $x = 2.5$ and $x = 9.5$, so the centers are 7.0 m apart. Each wave will cover half this distance, so we need to find the time for the pulses to travel 3.5 m: $t = d/v = 3.5$ m/5.0 m/s = about 0.7 s.

356. (B) The peaks of the two pulses will completely overlap to produce a pulse of the greatest amplitude when each pulse has moved 0.75 m. This would put the peak of pulse A between $x = 1.25$ and $x = 1.5$ and the peak of pulse B between $x = 1.25$ and $x = 1.5$. They would overlap as they pass that position, producing a pulse of double amplitude. Since the pulses are both moving at the same speed, they will reach that position at $t = d/v = 0.75$ m/2.0 m/s = 0.375 s.

357. (C) The sound is a maximum at the first position because the waves have traveled the same distance from each speaker, are in phase, and constructively interfere. At the second position, the sound waves from the two speakers destructively interfere, so the waves are ½ wavelength or 180° out of phase. Then the wavelength must be some multiple of 1 m. The possible wavelengths are 1 m, 2 m, 3 m, etc.

358. (D) The standing wave produced in the open tube has antinodes at both ends and a node in the middle, so the fundamental standing wave in the tube is ½ wavelength. The fundamental wavelength is 2L. Use $v = f\lambda$ to find the frequency: $f = v/\lambda$. Substituting, $f = v/2L$.

359. (D) The standing wave produced in the closed tube has a node at the closed end and an antinode at the open end, so the fundamental standing wave in the tube is ¼ wavelength. The fundamental wavelength is 4 times the length of the tube. Use $v = f\lambda$ to find the frequency: $f = v/\lambda$. Substituting, $f = v/4L$. Using the same reasoning, the wavelength for the open tube was 2 times the length of the tube, so the frequency equals $v/2L$. We can see that the frequency for the closed tube is one-half the frequency for the original open tube. When we hear a frequency that is lower in number, we call it a lower pitch. In fact, when the frequency is half is much, we hear what we call an octave lower.

360. (D) The harmonics for the tube that is closed at one end—where the standing wave has a node at one end and an antinode at the other end—are

$$\lambda_n = \frac{4L}{n}, n = 1, 3, 5, \text{ etc.}$$

The harmonics in a tube that is open at both ends are calculated in the same way as the harmonics for a string that is attached at both ends:

$$\lambda_n = \frac{2L}{n}$$

You can see that the wavelength for the first harmonic for the closed tube is twice as long as the wavelength for the open tube. Thus, a closed tube that is half as long as an open tube would produce notes of the same wavelength and the same frequency.

361. (D) The general formula for wavelength related to the length on which the standing wave is confined (for a string that is attached at both ends or a tube that is open at both ends) is $\lambda = 2L/n$, where n is the number of the harmonic. The first and second overtones are the second and third harmonics (since the fundamental is the first harmonic). Since $v = f\lambda$, we can use the information given to find v for the string: $v = f\lambda = 2fL/n = 2(200)(0.4)/1 = 160$ m/s. Now we can use that value of v to find the other two harmonics. For the second harmonic, $160 = 2f(0.4)/2$ and $f = 400$ Hz. For the third harmonic, $160 = 2f(0.4)/3 = 600$ Hz. Now that we have derived that, we can just remember (for future reference!) that the harmonics for a string that is fixed at both ends or a tube that is open at both ends are just multiples of the fundamental.

362. (D) The general formula for wavelength related to the length on which the standing wave is confined for a tube that is closed at one end is $\lambda = 4L/n$, where n has to be an odd number. For the fundamental, $n = 1$, and $n = 3$ and then $n = 5$ for the next two overtones. Since $v = f\lambda$, we can use the information given to find v for the air in the tube: $v = f\lambda = 4fL/n = 4(100)(0.8)/1 = 320$ m/s. Now we can use that value of v for the other two harmonics. For the second harmonic, $320 = 4f(0.8)/3$ and $f = 300$ Hz. (Note: You don't have a calculator to do this; you just compare the fractions: n is 3 times as much, so f is 3 times as much.)

For the third overtone, $320 = 4f(0.8)/5 = 500$ Hz. Now that we have derived that, in the future you can just remember that the harmonics for a closed tube (open at only one end) are just the odd-number multiples of the fundamental frequency, so the harmonics for this tube are 100 Hz (fundamental), 300 Hz, and 500 Hz.

363. (C) The mixture of fundamental frequencies and overtones created by a musical instrument is called the quality. Quality describes the sound of a specific instrument, created by resonance of all parts of the instrument.

364. (C) An open tube has harmonic frequencies that are multiples of the fundamental frequency, so the next higher frequency at which the open tube will resonate is the second harmonic, which has twice the frequency of the fundamental (or first harmonic). A closed tube has harmonics that follow the odd numbers, so the frequency of the next harmonic is three times the frequency of the fundamental (or first harmonic), the next harmonic after that has five times the fundamental frequency, and so on. Interestingly, the harmonics for a string that is attached at both ends are identical to the harmonics for a tube that is open at both ends.

365. (C) Assume that the speed of sound is the same in both situations. For a tube that is closed at one end, the fundamental wavelength is $4L$. Since $v = f\lambda$, $f = v/\lambda = v/4L$. When the tube is cut in two, the length is $L/2$, so $f = v/4(L/2) = v/2L$. The second frequency is twice the frequency of the original tube.

366. (C) To increase the number of loops in the standing wave, measures need to be taken that would decrease the wavelength of the standing wave. Since $v = f\lambda$, this can be accomplished by any measure that increases the frequency while keeping the wave speed constant or decreases the wave speed while keeping the frequency constant. In the correct answer choice (C), loosening the string to decrease the tension will also decrease the speed of the waves on the string. (The speed of a wave on a string is directly proportional to the tension in the string and inversely proportional to the linear density of the string.) When wave speed is decreased, keeping all other factors the same, the wavelength will decrease, so more loops can be produced on the string. Answer choice A is not correct because decreasing the frequency will increase the wavelength if wave speed is kept constant. Answer choice B is not correct because a thinner string has a lower linear density, which increases the speed of waves on the string. This will increase the wavelength if frequency is kept constant. Answer choice D is not correct because moving the supports apart will not change the number of loops.

367. (A) As the two frequencies superimpose, there are positions where the waves meet in the same phase, reinforcing and producing constructive interference—four times per second. In between, the waves from the two tuning forks are not in phase and destructively interfere, producing sound that is partially or completely "canceled." This pattern of higher-amplitude constructive interference six times per second is called the beat frequency. The beat frequency is the difference in the frequencies of the interfering waves.

368. (C) When clay was added to the tuning forks, it increased the period and decreased the frequency—much like lengthening a pendulum. The difference in frequency between the modified tuning fork and the original will be the number of beats heard per second. Five beats per second between X and modified Y indicate that Y has a frequency that is 5 Hz less than that of X. A beat frequency of three beats per second heard between Y and Z means that Y and Z are 3 Hz different in frequency, but without knowing how much clay was added to Y and Z, we don't know which has the higher or lower frequency. Thus, Z could be lower in frequency than Y and a total of 8 Hz lower than X, or Z could be higher in frequency than Y, putting it 3 Hz from Y and 2 Hz lower than X.

369. (A) As the truck approaches, the perceived frequency of the sound produced by the saxophone will increase, so the frequency of the A note played by the trombone in the truck will be higher than the A note being played by the saxophone on the street corner. The beat frequency is the difference in frequency of the two notes being superimposed, so the note played by the trombone in the truck must be 4 Hz higher, or 444 Hz. This is an example of the Doppler effect.

370. (C) If 4 beats per second are heard, the pipes are producing frequencies that differ by 4 Hz. The shorter pipe will produce a higher frequency, so the frequency produced by the shorter pipe must be 264 Hz.

371. (A) When the instrument is tuned, the length of the air column inside the instrument is set, so the fundamental wavelength for that note does not change until the instrument is tuned again. However, as the air in the clarinet becomes warmer, the velocity of the sound becomes greater, using the equation $v_{air} = 331$ m/s $+ 0.6T_C$. Apply the equation $v = f\lambda$, where v is the speed of sound, f is the frequency of the note played, and λ is the fundamental wavelength of that note. If wavelength is constant, then frequency must increase as the temperature and velocity increase. As a result, a wind instrument will tend to go up in frequency—or play the notes "sharp" and with a higher pitch—unless the instrument is warmed up well before playing.

372. (D) As sound travels from one medium to another in which the speed of sound is different, the waves may change direction, which is termed *refraction*. This happens at night, for example, near the surface of Earth over bodies of water. The air is cooler over the water, and sound travels more slowly in cooler air. Sounds traveling away from a source bend downward toward the cooler air near the surface, so sounds may seem to be amplified.

373. (B) Attenuation of sound in fluids is directly proportional to the viscosity of the medium and the frequency of the sound (actually, it is usually proportional to the square of the sound frequency). Attenuation varies inversely with the density of the medium and the speed of sound in that medium.

374. (D) The speed of sound in air increases with elasticity and decreases with increasing density, according to the equation below. Since increasing the temperature makes air more elastic and decreases its density, a temperature increase directly increases the speed of sound.

$$v = \sqrt{\frac{B}{\rho}} \quad \text{where } B = \text{elastic modulus and } \rho = \text{density}$$

375. (B) The diffraction, or bending, of sound waves around the corner of a building allows you to hear sounds from objects that you are not able to see. (Light also diffracts, but the much shorter wavelengths for light make this phenomenon of a much smaller magnitude.) Answer choice A is an example of the attenuation of sound as it is absorbed and scattered by the medium. Answer choice C is an example of the Doppler effect, or an increase in frequency when a sound source moves toward a stationary observer. Answer choice D is an example of the decrease of sound speed in colder air; this effect is much less noticeable on a warm day, when sound travels faster.

376. (B) The attenuation coefficient varies widely for different materials, so ultrasonic signals can be used to reveal structural information in many different contexts, from the human fetus to the chemical composition of solutions.

377. (C) The Doppler effect will be greatest when the relative velocity between the sound source and the observer is the greatest. For answer choices A and B, the perceived frequency is higher than the siren frequency in A (where the siren is moving closer) and the perceived frequency is lower than the siren frequency in B (where the siren and the observer are separating at the same speed as in A). Generally speaking, however, the Doppler effect is greater when the source is moving relative to a stationary observer than when the observer is moving relative to a stationary source. In answer choice C, the siren and the observer are each approaching the intersection at a speed of 30 m/s; using a right-triangle relationship, these speeds are the legs of a triangle with a hypotenuse of 42. Therefore, the observer and the siren are approaching each other at a rate of 42 m/s, which produces the greatest effect. In answer choice D, the observer is moving away from the intersection at 30 m/s and the siren is moving toward the intersection in the same direction at 30 m/s. In this case, they are not closing in or receding from each other, so the relative velocity is zero and there is no Doppler effect.

There is another way to make the calculation for answer choice C. In answer choice C, the difference is the resultant of the siren vector (from the east) and the negative of the observer vector (toward the south), which is shown in the figure below.

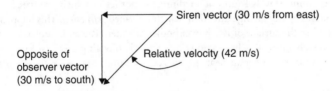

Siren vector (30 m/s from east)

Opposite of observer vector (30 m/s to south)

Relative velocity (42 m/s)

378. (C) You will hear a higher frequency from the siren when the two vehicles are moving toward each other with the highest relative speed. When the vehicles are moving away from each other, you will hear a lower frequency than the siren is emitting. In this case, the highest relative speed occurs when you are moving toward the siren and the siren is moving toward you. In answer choice D, the two vehicles are moving in the same direction at the same speed, so there is no relative speed, and you will hear the same frequency that the siren is emitting.

379. (D) Answer choice A is not possible since the wavelength range for sound, even for very high frequencies, is still many orders of magnitude too large to interact directly with molecules. Answer choices B and C are both viable possibilities.

380. (A) Ultrasonic has all the properties of sound, except that it is in the frequency range higher than 20,000 Hz—beyond the range of human hearing. It should not be confused with supersonic, which means "traveling faster than the speed of sound" in a given medium.

Chapter 9: Electromagnetic Radiation and Optics

381. (C) Since $c = f\lambda$, where the speed of light, c, is constant, the frequency must be inversely proportional to wavelength. Indeed, all the other statements are true: all forms of electromagnetic radiation do travel at the same speed (c) in a vacuum, all can be polarized, and all are formed of mutually perpendicular oscillating electric and magnetic fields.

382. (B) The lowest-frequency forms of electromagnetic radiation have the longest wavelength and the lowest energy—which starts at the radio-wave end of the spectrum. Listing various types of electromagnetic radiation, in order from lowest frequency and longest wavelength to highest frequency and shortest wavelength: radio, infrared, red, orange, yellow, green, blue, violet, ultraviolet, x-rays, gamma. Answer choice B has a listing in the correct order within these choices. Notice that within the visible range of electromagnetic radiations, the color red has the longest wavelength, the lowest frequency, and the lowest energy. The visible colors, in order from longest wavelength to shortest wavelength, are R-O-Y-G-B-V ("Roy G. Biv" without the indigo, which is not considered a distinct color).

383. (B) It's a good idea to remember that visible light falls within a range of about 400 nm (at the violet end of the visible range) to 750 nm (at the red end of the visible range). Ultraviolet light has a higher frequency and a shorter wavelength than violet, so it would be in a range shorter than is visible to us, or in the 250–300-nm range. Answer choice (A) falls within the visible range—green to yellow. Answer choice (C) falls within the visible range—green to blue. Answer choice (D) is within the red visible range. Light wavelengths longer than about 750 nm would be in the infrared range and not visible.

384. (D) Diffraction of light is evidence of the wave nature of light. Light has a dual nature: as photons that behave as particles and as waves that can interfere constructively when they are in phase and interfere destructively when they are out of phase (e.g., the crest of a wave pattern from one slit superimposed on a trough of the wave pattern from the second slit). The other statements are really just nonsense. Light does have a particle nature, and photons do have momentum, but they can't cancel when they collide because energy would not be conserved. In answer choice B, light is attenuated, or absorbed, by the region around the slits, but the remaining light would still create an interference pattern. In answer choice C, it is the wave nature of light that causes diffraction of wave fronts as they pass through the slits—and those diffraction patterns interfere to produce a pattern.

385. (A) Geometrically, the distance from each slit to the center of the diffraction pattern is the same, so the path length difference is zero. Since there is only one monochromatic light source, we can assume that the waves pass through the slits in the same phase. Since they travel the same distance to the center of the pattern and start in the same phase, they will be in the same phase to produce constructive interference at the center of the pattern, which is called the "central maximum."

386. (C) First, consider that green light will change phase upon its first reflection from the upper surface of the film since the film has a higher index of refraction than air. Also, green light will change phase after it goes into the film and reflects from the interface between the film and the glass. Since both reflections change phase, they will be in phase with each other and will constructively interfere with each other as they reflect back out into air, *as long as* the trip of the light for the second reflection does not change the phase. Therefore, the trip down into the film and back out to air (which is twice the thickness of the film) must be an integral number of wavelengths of the green light *in the film*. If $2d = \lambda$, then $d = \lambda/2$.

387. (A) The various colors seen on a soap bubble result from the interference of reflected light from the top surface of the film with reflected light from the bottom surface of the film. The film has various thicknesses, so the colors are a result of constructive interference of the reflected light rays from the two surfaces of the film.

388. (A) Diffraction is the bending of waves as they pass through an opening or around an obstacle. Diffusion is the scattering of waves as they interfere with a medium. Reflection is a reversal in path as a wave strikes a boundary between two different media. Refraction is a change in path and wave speed as a wave moves from one medium into another. Dispersion is the separation of white light into its component colors as a result of differences in the refractive index for different colors.

389. (C) When applying the equation to a single slit, the integer designated by m applies to the dark fringes. When applying the same equation to a double slit, the integer applies to the bright fringes.

390. (B) Use the equation $m\lambda = d \sin \theta$, where m is the number of the dark fringe, λ is the wavelength of the light, d is the aperture width, and θ is the angle for fringe spacing. As the wavelength is increased (on one side of the equation), we assume that d stays the same, and as a result, θ increases (on the other side of the equation). This will spread out the pattern of bright and dark fringes.

391. (A) Use the equation $m\lambda = d \sin \theta$, where m is the number of the bright interference pattern from the central maximum, λ is the wavelength of the light, d is the spacing between lines on the grating, and θ is the angle swept by the bright lines from the central maximum to the bright line designated by m. If other factors remain the same, changing to green light substitutes a smaller wavelength. By examination of the equation, the angle θ would also have to become smaller, resulting in a compression of the pattern on the screen.

392. (A) Indeed, when the angles are very small (as in the case where d is proportionally large), the approximation shown in answer choice A is acceptable. For very small angles (in radians), the angle measurement is very close to the sine of the angle. This small angle approximation can be used in such cases, where $\theta = \dfrac{m\lambda}{d}$.

393. (D) Electromagnetic radiation is polarized as the electric field component of the radiation is affected by some materials. Answer choices A, B, and C are all electromagnetic. Sound waves are longitudinal waves that travel only through a medium, are not electromagnetic, and cannot be polarized as they travel through a fluid (such as a gas or a liquid).

The direction of travel and the direction of oscillation are the same—not perpendicular, as in electromagnetic oscillations.

394. (C) The intensity of light is reduced by half as it passes through a polarizer since the electric field portion of the light is cut out, leaving only the magnetic field to contribute to the energy of the light.

395. (C) When the beam reflected from a surface is perpendicular to the refracted beam, the reflected beam is completely polarized in a direction parallel to the reflecting surface. This will happen when the incident angle is a special angle called "Brewster's angle," on the condition that the incident angle (Brewster's angle) plus the refracted angle must be 90 degrees. Polarization of light by reflection occurs on nonmetallic surfaces.

396. (B) As distant objects (such as quasars) move away from Earth, light from the objects undergoes a "red shift," which is a decrease in frequency or increase in wavelength that makes the light from the objects shift toward the red end of the visible spectrum. This would be true for any radiation coming from those distant objects—that is, observed radiation that is of longer wavelength than the radiation at the source.

397. (D) As the light enters the prism in what seems to be a path perpendicular to the left side, it does not change direction. However, when the white light exits on the right side, the light will bend away from the normal as it travels from glass to air. Path B seems to be along the normal, so both paths C and D could be possible rays refracted along the right side. Assuming that violet light refracts more than the other colors, D is the best answer.

398. (C) If a light wave is propagated in the positive x direction and the electric field oscillates in the y direction, then the magnetic field is in the z direction. The direction of propagation is found by the vector cross product $E \times B$.

399. (A) Red, blue, and green are the three primary colors of light, so all three of these colors must be present to produce white. Cyan is a mixture of green and blue, yellow is a mixture of red and green, and magenta is a mixture of blue and red. Answer choice A does not have green in any component, so it will not work. All the other three choices have red, blue, and green in some proportion.

400. (C) If light is incident upon an interface from a lower index of refraction to a higher index of refraction, the light will change phase by 180 degrees upon reflection from the surface. Light does not change phase upon refraction from one medium to another.

Chapter 10: Absorption Spectra

401. (C) First, since we are looking for the energy of an emitted photon, only the transitions in answer choices A and C will qualify. The transitions in answer choices B and D are absorptions since they represent transitions from lower-energy states to higher-energy states. The highest-frequency photon would be emitted for the transition of highest energy since $E = hf$. The energy emitted, ΔE, is equal to final energy minus original energy. By inspection, the change in energy from $n = 3$ to $n = 1$ is greater.

402. (D) In the derivation of energy states for the Bohr model of the atom, the energy of the lowest-energy state, or ground state, is represented by E, or $n = 1$. The higher-energy states for the electron are numbered consecutively and have energies equal to E/n^2. For example, if the energy for the ground state is -13.6 electron volts (eV), then the energy for the next higher state, which is $n = 2$, must be equal to $-13.6/2^2$, or -3.4 eV.

403. (D) The energy states of the Bohr model of the hydrogen atom have the ground state, or lowest-energy state, labeled $n = 1$. Each subsequent higher allowed energy state has energy proportional to the square of the level number. For example, the next higher energy state from the ground state, which is $n = 2$, has one-fourth the energy of the ground state, and the third energy state, $n = 3$, represents an energy that is one-ninth that of the ground state. The average energy is also proportional to the inverse square of the distance from the nucleus, so the third energy state ($n = 3$) has one-ninth the energy of the ground state, and the electron would be nine times as far (average) from the nucleus.

404. (C) The Rutherford model, which was developed previous to the Bohr model, emphasized the structure of the nucleus. The Bohr model (proposed in 1915) improved upon this by emphasizing that (1) electrons orbit only at discrete energies and distances from the nucleus; (2) the energy of each orbit is related to its size, with smaller orbits having lower energy; and (3) radiation is emitted or absorbed when electrons make a transition from one energy state (or orbital) to another. The Bohr model is inaccurate in many ways—and is now considered obsolete—but it is useful as a tool for calculating quantum transitions of electrons between energy levels.

405. (A) For angular momentum to be conserved, an integral number of electron wavelengths must "fit" into the orbit. The circumference of the orbit is $2\pi R$, so only an integral number of wavelengths (nR) will fit into that orbit without the electron wavelengths undergoing destructive interference, according to the Bohr model. For the next energy level ($n + 1$), the allowed orbital has a radius and electron energy that must agree with the condition $2\pi R_{new} = (n + 1)\lambda_{new}$.

406. (A) One way to determine the correct answer is to substitute $E = hf$, which we know is the expression for energy related to frequency using Planck's constant (h). Doing that, answer choice A becomes hc/hf, which reduces to c/f. When we look at $\lambda = c/f$, the expression $c = f\lambda$ becomes apparent—a true statement. Cross-multiplying the other answer choices does not produce anything reasonable. For example, we can see in answer choice D that hf in the numerator is equal to E; then we have $\lambda = E/E = 1$, which is not a reasonable solution.

Considering the expression in the correct answer choice (A), it becomes apparent that as the energy level increases, the wavelength must decrease (since h and c are constants). This makes senses. Electrons in higher energy states do not have higher energy, they have higher frequency ($E = hf$)—and higher-frequency waves have longer wavelengths.

407. (D) Only the energy transitions shown are allowed. The arrows here are the possible energy state transitions for absorbed photons—and their reverse in each case would be an emitted photon. The energy for each emission is $\Delta E = E_{final} - E_{initial}$. The smallest change possible is from the $n = 4$ state to the $n = 3$ state. Calculating this change:

$$\Delta E = E_{final} - E_{initial} = -1.51 - (-0.85) = -0.66 \text{ eV}$$

The negative value on this change means that the energy is emitted in the form of a photon of this energy. We could calculate the frequency of this photon using the equation $E = hf$, where h is Planck's constant.

408. (C) The diagram is constructed so that the spacing gives an indication of the amount of energy between the energy states. The transition from $n = 4$ to $n = 1$ is an allowed energy transition, and that transition would give off energy ($\Delta E = E_{final} - E_{initial} = -13.6 - (-0.85) = -12.75$ eV). The energy is directly proportional to frequency and inversely proportional to wavelength. Thus, this high-energy transition will emit a photon with high energy and short wavelength.

$$\Delta E = hf = \frac{hc}{\lambda}$$

$$\lambda = \frac{hc}{E_2 - E_1}$$

409. (B) Referring to the equation in the previous explanation, a change in energy state, ΔE, is equal to the energy of the final state minus the energy of the original state. If the transition is from higher energy to lower energy, the energy change is negative, meaning that energy is given off in the form of light—as in this case. If the final energy state is higher than the original energy state, the net change is positive, meaning that energy is absorbed as photons of light. In the equation, h is Planck's constant. The substitution is based on the equation $c = f\lambda$, where c is the speed of light.

410. (C) The force on the protons as they enter the magnetic field is described by a vector cross product: $\mathbf{F} = q\mathbf{v} \times \mathbf{B}$. Only the component of the velocity that "crosses" the field lines will produce a force. Using a right-hand rule, the index finger (representing velocity) points to the right, and the other fingers (representing the B field) point down on the page, so the thumb (representing force) points into the page. (Make sure the index finger, the other fingers, and the thumb are all mutually perpendicular.)

411. (C) The centripetal force to keep the charged particle moving in a circle is provided by the magnetic force in this course. Set the two expressions equal and solve for mass, m, using $2e$ for the charge q and noting that the particle's motion is perpendicular to the field, so maximum force is exerted on the particle:

$$F_B = qvB$$

$$F_{cent} = \frac{mv^2}{R}$$

$$2evB = \frac{mv^2}{R}$$

$$m = \frac{2eBR}{v}$$

412. (C) First, use the right-hand rule to determine the charge on the particle. If the force is down on the page in the $-y$ direction, the magnetic field is into the page in the $-z$ direction, and the velocity is to the right in the $+x$ direction, the only way this can work is if you use your left hand. This means that the particle is negative. The negative particle has a magnetic force on it downward on the page, so there must be an electric force upward on the page in order to balance the forces so that the particle can move in a straight line. Using the equation $F = qE$, the force and electric field are in the same direction for a positive particle. For this negative particle, the force is in the opposite direction from the electric field. Therefore, for the electric force to be upward, the electric field must be downward on the page, or in the $-y$ direction.

413. (B) For the electron to move in a straight line across the page, the net force on the charge should be zero. We can see that the magnetic force on the electron is upward on the page, so the electric force should be downward on the page. However, for the electric force to be downward on the page, the electric field needs to be upward on the page since electric force on a negative charge is in the opposite direction from the electric field: $\mathbf{F} = q\mathbf{E}$. (Force on a positive charge is in the same direction as the electric field in this vector equation.) This is the "crossed fields" effect, that is, that crossed electric and magnetic fields can apply equal force on a charge so that the charge moves in an undeflected path.

414. (D) Using the right-hand rule and then reversing direction for the negative charge (or using the left hand in the first place), we find a magnetic force directed into the page. The electron will experience a force into the page and then continue in a circular motion, with the magnetic force providing the centripetal force: $\mathbf{F} = q\mathbf{v} \times \mathbf{B}$.

415. (B) First, you have to recognize that the charge, q, on a proton is the same as the charge on an electron, except that it is positive. This charge, which is 1.6×10^{-19} C, is often just called e. Then apply the equation $\mathbf{F} = q\mathbf{v} \times \mathbf{B}$, where q is the charge (e, the charge on an electron, in this case), $\mathbf{v}$ is the component of the velocity that is perpendicular to the field lines ($v \sin 60°$), and $\mathbf{B}$ is the magnetic field.

416. (D) Use the right-hand rule to determine that if the charges were positive, they would curve outward on the page, toward the curved end of the magnet. Since these are electrons, the rule is opposite, so the electrons curve inward on the page, toward the open end of the magnet and away from the magnet. To use the right-hand rule, point your index finger in the direction of velocity and extend your other fingers perpendicular to velocity to represent the magnetic field (which is from north to south). Then extend your thumb to show the direction of the magnetic force. This magnetic force changes the direction of the motion of the charged particles but does not change their speed.

417. (D) Since the wire is stationary and the magnet is stationary, there is no relative motion between the electrons in the wire and the magnetic field. Therefore, there is no force from the magnetic field on the electrons, and no current is produced: $F = qvB \sin \theta = qv \times B$.

418. (C) With a greater speed, the second particle will move in a larger radius. This can be proved by setting the magnetic force on the particle equal to the centripetal force and examining the effect on speed, v:

$$F_B = F_C$$
$$qvB = \frac{mv^2}{R}$$
$$v = \frac{qBR}{m}$$

419. (D) The charge will not move. In order for a magnetic force to be exerted on a charged particle, the particle must be in motion: $F = qv \times B$.

Chapter 11: Geometric Optics

420. (C) The red-light wavelength is reduced by a smaller amount, so red light has a smaller refracted angle than blue light. The light frequencies do not change as light enters a different medium, but both speed and wavelength are reduced when light enters glass from air.

421. (B) The image formed by a plane mirror by a real object is the same size as the object and upright relative to the object You see this when you look at your own image in a flat mirror. Your image is upright and appears to be twice as far from you as you are from the mirror—or the same distance behind the mirror as you are in front of the mirror.

422. (D) The image formed by a convex (diverging) mirror by a real object is smaller than the object and upright relative to the object. We don't need to prove this mathematically since we see it every day. The large mirrors in the upper corners of some stores and the side mirrors of your car are convex mirrors that show real objects (or people) as smaller and upright. These are virtual images. The purpose of such mirrors—even though they show images that make the object seem farther away—is to gather images of objects from a wider area.

423. (D) The image formed by a convex (converging) lens by a real object located inside the focal length of the lens is larger than the object and upright relative to the object. A quick examination of the thin-lens equation, with f equal to focal length and $f/2$ equal to the object distance, can show this. Let's say we have a convex lens of focal length +10 cm and an object placed 5 cm from the lens. (Note that the focal length is positive since this is a convex lens.) The calculations shown below help to verify that the image is virtual (upright) and larger than the object.

$$\frac{1}{d_o} + \frac{1}{d_i} = \frac{1}{f}$$

$$\frac{1}{5\,\text{cm}} + \frac{1}{d_i} = \frac{1}{10\,\text{cm}}$$

$$\frac{1}{d_i} = \frac{1}{10} - \frac{1}{5} = -\frac{1}{10}$$

The negative image distance indicates that the image is virtual and that the image distance is larger than the object distance, so the magnification is greater than 1, and the image is larger than the object:

$$M = d_i/d_o > 1$$

424. (D) The image formed by a concave (converging) mirror by a real object located inside the focal length of the mirror is larger than the object and upright relative to the object. An example of this is a shaving or makeup mirror that magnifies a person's face so that the person looking into the concave mirror appears to himself as being larger and right side up. If the person then moves the mirror away so that his face is located outside of the focal length of the mirror, his face will appear upside down (a real image is formed).

425. (C) Wearing concave lenses will extend the focus farther from the lens, placing the image on the retina and in focus.

426. (C) Different color components of white light have different focal lengths since each color has a unique index of refraction. Each color refracts at a slightly different angle, separating the white light into its color components and causing the colors to appear as rings around a circular lens.

427. (D) The three primary colors of light are red, blue, and green. Mixed in the correct proportions, they will produce white light.

428. (B) Each color of light has a different index of refraction, so each color bends a different amount when entering the glass from air. This is called dispersion.

429. (D) Rays passing from the object through the lens will be directed parallel to each other on the other side of the lens, so they will not converge to form an image. We can confirm this by applying the thin-lens equation for the case where the object distance is equal to the focal length:

$$\frac{1}{d_o} + \frac{1}{d_i} = \frac{1}{f}$$

$$\frac{1}{f} + \frac{1}{d_i} = \frac{1}{f}$$

$$\therefore \frac{1}{d_i} = 0$$

There is no real value for the image distance.

430. (C) First, we know that a diverging (concave) lens cannot create a real image. (The only two possibilities for real images are when an object is positioned outside the focal length of a convex lens or a concave mirror.) A negative focal length is substituted into the thin-lens equation:

$$\frac{1}{d_o} + \frac{1}{d_i} = \frac{1}{f}$$

$$\frac{1}{12} + \frac{1}{d_i} = \frac{1}{-6}$$

$$\frac{1}{d_i} = -\frac{1}{6} - \frac{1}{12} = -\frac{3}{12}$$

$$d_i = -4$$

The image is located 4 cm from the lens, on the same side of the lens as the object, and is a virtual image. All virtual images are upright.

431. (D) Use the thin-lens equation:

$$\frac{1}{d_o} + \frac{1}{d_i} = \frac{1}{f}$$

$$\frac{1}{1.5f} + \frac{1}{d_i} = \frac{1}{f}$$

$$\frac{2}{3f} + \frac{1}{d_i} = \frac{1}{f}$$

$$d_i = 3f$$

432. (B) The index of refraction, n, is the ratio of the speed of the electromagnetic radiation in a vacuum to the speed of the radiation in the medium: $n = c/v$. Answer choice B is correct because if $n = 1.5$, or 3/2, then the ratio c/v equals 3/2, and the ratio $v/c = 2/3$. Answer choice A is not correct because frequency remains constant. Answer choice C is not correct because a ray of light entering a medium along a perpendicular line (or normal line) changes speed and wavelength but does not change direction. Answer choice D is not correct because it would imply that light entering the medium travels at a speed faster than the speed of light.

433. (C) Use the thin-lens equation, remembering to use a negative value for the focal length:

$$\frac{1}{d_o} + \frac{1}{d_i} = \frac{1}{f}$$

$$\frac{1}{1.5f} + \frac{1}{d_i} = \frac{1}{-f}$$

$$\frac{2}{3f} + \frac{1}{d_i} = \frac{-1}{f}$$

$$d_i = -\frac{3f}{5}$$

The negative value for image distance indicates that it forms on the same side of the lens as the object.

434. (B) If the object looks blue under a white light source, then the object reflects blue and absorbs all other visible colors. We describe the object as blue. Then when the object is illuminated by only yellow light, the yellow light is absorbed and the object reflects no visible colors and appears black.

435. (D) Each color of light has a different index of refraction in glass. Index of refraction relates the speed of light in a vacuum to the speed of light in a medium ($n = c/v$), with light of high frequency having a higher index of refraction. Frequency remains the same as each color travels into the glass, but both the speed and the wavelength decrease, depending on the index. Thus, the blue end of the spectrum changes more—in speed, wavelength, and direction. The red end of the spectrum changes less. The correct answer is D because blue light has a higher frequency than red and will have a higher index, reducing its speed more than that of red.

436. (B) Total internal reflection occurs when light from a material with a higher index of refraction crosses an interface to a material with a lower index of refraction. In this situation, the light will refract away from the normal in the second medium, while some light reflects back into the original medium. As the incident angle is increased in size, the refracted angle also increases, and more of the light is also reflected back into the medium. When the incident angle is the critical angle, the refracted angle is 90 degrees. Beyond that point, as the incident angle increases beyond the critical angle, all the light is reflected back into the original medium.

437. (B) The image of a person standing in front of a plane (uncurved) mirror appears to that person to be "flipped" horizontally but not vertically, so it appears to be an upright image. Since the image appears to be the same distance behind the mirror as the person is standing in front of the mirror, the distance of the image behind the mirror is d, and the distance of the image from the person is $2d$. Since the light rays don't actually pass through the point where the image appears (behind the mirror), the image is virtual.

438. (B) Ray B does not follow a valid path after reflection from the mirror. Ray C follows an incident path parallel to the principal axis, so it correctly reflects through the focal point. Ray A correctly follows an incident path through the focal point, so it correctly reflects parallel to the principal axis. And Ray D follows an incident path to the center of the lens, so it reflects at an equal angle to the principal axis.

439. (B) The index of refraction, n, is the ratio of the speed of the electromagnetic radiation in a vacuum to the speed of the radiation in the medium: $n = c/v$. As radiation travels from a medium of lower index to a medium of higher index, the speed at which the radiation travels decreases, and so does the wavelength. The frequency does not change.

440. (D) Concave, or diverging, lenses cannot produce real images.

441. (D) Use the thin-lens equation with the quantities given to find a value for f in terms of d_o. If the magnification is ½ (i.e., the image is ½ as tall as the object), then the ratio of the image distance, d_i, to the object distance, d_o, is ½.

$$\frac{1}{f} = \frac{1}{d_o} + \frac{1}{d_o}$$

$$\frac{1}{-f} = \frac{1}{d_o} + \frac{1}{\frac{1}{2}d_o}$$

$$\frac{1}{-f} = \frac{3}{d_o} \qquad d_o = -3f \qquad -f = \frac{d_o}{3}$$

442. (D) Total internal reflection can occur only at an interface where the light is traveling from a medium with a higher index of refraction to a medium with a lower index of refraction. Under that condition, the incident angle must be greater than the critical angle: $\theta_c = \sin^{-1}(n_2/n_1)$, $n_1 > n_2$.

443. (C) Power in diopters is the reciprocal of focal length in meters. The first lens has power 1/0.5, or 2 diopters, and the second lens has power 1/0.25, or 4 diopters. Power in diopters is additive (which is the advantage of using diopters), so the power of the combination is 6 diopters.

444. (D) Spherical aberration is produced when a spherical lens bends light from the edges to a closer focal point than light passing through closer to the center. Making the lens nonspherical will allow focus. Aberration caused by separation of colors (blue bending more than red toward a focal point) is called chromatic aberration.

445. (D) In nearsightedness (myopia), light from a distant source is focused at a "near" point after passing through the lens of the eye—the light is focused in front of the retina, making the image fuzzy to the person. A concave lens diverges the light, moving the focal point closer to the retina and helping the image to appear clear. Conversely, people who are farsighted (hyperopic) use convex lenses to focus light on the retina when the light naturally focuses behind the retina (generally due to an eye structure that is "short" with respect to the shape of the lens or a lens that is unable to change shape to focus on the retina).

446. (C) The magnification of a microscope is determined by multiplying the magnifications of the eyepiece and the objective lenses. In this case, the magnification is 50 times. The object on the slide is then seen as 50 times 0.3 mm, or 15 mm. Since there are 10 mm per centimeter, the object appears to be 1.5 cm in diameter.

447. (C) Light from distant objects will focus from the objective lens at a point 15 cm from the lens and then serve as a real object for the eyepiece lens. If this image is at the focal point of the eyepiece lens, then the observer can view the image as if it were an infinity—but the image is now enlarged and can be viewed with a relaxed eye. Therefore, the sum of the focal lengths will be the length of the tube.

PART 5: ATOMS, NUCLEAR DECAY, ELECTRONIC STRUCTURES, AND ATOMIC CHEMICAL BEHAVIOR

Chapter 12: Atomic Nucleus

448. (C) This notation shows the composition of the nucleus of the atom. The lower number (on the left or right) is the atomic number, which is the number of protons in the nucleus. This identifies the element. The upper number (on the left or right) is the mass number, which is the number of nucleons, or the number of protons and neutrons in the nucleus. In a neutral atom, the number of electrons in the atom would be equal to the number of protons in the nucleus.

449. (D) Protons and neutrons, which make up atomic nuclei, are called nucleons, so answer choice A is a true statement. Atomic nuclei increase in radius as they increase in mass, so the density of atomic nuclei remains approximately constant, and answer choice B is true. The number of protons in the nucleus identifies the element, so answer choice C is true. However, the nuclei of atoms of the same element may vary in the number of neutrons, so the total number of nucleons in nuclei of the same element may vary, and therefore answer choice D is not true. Elaborating on this, when the number of neutrons in an element's nucleus vary, the variations are called isotopes of each other.

450. (C) The proton and neutron are both nucleons, or particles found in the nucleus of the atom, and both are composed of quarks, so neither is a fundamental particle. Fundamental particles, such as the electron or the neutrino, do not have internal structure (as far as we now know). A deuteron is a nucleus composed of a proton and a neutron held together by nuclear forces and thus is not a fundamental particle. Another name for a deuteron is a deuterium nucleus, that is, an isotope of hydrogen that has a mass number of 2 owing to the presence of the neutron.

451. (D) Hydrogen has three isotopes, that is, forms of hydrogen that have one proton in the nucleus (which identifies it as hydrogen). The isotope deuterium has one proton and one neutron in the nucleus, and the isotope tritium has one proton and two neutrons in the nucleus. These are the three isotopes of hydrogen: protium ($_1H^1$), deuterium ($_1H^2$), and tritium ($_1H^3$).

452. (D) Answer choices A, B, and C are all possible transformations within the nucleus. In each case (A, B, and C), the charge before and after the reaction is the same. However, in answer choice D, the charge before the transformation is positive, and the total charge afterward is negative—which does not conserve charge.

453. (B) For smaller elements, the ratio of neutrons to protons in stable nuclei tends to be 1 to 1. However, as the nuclei get larger in elements with increasing atomic number, stable nuclei tend to have a slightly larger ratio of neutrons to protons—closer to 1.6 to 1.

454. (D) The weak nuclear force is generally defined as the fundamental force responsible for beta decay (radioactivity). The force that causes electrons to be attracted to the positively charged nucleus is the electromagnetic force. The force or interaction that causes nucleons to attract and thus holds the nucleus together is the strong force. The force that causes protons to repel other protons is the electromagnetic force.

455. (C) At short ranges, that is, within the nucleus, the strong nuclear force is considered to be the strongest. The gravitational force is by far the weakest.

456. (B) The emission of an alpha particle ($_2He^4$), which is a helium nucleus with 2 protons and 2 neutrons, will result in a new nucleus that has 2 fewer protons and 2 fewer neutrons. Reducing by 2 protons and 2 neutrons reduces the mass number by 4.

457. (B) A beta particle is a high-speed electron, which has an atomic number of –1 and a mass number of 0: $_{-1}e^0$. To conserve charge, the new nucleus must have a higher atomic number by +1 to balance the –1 charge of the emitted electron. To conserve mass, there is no change in mass number for the new nucleus since the emitted electron has a mass number of 0.

458. (C) Emission of only one gamma photon would defy conservation of linear momentum. When two photons are emitted, they have components of momentum in opposite directions that add to zero so that no "new" momentum is created in a particular direction.

459. (C) The half-life is a probability of decay, so if there is only one nucleus, either it will have decayed or it will not, so the probability is 50%.

460. (C) A beta⁻, or high-energy electron, would be produced from a nuclear neutron decay that also produced a proton. This is the only answer choice that is a decay, or breakdown of larger particles into smaller particles. It is also the only answer choice that obeys conservation of charge; that is, the total charge before the decay equals the total charge after the decay. In answer choice C, the neutron has no charge before the decay, and the proton and the electron have positive and negative charges, respectively, that add to zero. Even though the proton and the electron are quite different, with very different masses, their charges are equal and opposite.

461. (D) This half-life curve shows the probability of the amount of the original material that is radioactive after a given length of time. If the original 100-g sample is initially radioactive, the plot would predict that after one half-life, only 50 g of the sample would be radioactive. Interpolating from the graph, the curve is at 50 g at close to 140 days.

462. (A) Positrons are the antiparticles of electrons; they have the same mass as electrons, but each positron has a positive charge. Positrons may be given off during radioactive decay of the nucleus. Beta particles, which are electrons, may be given off during the process of radioactive decay. Alpha particles, which are helium nuclei consisting of 2 protons and

2 neutrons, are certainly radioactive decay products. However, gamma rays are not particles with mass, even though they are given off during radioactive decay. Gamma photons have energy but do not qualify as particles with mass.

463. (B) Starting with the atomic number of bismuth (83), the emission of an alpha particle ($_2He^4$) would reduce this number by 2, leaving it at 81. Then the emission of an electron ($_{-1}e^0$) would increase the atomic number by 1, bringing it to 82. This is answer choice B. We can check this answer by determining the mass number changes. Starting with a mass number of 215, giving off an alpha particle would reduce the mass number by 4, leaving the product with a mass number of 211. Giving off the electron does not change the mass number, so the final mass number is still 211, or answer choice B.

464. (C) Alpha particles and positrons, which are positively charged, and beta particles, which are negatively charged, would all have a magnetic force exerted on them by the magnetic field, causing them to change direction: $F_B = q\boldsymbol{v} \times \boldsymbol{B}$. The gamma rays do not carry a charge, so they would pass undeflected through the magnetic field.

465. (D) The atomic charge (the bottom numbers) on both sides of the equation must balance due to conservation of charge, and the atomic mass (the top numbers) on both sides must also balance due to conservation of mass. We can see that the total charge (92) is already the same on both sides, so the last product can't have any charge. That eliminates the other three answer choices, all of which have charges. Then we check the atomic mass on both sides. On the left, the total mass is 236. On the right, the total of the first two products is 233, so a mass of 3 is needed to balance. Three neutrons would have this mass, as we can see from the neutron on the left.

466. (C) The atomic charge (the bottom numbers) on both sides of the equation must balance due to conservation of charge principles, and the atomic mass (top numbers) on both sides must also balance due to conservation of mass principles. We can see that the total charge on the left side is 4, so we need two more positive charges on the right side to balance. That eliminates answer choice D. Then we check the atomic mass on both sides. On the left, the total mass is 4. On the right, the total of the first two products is 4, so the final product must have zero mass. Only the positrons have a mass number of zero.

467. (B) First, balance the charge on both sides of the equation (the bottom numbers). Since the total is already 2 on both sides, the unknown particle must have zero charge (which can be only the neutron). We can check by balancing the nucleon numbers (or mass numbers) on both sides, which are the top numbers. The total on the left is 5. We see only 4 on the right side, so the unknown particle must have a mass number of 1. Only the neutron has no charge and a mass number of 1.

Chapter 13: Electronic Structure

468. (D) The photoelectric effect is an example of conservation of energy. The energy of the light photon absorbed (hf) is equal to the work necessary to strip each electron (called the work function, Φ) plus leftover energy used to give the electron kinetic energy: $hf = \Phi + K$. The point at which the line intercepts the x axis is the lowest possible frequency that can result in electron emission; it is called the cutoff frequency or threshold frequency.

That frequency will supply enough energy to free the electron but supply it with kinetic energy. That value is closest to 1.0×10^{15} Hz.

469. (A) A proton moving from the left with respect to the magnetic field directed into the page will experience a force upward on the page, since $\boldsymbol{F_B} = q\boldsymbol{v} \times \boldsymbol{B}$.

470. (A) The equation for momentum of a particle is $p = mv$. For a photon, all of its mass is in the form of energy, $E = mc^2$. Also, the speed of the photon is the speed of light, c. We recognize that the energy of a photon is $E = hf$. Substitute these into the momentum equation:

$$p = mv = \left(\frac{E}{c^2}\right)(c) = \frac{E}{c} = \frac{hf}{c}$$

471. (C) The Heisenberg Uncertainty Principle states that since particles can behave like waves, if the momentum of a particle is known with great precision, it is impossible to know the particle's position with the same great precision.

472. (C) Only photons have zero rest mass so particles do not have zero rest mass. Anything with mass has a rest mass equal to the inertial mass of the object when it is at rest. The relativistic equations applied to photons assume that $m = 0$.

473. (A) Only one electron at a time may have a specific set of quantum numbers that identify the energy state in an atom. Thus, when an atom is in its ground state, not all electrons may occupy the lowest-energy states. This is a partial statement of the Pauli Exclusion Principle.

474. (D) As the wavelength of a photon increases, its momentum decreases since photons of longer wavelength have lower energy:

$$E = hf$$
$$p = \frac{h}{\lambda}$$

475. (C) Materials that have no net magnetic field but that can become magnetic if they are placed in an external magnetic field—with the magnetic alignment in the same direction as the external field—are called paramagnetic. The magnetism of the material is not retained once it is removed from the external magnetic field. Most elements are paramagnetic.

476. (B) Materials that have no net magnetic field but that can become magnetic if they are placed in an external magnetic field—with the magnetic alignment of domains with the material in the opposite direction from the external field—are called diamagnetic.

477. (D) Answer choices A, B, and C all describe Earth's magnetic field. A magnetic compass has a defined north pole, and this end of the compass needle points toward geographic north. Since a north pole is attracted to a south pole, the north end of the compass must point toward Earth's south magnetic pole, placing that pole near Earth's north geographic pole.

That would mean that Earth's magnetic field lines emerge from its north magnetic pole in Antarctica and go back in at its south magnetic pole in northern Canada. Magnetic field lines make continuous loops, and a magnetic compass needle will align itself along those lines.

478. (D) The magnetic fields in materials depend upon the spin nature of electrons, the pairing of electrons, and the alignment of atoms within the materials, creating magnetic domains. All of the statements in answer choices A, B, and C contribute to the explanation of why some materials have magnetic fields. In most materials, the opposing electron spins of paired electrons effectively cancel each other, creating no net magnetic field. In some materials, not all electrons are paired, so there is a net magnetic field. In addition, the magnetic atoms tend to align strongly with each other, magnifying the magnetic effect.

479. (C) The mass of each particle is converted to energy, using the equation $E = mc^2$. Antiparticles have the same mass, so the total energy converted from the mass of the two particles is $2mc^2$. This energy is the energy of the two gamma photons that are produced—each of which has the same energy. The energy of a photon is $E = hf$, where h is Planck's constant and f is the frequency of the photon. Since there are two photons produced due to the described pair annihilation process, the total energy of the photons is $2hf$, where f is the frequency of each photon. Setting the two expressions equal to each other and solving for f:

$$2hf = 2mc^2$$

$$f = \frac{mc^2}{h}$$

480. (C) A magnetic field exerts a force on a moving charged particle of a magnitude that depends on the size of the charge on the particle, the component of the velocity that is perpendicular to the magnetic field, and the strength of the magnetic field. In answer choice A, there is no force because the charge is not moving. In answer choice B, the charged particle is moving along the field lines, so it has no velocity component perpendicular to the field—and the force is zero. Answer choices C and D are both situations in which the magnetic field would exert the force, but the velocity is entirely perpendicular to the field in answer choice C, so the largest force is exerted in situation C.

481. (D) A charge at rest with respect to a uniform magnetic field will not experience a force and thus will not move since $F_B = qv \times B$. A charge at rest in an electric field, however, will experience a force: $F_E = qE$.

Chapter 14: Thermochemistry and Thermodynamics

482. (C) The first law of thermodynamics is $\Delta U = Q + W$, where U is the internal energy of the system, Q is heat transfer to or from the system, and positive work W is work done on the system. If the process is adiabatic, by definition Q is zero. Then $\Delta U = W$. Internal energy, U, is proportional to the temperature of the system, so an increase in temperature (which also indicates an increase in the kinetic energy of molecules) means that work has been done on the system.

483. (B) Using conservation of energy (the first law of thermodynamics), an increase in the internal energy of the system (ΔU) is equal to thermal energy added and/or work done on the system. The term *isothermal* means "no temperature change." Since internal energy is proportional to temperature, there is no change in internal energy during an isothermal process. Thus, an amount of thermal energy must be added that is equal to the work done by the gas.

484. (A) Use the ideal gas equation: $PV = nRT$. Recognize that the term *isothermal* means that there is no change in temperature during the process. Assume that no molecules of the gas enter or leave the container; that is, the value of n (the number of moles of gas) does not change. We conclude that P and V must be inversely proportional since the value of nRT is constant. As P doubles, V is halved.

485. (C) By conservation of energy, described by the first law of thermodynamics, any change in internal energy is due to energy (Q) added or removed and/or work (W) done on or by the gas: $\Delta U = Q + W$. Using the equation in this way, work done on the system is considered to be positive—and increases the internal energy of the gas. Summing the changes during this set of processes, 80 J of work done on the gas increases the internal energy by that amount. When the gas gives off 25 J of energy, that amount is subtracted from the internal energy. Then, when the gas does work on its surroundings, it uses its internal energy so that it decreases by 40 J. The net change is internal energy is $\Delta U = +80$ J $- 25$ J $- 40$ J $= +15$ J.

486. (C) The internal energy of an ideal gas is proportional to the temperature and the average kinetic energy of gas molecules. The first law of thermodynamics is the conservation of energy statement: $\Delta U = Q + W$, where U is internal energy, Q is heat, and W is work. An increase in internal energy would definitely be the result of heat being added to the system and work being done on the system since each would increase internal energy. Answer choice A is not a correct choice because *isobaric* means that the pressure remains constant, which could be true when work is done ($W = P\Delta V$); however, if more heat is removed during the process than work done on the system, internal energy would decrease. Answer choice B is not a correct choice because no work is done if there is no change in volume (*isovolumetric*). Answer choice D is not correct because by definition an isothermal process means that there is no change in temperature, and thus ΔV is zero.

487. (B) The change in entropy for each chamber can be estimated as heat transfer divided by average absolute temperature over which the transfer takes place: $\Delta S = Q/T_{ave}$. Since the reservoirs are large, the transfer of just 500 J of energy in or out doesn't appreciably change the temperature of either chamber. Thus, we can assume that the value of T_{ave} doesn't change during the transfer. The hotter chamber has a higher average temperature; when T is larger, ΔS is smaller (since Q is the same for both). The hotter chamber, then, undergoes a smaller change in entropy, and the cooler chamber undergoes a larger change in entropy. Additionally, the net change in entropy of the universe is the sum of the two entropy changes. The cooler chamber has heat transferred in, so the value of Q is positive, and the value for entropy change is positive. The entropy change for the hotter chamber is negative since heat is transferred out. The sum of the entropy changes is positive, so the net entropy change for this situation is positive. The entropy of the universe increases as a result.

488. (D) Without using calculus, the change in the entropy of a system is estimated as heat transferred into or out of the system divided by the average Kelvin temperature over which the process takes place:

$$\Delta S = \frac{Q}{T_{ave}(K)}$$

The change in entropy for chamber X is $-Q$ divided by T_1. Q is negative here because the heat is transferred out—from higher temperature to lower temperature. The change in entropy for chamber Y is $+Q/T_2$. The value for Q is the same for both chambers. However, since T_1 is higher than T_2, the change is entropy in the first case is lower. We are concerned only with magnitudes, so we can ignore the negative sign. Thus, chamber X loses the same amount of heat as chamber Y gains, but the change in entropy for chamber X is less than the change in entropy for chamber Y.

489. (A) The boiling water inside the beaker will stay hot the longest when the product of the conductivity (k) and the thermal gradient (ΔT) is the least. Considering all the other parameters to be about the same, we can see these two variables in the following equation:

$$\frac{Q}{t} = \frac{kA\Delta T}{L}$$

So we select the liquid for the "bath" such that the product of k and ΔT (the difference between the temperature of the liquid and the temperature of boiling water at 100°C) is the smallest. In answer choice A, the product is 0.145 W/m·C° times 10 C°, or 1.45 W/m. In answer choice B, the product is 0.202 W/m·C° times 20 C°, or 4.03 W/m. In answer choice C. the product is 0.609 W/m·C° times 10 C°, or 6.09 W/m. In answer choice D, the product is 0.609 W/m·C° times 20 C°, or 12.18 W/m. Of these, the smallest heat transfer rate (in joules per second per meter of liquid surrounding the beaker) is to the oil in answer choice A.

490. (B) Convection takes place in fluids, that is, in liquids and gases. As the fluid is heated, it expands, becomes less dense, and then rises—allowing cooler, more dense fluid to sink under the influence of gravity (since it is more dense).

491. (C) The rate at which heat is transferred from a higher-temperature reservoir to a lower-temperature reservoir is:

$$\frac{Q}{t} = \frac{kA\Delta T}{L}$$

where Q/t is the rate of heat transfer, k is the conductivity of the material used (in this case, silver, which has high conductivity), A is the cross-sectional area through which energy is transferred by conduction, ΔT is the temperature difference between the hot and cold regions, and L is the length through which the energy is transferred. Doubling A would increase the rate of transfer, and doubling L will increase not only the surface for absorption of energy in the hot liquid by the rod but also the surface area for dissipation of energy to the air for the portion of the rod sticking out of the liquid.

492. (C) The rate at which heat is transferred by conduction through something like a steel rod is directly proportional to the thermal conductivity, cross-sectional area, and difference in temperature between the two chambers and inversely proportional to the length of the rod. Answer choice A is incorrect because specific heat is not the correct quantity to use here. Answer choice B is incorrect because making these changes in temperature in the two chambers will decrease the temperature difference between the chambers, which will decrease the rate of heat flow through the rod. Answer choice D, in which cross-sectional area is decreasing, is a change that will decrease the rate of heat transfer by conduction.

493. (B) Infrared radiation is electromagnetic radiation. When you put your hand near a warm stove, you are sensing infrared radiation—which is not within the visible range.

494. (D) The mechanism is described in the answer. It's important to realize that the energy is transferred by conduction, but the molecules do not actually travel from one end of the spoon to the other.

495. (D) Calculate the rate of energy transfer through the door by conduction, using Q for heat, t for time, k for thermal conductivity, A for area of the door, T for temperature, and d for the thickness of the door:

$$\frac{\Delta Q}{\Delta t} = \frac{kA\Delta T}{d} = \frac{(0.1 \text{ W/m} \cdot \text{C}°)(2.0 \text{ m})(1.0 \text{ m})(50 \text{ C}°)}{0.02 \text{ m}} = 500 \text{ W}$$

This answer, 500 W, is the same as 500 J/s. As the formula shows, the rate at which heat is transferred through the door by conduction increases with the area of the door and the temperature difference between inside and outside. Heat transfer decreases as the thickness of the door increases.

496. (C) Electrical resistance increases with temperature for most materials. The speed of sound in air increases with temperature. As temperature increases, the volume of a gas is expected to increase; however, if the number of molecules is kept constant, mass is constant, so density (mass/volume) would be expected to decrease with temperature. Using $PV = nRT$, if volume is kept constant, pressure would be expected to increase with temperature. Most solid objects increase in length with temperature.

497. (B) Since the ball and the ring are made of the same material, they have the same coefficient of expansion and thus expand at the same rate. The diameter of the ball and the diameter of the ring increase the same amount, so the ball will fit through the ring as the two are heated together.

498. (C) The formula to determine the change in length of an object when it expands during heating is:

$$\Delta L = \alpha L_o \Delta T = (12 \times 10^{-6}/\text{C}°)(1 \text{ cm})(30 \text{ C}°) = 0.00036 \text{ cm}$$

$$\% \text{ change} = \frac{\Delta L}{L_o} = \frac{0.00036}{1} \times 100\% = 0.036\%$$

499. (B) The key to solving this problem is the approximation that the coefficient of area expansion for a material is twice the coefficient of linear expansion. The original area of the plate is equal to $(0.1 \text{ m})^2$, or 0.01 m^2. Apply this to the formula for expansion:

$$A_{final} = A_{original} + \Delta A = A_{original} + 2\alpha A_o \Delta T$$
$$A_{final} = (100 \text{ cm}^2) + (10 \times 10^{-6} /C°)(100 \text{ cm}^2)(10 \text{ C°}) = 100.01 \text{ cm}^2$$

500. (A) Work done on an ideal gas causes a compression, or decrease in volume, of the gas ($W = -P\Delta V$). There is no change in volume in steps II and IV, so no work is done on or by the gas molecules during those steps. In step III, the gas expands, so work is done by the gas in expanding itself. Only step I shows a decrease in volume, which means that work was done by an external force in compressing the system of gas molecules.